How to Use the Computer in Business Planning

Henry F. Lande

How to Use the Computer in Business Planning

Prentice-Hall, Inc.
Englewood Cliffs, N.J.

PRENTICE-HALL INTERNATIONAL, INC., *London*
PRENTICE-HALL OF AUSTRALIA, PTY. LTD., *Sydney*
PRENTICE-HALL OF CANADA, LTD., *Toronto*
PRENTICE-HALL OF INDIA PRIVATE LTD., *New Delhi*
PRENTICE-HALL OF JAPAN, INC., *Tokyo*

© 1969, BY

HENRY F. LANDE

ALL RIGHTS RESERVED. NO PART OF THIS
BOOK MAY BE REPRODUCED IN ANY FORM
OR BY ANY MEANS, WITHOUT PERMISSION
IN WRITING FROM THE PUBLISHER.

LIBRARY OF CONGRESS
CATALOG CARD NUMBER: 69–12822

PRINTED IN THE UNITED STATES OF AMERICA
B & P

L25

HQ9969

"The formulation of the problem is often more essential than its solution, which might be merely a matter of mathematical or experimental skill. To raise new questions, new possibilities, to regard old problems from a new angle requires creative imagination and marks real advance in science."

Einstein and Infeld, *The Evolution of Physics*, (New York: Simon & Schuster, 1961), p. 92. Reprinted by permission of the Estates of Albert Einstein and Leopold Infeld.

———— **This book is dedicated**
———— **to my entire family.** ————
————

About the Author

Henry F. Lande is Manager of Planning Systems Development at the Corporate Headquarters of IBM. He received his M.S. degree in Engineering from the Technical University of Berlin, Germany, and his Ph.D. degree in Economics from Western Reserve, Cleveland, Ohio.

His prior experience includes industrial engineering and labor relations management as well as controllership. Since 1956, when he joined IBM, he has been Manager of Divisional Planning in the Office Products Division and the Data Systems Division and Manager of Planning Services in the Data Processing Group Staff. He assumed his present position in the spring of 1966. Since 1961 Dr. Lande has been responsible for the design and installation of computerized systems for business planning.

Dr. Lande is a member of the American Management Association, the American Economic Association, Verband Deutscher Wirtschaftsingenieure, the National Planning Association, and other professional associations interested in planning.

Acknowledgments

The concepts and procedures described in this book began to take shape in the late fifties when the computer first appeared to offer a medium to develop new messages for business management. Since then many aspects of the basic idea have been molded by the IBM environment. Two types of contributions must be acknowledged. One deals with the allocation of resources—not just money, but talented associates and accessible machines. In both respects IBM has been a most favorable environment.

Those who have directly contributed to the success of this planning systems approach (division general managers, controllers at the divisional and corporate level, directors of planning and directors of budgets, managers of financial planning, and the many analysts and programmers who did the legwork) know of their contribution because it became a part of their working environment. However, I want to acknowledge also the important role of those who through the years were nonsupporters, if not outright detractors, of this development effort. They saw to it that the approach and working system remained realistic and practical and prevented it from becoming an elegant, theoretical exercise.

Since mentioning any names on either side of the fence could never be complete, I am restricting myself to mentioning only a few who have directly furthered the writing of this book itself: Mr. Paul Rizzo, IBM vice-president and Corporate Controller; Mr. W. W. Simmons, IBM Director of Planning Systems and Mr. Allan Krowe, Director of IBM Information Systems, for giving me moral support and allowing me to use IBM resources; as well as Mrs. Virginia Garrahy and Miss Linda Lepore for helping me with the preparation of the manuscript and its many figures and exhibits.

I should not forget to mention my longtime associate, Robert S. Weinberg, who by his friendly critiques kept the project alive.

My wife Marlies did a marvelous job editing large portions of the manuscript, as well as tolerating the commotion and tension created by writing a book in addition to holding down a full-time job.

The Purpose of This Book

This book deals with the general management problem of planning for the future. In practice this task is being handled by more or less formal methods and procedures in every business, large or small, at all times. Planning for the future is one of the chief responsibilities of general management, the performance of the entrepreneurial function in our economy. Both skill and good fortune determine success or failure.

We may assume that having been planned in the same organization, both the Ford Edsel and the Ford Thunderbird were given the same skillful planning. But one failed and the other became a successful venture. Therefore, we must be careful not to overstate the case for skill and skill, alone, in planning. Let us not forget the old adage, "Forecasting is very difficult, especially about the future."

While a large part of planning involves management in making forecasts or predictions about the future, business planning is also a formidable administrative task. In other words, planning for the future presents management both with a substantive and a procedural problem. In the many years in which the writer has been involved with the question of how management originates and achieves planned goals, he has come to the conclusion that more often than not it is the lack of procedure which imposes rather severe limitations on substantive planning. Therefore, he submits that for management to improve its ability to establish and achieve planned goals, management must take part in the development of sound planning and control procedures. These procedures must become an integral part of the management process or management system through which the business is operated.

A great deal has been said and written about what management should do or not do when planning for the future, but the question of how to do it has usually been left to the reader's imagination. One of the reasons for this situation may be found in the fact that a successful planning and control system cannot be easily generalized. In a way it is an organic part of the successful business and its organization. The adoption of another organization's planning system may be as dangerous as a transfusion of incompatible blood. In addition, many executives, who after years of hard work have arrived at what they consider a proper planning and control system, cherish it as a competitive advantage and are reluctant to release details about their struggle or the key features of success for general publication.

This book is intended to help bridge the gap between the many general prescriptions for business planning and a specific, practical planning system. Since such a system for business planning must be tailored to the needs of the particular business in question—as we said, there is no valid general solution—this book will deal principally with an approach, with the architecture of the system. This approach, making use of today's information technology, has general validity and would readily yield a specific solution for any given business. Electronic information technology, still just in its teens, represents a "mutational change." Its impact on management systems and especially on business planning and control is becoming more and more pronounced. This involves technical, organizational, political, as well as economic problems, all of which will be addressed in this book.

The interest in a frank discussion of the procedural aspects of planning for the future has been growing stronger over the years. In the past the staff planner's primary task was to sell line management on the need for a new look at the overall question of management systems and business planning. Management for years, sometimes *ad nauseam*, has been told what to do and is turning around asking the counter question "How?". This has on occasion become a source of embarrassment and annoyance to the staff planner—the more so, the higher powered his sales talks had been in previous encounters with management.

He is now being asked to deliver and finds himself confronted with a new type of frustration. Instead of not getting management's ear and support, he is now stymied by not really knowing how to go about doing the job in the administrative and procedural reality of a business organization.

In the future, then, the staff planner's primary task will become one of furnishing management with the means with which to do an effective planning job. This calls for some kind of a system that answers the question of how to originate and achieve planned goals. This book should give the staff planner and his management ample material to consider in such a systems development effort, as well as a result-minded, tested approach for immediate implementation.

In writing a book under the subject of *How to Use the Computer in Business Planning* most authors would follow the traditional road of surveying the field by interviewing the authorities and then presenting to the reader a symposium of their findings with careful analysis and conclusions. In contrast, this book will be based primarily on the specific approach taken by the writer himself, in developing systems for comprehensive business planning in the IBM Corporation at the divisional and corporate staff levels. It will draw on the writer's extensive exposure to corresponding efforts in other American and European corporations, only to emphasize specific points and illustrate possible alternative solutions as well as the reasoning for not having gone that road. On the one hand, this makes the book an attempt to present a subjective experience as a normative structure. On the other hand, it allows the reader, within the scope of a single book, to examine the exhaustive statement of at least one practical and operational solution which is capable of being implemented in his own business environment. It is suggested that the reader will benefit more from sorting out his thoughts in front of a frank expression of conviction, backed by the description of specific workable solutions, than by perusing a menu of problematical alternatives.

List of Figures

List of Exhibits

10. PLANNED GOALS

Contents

1

The Subject of
Business Planning

Since World War II economic planning has become a more and more accepted activity in our society. This may seem paradoxical because our society is based on the philosophy of free enterprise and competition in a market where prices are supposed to regulate transaction volumes. This paradox, however, dissolves itself when we recognize that the term "planning" is so broad as to be almost meaningless as a description of any specific planning activity or process.

Some economic theories deal with a fourth factor of production besides land, labor, and capital, and identify it in various ways, such as organization, or planning, or enterprise. Let us accept this concept of planning as the entrepreneurial function in business in contrast to national economic planning, as a first step towards defining

1

what type of planned goals we are talking about. Of course, this book is not concerned with national economic planning. On the other hand, as it relates to entrepreneurial planning or business planning, further distinction and refinement of our definition will be necessary.

SMALL BUSINESS

The so-called small business is usually owned and operated by an individual combining enterprise, organization, and planning in one person. He is the personification of the entrepreneur of classical economic theory. Most of his decisions deal with the relationship of his products or services to the market upon which he has absolutely no influence. He plans his business under the assumption that there will continue to be a market just as a tourist in a car driving uphill on an unknown road presumes that past the crest of the hill the road will continue. He will most likely worry and fret about whether or not he is doing the best possible job with the resources available to him and the customers or clientele whose demand he is attempting to satisfy. But the whole process of his planning is thoroughly intertwined with his personal goals in terms of values, utilities, ego, etc.

Of course, this type of individualistic business would not be representative of a business which is in need of a systematic planning effort of the type which is the subject of this book. However, there are many such individualistic businesses which have grown large enough to require systematic planning. At what size—which would, of course, vary from industry to industry—a business loses its individualistic nature and becomes a collective undertaking is not clear. The break would also depend upon the ability of the entrepreneur himself.

LARGE-SCALE BUSINESS

Nevertheless, somewhere there is a size and complexity of business operation where "more of the same" converts into "a different ball game," where a business changes its character from an individualistic to a collectivistic undertaking. In the current literature, the distinction is often made on the basis of legal form. It is usually the corporation as distinct from the proprietorship. Therefore, we often talk about corporate planning. It is suggested that not so much the legal form, but the size and scope of the operation to be planned for is the decisive criterion for the determination of whether or not systematic business planning is necessary and, if so, how it might be accomplished. In order for formal comprehensive business planning to be needed, there must be a sufficient number of internal conflicts of interest, and physical and organizational limitations to the free exercise of the entrepreneurial function within the business. Perhaps the most readily discernible characteristic of such a business is several layers of management.

DECISION HIERARCHY

In businesses whose scope and size of operation require several levels of management, planning takes place at each of the different levels of management as well as in different contexts. In order to clarify this point, let us visualize a business stratified into the following levels:

(1) Corporation (multiple lines of products and markets)
(2) Division (specialized product and/or market)
(3) Function (major activity such as manufacturing, marketing)
(4) Department (such as advertising, assembly, accounts payable)
(5) Operation (such as copywriting, plant layout, payroll check issuing).

For instance, at the operational level the rearrangement of factory space in connection, say, with the installation of a large-scale transfer tool is a typical operational planning problem. The request for additional equipment from the department (machining) level may have triggered a study at the functional (manufacturing) level to determine how to increase departmental capacity.

At the functional level the decision whether or not to use a large-scale transfer tool will be based on assumptions about business volumes and related production requirements furnished from the divisional or corporate management levels. In some cases, they may be determined within the function based on past experience and trends developed from that experience, without considering the total business and the consequences of the proposed action on it. The inputs to such a comprehensive view of the decision are so complex and far reaching that the procedural problem of collecting the data becomes more difficult than the substantive problem of making a decision.

As we ascend the levels of management, it becomes a matter of major concern whether or not the decision at the functional level is subject to review at the divisional level only or both at the divisional and corporate levels. If the expenditure or investment involved is large enough, the control procedures usually require approval at the corporate level. However, the decision process related to this approval is really not based on a corporate view and in some cases not even on a divisional view of the situation. It is in effect only a substitution of corporate decision makers for the respective functional managers with information usually no more comprehensive than that available to the functional manager in the first place.

INFORMATION TECHNOLOGY

Information is the lifeblood of any human organization. The larger the organization is the more important information becomes. Hence, information technology is the chief factor which determines the practicability of large-scale organizations. On the one hand, information technology may be a limiting factor, a constraint. On the other hand, it may become the driving force behind major organizational upheavals and the development of new structures. The Roman Empire would not have been possible without its efficient communications system consisting of an extensive network of roads and Mediterranean seaways, combined with written messages backed by an extensive legal structure. Military prowess alone would not have done it.

Since the invention of paper and printing, the most important innovation in information technology has been electricity and its more recent offshoot, electronics. Within the area of electronics technology, most recently the computer has introduced what we might call a mutational change in information development. While telegraph, telephone, and radio technology has shaped the organizational structures of the first half of the twentieth century, television and the computer are about to reshape it in the second half.

The enormity of this reshaping, which is taking place at a very rapid pace, can only be appreciated when we recall consciously to our minds that both television and the computer are Post-World-War-II phenomena. As far as age is concerned they are still in their teens. What this technology will accomplish when it reaches adulthood we may dream about in awe and sometimes in fear. Some of the things to come are already discernible in broad outline.

This book will fill in some details for one area of application, the planning and controlling of a large scale business. It will do so not in terms of things that might be possible in five, ten, or 15 years from now, but in terms of what can be and is being done today. No doubt, the use of computers is having a revolutionary impact on management systems, and its most pronounced influence will be felt in the area of how management originates and achieves planned goals.

POLITICAL CONSTRAINTS

As a student at the Technical University of Berlin, first under Soviet and later under British occupation following World War II, the writer took part in many a heated discussion about planned vs. free market economies. The theory of a planned economy often sounded attractive, but a nagging doubt continued as to its practice. How was the concept of centralized planning going to be translated into administrative methods and procedures? Even the technocrats among the supporters of the view of a planned society had no plausible answer.

It is of great significance to observe what has happened in the Communist world since then. The planning process has become stratified by levels of managerial responsibility in a realistic attempt to balance the degree of participation in goal setting with the ability to achieve the agreed upon objectives. The scope or span of managerial effectiveness, though by no means clearly understood, constrains the size of the planning unit.

Computer application in planning may tend to support larger planning units, but in the end economic planning will become limited by the sociopolitical aspects of dealing with the judgment, ambitions, and ideas of large groups of people. Participation in the decision-making process, however, recognized as a key motivator toward achievement, opens up Pandora's box for individual systems, each with its own subsets and decision variables.

While we may observe a gradual disaggregation or decentralization of the planning process in so-called planned societies, Western corporations have not developed much understanding of the sociopolitical forces either. It is generally agreed that a corporation is a legitimate planning unit within the larger system of a competitive free market. It is beyond the scope of this book to deal with the question of how the USA, the most important of the Western economies, originates and achieves planned goals, but some of the issues raised certainly also apply to the larger economic decision-making process of our nation.

Returning to the subject of management of a legitimate planning unit, the situation is no less schizophrenic than on the national scale. Most people see the trend toward centralized government or management assisted by computerized information processing, as a threat to freedom. Hence they oppose it. Management, on the other hand, recognizes the limits of centralized power in their own areas of complete legal competence and try to decentralize, to get lower levels of management involved in the decision-making process. At least so they say.

In the middle of all this, and confusing the issue, appears the computer as a new information technology tool feared by some as the ultimate device for centralized management and control. In this crosscurrent of emotion and prejudice the architect of a planning system is wrong almost by definition, whichever way he turns. To the senior executive in power he offers a road toward specific and unequivocal decentralization, when the computer has just raised the hope and whetted the appetite for recentralization. To the junior executive he offers a reduction in confusion and ambiguity, when those conditions are recognized as a major source of job security and protection against failure.[1]

The development of a planning system which reaches through several levels of management might perhaps be accomplished by gradual evolution. Peripheral subsystems might be incorporated into a well-established and fully integrated nucleus. It is not clear, however, why such an all-pervasive planning system should be desirable. It would tend to stifle initiative and creativity. Politically, therefore, it appears preferable to visualize the managerial decision process operating through a network of independent planning systems, each designed to serve its respective level of management.

---

[1] Cf. Charles H. Granger, *The Hierarchy of Objectives*, HBR, May-June, 1964.

2

The Planning Process

Any human action implies some plan. In this sense, planning represents the universal effort of matching aspirations with capabilities, or in other words, of establishing attainable objectives and goals.

The degree to which such efforts are systematized and formalized varies considerably. Likewise, the success or failure of the planned venture may be independent of the planning effort. Economic history teaches us many lessons about thoroughly planned ventures which failed and bungled gropings in uncharted territory which were carried to great success.

We must be careful not to confuse planning with risk taking. The management of economic affairs will continue to require the taking of risks. But we may be justified to profess a conviction, perhaps a faith, that formal planning will increase the likelihood of success. In addition, we may have no choice in the matter. Circumstances or technological conditions may force management to move toward formal planning,

7

whether they like it or not. In this sense, the alternative to formal planning is organizational disintegration and chaos.

As long as a business is small and run by the owner-operator as an extension of the family household, some formal planning may be helpful, but it is not yet characterized by issues which require the type of system proposed in this book. The small entrepreneur plans primarily in relation to his external environment: customers, suppliers, the labor market, and the money market.

As soon as a business becomes large enough to require several levels of management, each with a fair degree of bargaining power, management faces a new phenomenon. In a large-scale business we also need to plan the internal environment, not just technically but politically. The new phenomenon facing management is the fact that each organizational unit has its own ideas about what to do, when, and how to do it, and the power to bargain about its point of view.

In a large business, planning consists of management's efforts to balance objectives and resources not only in relation to the outside world, but also in relation to the internal world of motivation and power to operate. It is for this purpose that a formal business planning system becomes a necessity.

Figure 1 shows the size distribution of U. S. corporations by major industry. From this it appears that between 3,000 to 6,000 corporations are large enough to need some formal business planning effort.

PLANNING BY MANAGEMENT RESPONSIBILITY

In response to the challenges posed by continuity in growth and profitability in an expanding economy, many of these corporations have, in the past ten years, established some separate and distinct comprehensive planning effort. Because a longer-range view is called for, long-range planning is often used as a synonym for business planning. Just as often, this led to organizational confusion. Planning does not partition well into a short and long range, and if nevertheless so divided, tends to fall apart at the seams between the two time ranges.   It appears more appropriate to identify planning with the level of management that is responsible for it, such as corporate planning, divisional planning, functional planning (research, development, manufacturing, or marketing), etc.

Incidentally, the terms "strategic," "tactical," or "operational" planning are not very helpful either. They label differences in the planner's thinking, rather than differences in the planning process. Strategic, tactical, and operational points of view enter the planning-bargaining process at all levels of management responsibility.

The current situation is perhaps best summed up in a quotation from Dean E. Wooldridge, who says, "Debates on the subject of planning, insofar as there are any, have to do not with whether but with how and how much."[1] In other words, not

---

[1] Melville C. Branch, *The Corporate Planning Process,* American Management Association, 1962, Introduction by Dean E. Wooldridge, page 13.

ACTIVE CORPORATION INCOME TAX RETURNS
BY ASSET SIZE-CLASS AND INDUSTRIAL DIVISION
1965

	Millions of Dollars				
	250 and Over	100– 249	50– 99	25– 49	Under 25
Agriculture, Forestry, and Fisheries	1	1	4	7	27,517
Mining	11	18	14	49	13,193
Construction	1	8	16	26	113,233
Manufacturing	198	234	317	581	184,594
Transportation, Communication, Electric, Gas & Sanitary Services	129	91	82	110	59,264
Wholesale & Retail Trade	25	42	61	158	440,018
Finance, Insurance, and Real Estate	451	671	976	1,879	384,451
Services	6	14	30	47	188,080
Other	—	—	—	—	7,372
Total	822	1,079	1,500	2,857	1,417,722
Cumulative Total		1,901	3,401	6,258	1,423,980

Source: Stat. Abstract of the U.S. 1968, p. 481.

Figure 1

enough planning and too much action might be as detrimental as too much planning and not enough action. Therefore, the key procedural problem for planning is to determine the how and how much as it relates to decision making and action.

COMPREHENSIVE VIEW OF THE BUSINESS

Traditionally, in most corporations it is the financial function which maintains a comprehensive view of the business. Under the rules of financial accounting, the corporation pulls together a comprehensive view of past period activities and current status of resources. The typical annual report contains a profit and loss statement and a balance sheet. Resources such as inventories, plant, and equipment are shown by the financial value at which they are carried on the books. Manpower, skills, capacities, capabilities, as well as plans for the future, are covered by narratives and some

S. U. Libraries

subsidiary statistics. It would certainly be a revolutionary move by any corporation if it were to publish in its annual report the objectives for the profit and loss statement and balance sheet of the next five years, rather than the history of the past ten years as is usually the case.

Suppose, such publication were required by law. Most corporations would not be able to comply. However, from the point of view of what is important, it is just this projection of current positions of strength and weakness, of current capabilities and capacities, together with the plans and programs to be pursued in the immediate future that must be made available to senior management. They are the first steps towards identifying the need for change and achieving any progress. This is more and more recognized by management as attested to by the fact that most large corporations are engaged in some five-year planning efforts or are getting ready to do so.

PLANNING, NOT BUDGETING

At this point, it is necessary to make a clear distinction between the standard practice of preparing budgets for the immediate future and business planning as we understand it in this book. While the word budget is often replaced by euphemisms such as profit plan and operating plan or other less oppressive terms, essentially next year's budget is an authorization for the expenditures of money, for the entering of commitments in terms of hiring people, building plants, acquiring machineries, and producing goods and services. In this sense, the budget is a control mechanism that enables senior management to delegate operational authority within clearly prescribed limits to the various lower levels of management. Without a budget the modern corporation could not operate.

Due to the fact that the financial function within a corporate structure has been the only one which develops comprehensive views of the business and because the financial function is the custodian of the budget, many corporations when confronted with the necessity of business planning have assigned this task to its financial function. As a result, business planning often has been oriented to satisfy financial considerations and has been treated as a long-range extension of the budget. A long-range budget is a paradox. The budget which is tied to the structure of the financial accounting system by necessity must follow current organizational structure. It requires numerical values for every operational detail because it is these operational details which are to be authorized and controlled by the budget. To employ this methodology for a longer-range view of the future becomes self-defeating. Longer-range projections are usually based on assumptions which are subject to frequent change. If every change in assumption is to be reflected in all budgetary details, the resulting deluge of planning data becomes unmanageable. The purpose of planning is to establish new directions and to evaluate changes and alternate courses of action. This does not require the numerical support of budgetary details. On the contrary, to carry such budgetary detail, in, say, a five-year plan might be dangerous inasmuch as it gives an illusion of legitimate accuracy and validity, thus clouding the issues of risk and judgment in all data about the future.

COMPUTERIZED BUDGETING

The use of computers in budgeting and subsequently in business planning tends to increase this danger because it offers the technical feasibility of carrying out such a long-range budgeting process. In this context, the computer is used to digest tremendous amounts of manually generated data and to consolidate them into the customary financial documents. The underlying assumptions are so detailed that they defy senior management review, and the introduction of alternate assumptions requires a recasting of all inputs at the lower operational level. Even if such a computerized long-range budgeting system were feasible it would not be of much help in bargaining about the probable consequences of alternate courses of action under consideration and in motivating people to new directions and commitments. As Russ Ackoff has pointed out, such a system would contain an overabundance of irrelevant information.

Fortunately, computerized long-range budgeting is running into some generic problems. Although the writer has rubbed elbows with many systems development experts who have been working on such systems for years, he has yet to see one in operation as specified in the original project proposal. Perhaps there is some information entropy at work which saves us from ourselves. As in the Greek myth about Sysiphus' stone rolling down the mountainside just before reaching the summit, those all-embracing, all-pervasive systems tend to disintegrate and turn into chaos just before the proposed final delivery date. In a way the substance of this book deals with just this problem of information entropy and proposes an approach to the development of planning data systems which consciously tries to avoid an entanglement with unmanageable data banks.

STATEMENT OF PLANNED GOALS (FORMAL BUSINESS PLAN)

Consider now what it takes to prepare a formal business plan. Perhaps a corporation's annual report to its stockholders and the investment community is as good a starting point as any. It contains a profit and loss statement, a balance sheet, and other financial data. Information on manpower, production capacities, and future business opportunities are covered by narrative text and subsidiary data. Also included in the annual report are statistics about the last five or ten years' history of accomplishments in terms of sales, investments, and earnings, together with customary ratios for evaluation.

As a minimum, a formal business plan should consist of something like annual reports for the next five or ten years. The documentation of such a view of the future is indeed the end product of the business planning process.°

The procedures followed in developing and maintaining this formal business plan are an expression of management philosophy. They affect not only the form but also the substance of the plan and its impact on business decisions and operations. Unfortunately, planning procedures have been given little if any attention in the literature. The limelight is on why to plan and what to plan for, rather than how to do it. Even publications entitled "How Companies Plan" or "How to Prepare a Profit Plan" tell us what is being done or ought to be done, not how one might go about doing it.

HIERARCHY OF SYSTEMS (NETWORK)

In order to make business planning effective, it is most important for senior management to become familiar with the planning procedures and to understand the planning logic which is employed in making projections. Consequently, the planning logic must be tailored to the management level which is going to use it. The planning logic at the corporate level would have to include major ingredients from the divisional level. It is of course essential that the divisional management understands and concurs with the representation of the division within the corporate logic and its use. Likewise, the divisional logic and its functional modules should be understood and concurred with by functional management. However, there would be no necessity for functional managers within a division to understand and concur with the divisional representation in corporate logic.°° Going further down the line, the functional planning logic would have to give proper attention to departmental detail. However, such departmental detail need not be part of the divisional logic.

Many years of practical experience in this area have convinced the writer that any attempt to develop a business planning system which integrates the planning logic across all management levels will not lead to useful results in the foreseeable future.

It is his contention that the need for using a computer in business planning does not arise because there is so much data to be digested and consolidated, but because a limited amount of data must be re-evaluated many, many times. The primary purpose of designing a system for business planning does not lie in the mechanization of accounting and budgetary procedures, but in the development and stabilization of planning procedures, i.e. the rationale or logic for the evaluation of alternatives.

° The document which emerges may consist of 50 to 300 pages, plus subsidiary working papers of undefinable volume and complexity. A variety of writing styles may be employed: from econometric science fiction by ivory tower professionals to trivial "for motherhood" statements by payroll-meeting line managers, and any editorial compromise hammered out between these two extremes.
°° This does not exclude the possibility of using the corporate model for training functional managers.

Planned goals cannot be generated, discussed, and agreed upon by looking at only one solution.

Different levels of management get involved and are being committed to action. In a larger divisionalized corporation, both corporate and divisional management get involved in the setting of corporate goals. In turn, divisional management must translate these goals into objectives by functional area. Therefore, the planning logic at the divisional level must include representation of all functional complexities within the divisional operations. As such, divisional planning tends to become more complex and demanding than corporate or functional planning. This raises the question as to whether or not divisional planning should deal with functional logic in the same degree of detail with which it would apply to planning at the functional level. Those who are intrigued by the potential of computers like to answer this question in the affirmative as follows: "Since the computer is fast and efficient in digesting tremendous amounts of data, we no longer need to abstract, but instead we can develop summary data by consolidation from the lowest operational denominators." This is a naïve and misleading proposition. With the use of computers we may be able to compress the time for calculations, but what cannot be shortened is the time it takes to prepare inputs to the calculations.

If the planning process requires myriads of inputs, it is easy to see how the evaluation of alternative sets of inputs will bog down before it reaches the computer. Stratification by management responsibility and abstract representation of decision criteria continues to be necessary. It is indeed the vital effort in designing a planning system.

3

Traditional Planning
Methods

When the management of a large company begins to consider the
problem of longer-range planning, it is faced with a serious dilemma. The organizational philosophy, which has been the governing factor in most of today's industrial
organizations, is functional. This philosophy emerged 50 years ago and may be traced
directly to the efforts of Frederick Winslow Taylor and his disciples and followers.
Before the introduction of functional management as a way of improving operational
efficiency, all supervision was general, i.e. management at all levels dealt with comprehensive problems in their entirety. The concept of functional management was
in keeping with the concept of the division of labor. In this case it represented the
division of intellectual labor, the bringing to bear of the advantages of specialization,

15

and more thorough knowledge of a given activity to the field of administering or managing this activity.

We must not overlook the fact that this philosophy of functional supervision was developed in an era of information technology which did not as yet include the telephone, radio, television, tabulating machines, and computers, as well as the pervasive use of intercom systems, loudspeaker and public address systems, remote data collection systems and vast information banks. In the days of F. W. Taylor, application of specialized knowledge required the employment of a knowledgeable specialist in direct contact with the physical work environment.

Whatever the historic reason for the development of functional structures of organization, the fact stands that they are predominant in industry today and that as a management system, today's functional organization structures represent an anachronism in today's information technology. All current efforts in the development of so-called management information systems—an unfortunate misnomer for an effort to establish new management systems in keeping with today's information technology—are continuously running into passive or active resistance based on signal reactions which emanate from the "territorial instincts" of functionally oriented organizational units.

Faced by this dilemma, many top managements of large businesses have chosen an easy way out. If there is a new job to be done in the development of coordinated companywide comprehensive plans, goals, and objectives, this is a new management function to require appropriate staffing. Therefore, a director of corporate planning or a director of long-range planning is named and given the thankless job of changing a management system in which all the participants don't want any real change. Hence, such stories as "The Short, Happy Life of the Long-Range Planner" as it appeared in the January 1967 issue of *Dun's Review*.

Many so-established, new long-range planning functions did not recognize or acknowledge the true nature of their assignments and preferred to do a politically reasonable job under the circumstances. Those circumstances clearly indicated that a broader view of the business planning process could be taken to mean a broader scope of activity for the financial function. Many articles in *Controllers' Magazine* express this point of view. Finance has traditionally been the function which did include the assembly of a comprehensive view of the entire business.

PLAN AS EXTENSION OF BUDGET

Under those conditions, it is most inviting to make the planning process an extension of the budgeting process. Supposing a company had a one-year budget and it is felt that there is a need for a longer-range view; then the first step is to extend the budgetary period to two years. Since the budgetary procedures and the personnel engaged in them are well established, this expansion of the budgetary period does not require a change in technique or methodology. At best, forms have to be redesigned for additional columns to provide spaces into which additional quantitative data have to be inserted on worksheets and report formats. At the same time, primary assumptions such as forecasts of business volume, payroll criteria, vacation and holiday policies would have to be issued for two years rather than just the immediate year ahead.

Should a need be felt for further long-range planning, say five years out, it is easy to visualize and call for a further extension of the budgetary period. Since the personnel who are assigned the job of preparing the data for the five-year plan are the same as those who prepare the two- or one-year budgets, five-year planning in fact becomes a perpetuation of budgetary thinking into a five-year time scale. The input requirements and data definitions as well as output documents stay the same. As a matter of fact, controllers may take the position that long-range programs and projects which have not yet been given a full financial evaluation and approval (funded only in development) should not be included in the five-year plan because "no reliable information" is available as yet. At most, these uncertain projects might be treated as an addendum in the form of an overlay over the profit and loss statement, balance sheet, and cash flow based on "reliable projection of current business and near future projects which had been fully evaluated."

It usually takes some time in negotiations and discussions until it will be accepted that a five year plan would have to include all projects and programs under consideration within these five years. At this point, there must be agreement that the long-range plan will contain information at substantially different levels of accuracy or reliability. It also will become apparent that long-range objectives place new demands on the resources of the business and call for some method of assigning priorities based on relative importance in the context of a going business.

In keeping with the leading role which the financial function plays in the traditional planning process, the responsibility for evaluating priorities is usually assigned to the pricing department. Of course, the rules and procedures for pricing are extremely detailed, as they should be, and the evaluation process is in trouble because such detailed information about long-range undertakings simply is not available. Also, pricing deals with individual products or groups of products by themselves, rather than in the context of a going business.

It stands to reason, that the demands on the functional planners issued by the financial planners for such detailed long-range planning information and the workload generated for all of them in preparing and consolidating these tremendous volumes of data do not make for the popularity of long-range planning. Justifiably, the people involved in this type of planning process question the validity of some of the data they are thus forced to generate, often against their better judgment.

TIMING AND CONSISTENCY

Apart from these objectives as to content, there is also the difficulty that this process requires such a lengthy time cycle. From the day the primary assumptions for the long-range plan (consisting of a definition of products and related forecasts in terms of sales, billings, and production demand) to the day when all departments and functions have submitted their respective long-range operating plans, several months have passed. Until it is finally possible to look at a consolidated income and expense statement for this first set of input assumptions, several of them have become outdated either by more recent business transactions or by changes in competitive or general economic conditions. Under those circumstances, it would be sheer co-incidence if the first consolidated statement of such a plan satisfied the long-range growth and profitability objectives of the business. As changes in input assumptions have to be made, all functional plans have to be adjusted accordingly. Considering the workload involved and the level of detail to which these functional plans have to be carried, such adjustments become a monstrous job. Of course, two or three such iterations—necessary because of the question of priority of competing projects some of which would have to be eliminated in order to satisfy profitability constraints —make the internal consistency of the entire plan more and more tenuous. After the original deadline for the preparation of "the" long-range plan has passed and several extensions have been given and used up, the iterations become more and more hectic. Management, as it should, continues to ask questions about alternatives—questions which result in a substantial effort to adjust planning data and maintain internal con-sistency at the same time. This creates not only a serious morale problem for those charged with the responsibility of generating planning data, but on occasion, it may even raise questions of ethics. When time for making changes is running out, when only summary data are adjusted on the basis of highly aggregated factors, and when the backup data no longer support the summaries, the system has factually broken down, but the breakdown does not show.

Thus the purpose of planning is defeated. Planning is supposed to facilitate the identification of business problems and their evaluation by management for appropriate action. Under time pressure, more often than not, particularly complex problems are pushed aside for consideration at a later date. This later date often does not materialize until a condition has become critical.

Anyone who has ploughed through several planning cycles under these traditional methods, will agree that some new way has to be found to furnish management with the information it needs to establish planned goals. The problem is not lack of information, but lack of a system for the specific purpose of processing information about alternate strategies with respect to existing products, planned new products, and long-range projects. Of course, the design of such a system would require the sifting of all possibly available information for what was really needed in strategic long-range planning. Since this information is subject to frequent modification, it should not be more voluminous than could be digested and effectively processed and reprocessed by the responsible managers or planners.

In order to gain the proper perspective for the information which such a planning data system would have to process, let us review typical ingredients and time schedules in the preparation of a comprehensive plan.

PLANNING INFORMATION

The packages of information which are prepared in the planning process—in the functional departments where the respective competence resides—consist of narrative text and numeric data. It is, of course, not possible to quantify all aspects of the process which leads to the determination of planned goals, but it stands to reason that only those aspects which are capable of quantification can be considered as valid input and output. Otherwise it is impossible to measure accomplishments against plan.

Quantification can be carried to excess, and there exists an innate resistance against quantification where it might run contrary to cherished management prerogatives or idiosyncrasies. This will be discussed later at length in the chapter on socioeconomic problems. As for now, let us include the descriptive titles and definitions of specific line items of quantitative data as part of the qualitative or narrative portion of planning information and restrict the term "quantitative" to refer to the actual numbers. In this way it will become apparent that a great deal of planning information, which might otherwise be considered quantitative, is really first of all qualitative, descriptive, and definitional, certainly until such time as the explicit quantification is added to it. For example, an income and expense statement format—without numbers—should be considered qualitative planning data; and after the numbers have been filled in, the resulting document should not be lumped into the category of quantitative information in its entirety. Instead, the conceptual difference between the form, including titles and line item descriptions, as qualitative data and only the numbers themselves as quantitative information, should be retained.

With this distinction between qualitative and quantitative planning information, the reader is asked to imagine some of the line item descriptions and numeric expressions which are implied in the following listing of typical planning information.

(1) **Key company policies**

These refer to broad-gauged business concepts such as mission and public image; growth, profitability, and pricing principles; organizational philosophy; labor relation and employment practices, such as wage and salary levels, benefits; etc.

(2) **General economic conditions**

These reflect the assumed state of the economy and, depending upon the scope of the business, may involve international, national, or regional factors in one or several industries and related government policies.

(3) **Product plans**

These deal with the specific products or services which the business will market, some old, some new. An assessment of the old and potential new products of the current competition must, of course, be taken into account, as well as the possible market entry of substitute products and new competitors.

(4) **Research and development programs**

This involves identification of those R&D efforts which directly support the product plans. The interconnection may be sheer hopes or specific commitments for marketable products based on design specifications furnished by market analysis. The coordination of the R&D efforts with the product plans is usually assigned to a Product Planning Department. Mergers or acquisitions may be included here as alternatives to internal development.

(5) **Forecasts of future business volume**

These represent a suitable measure of turnover by major product and service category within customer grouping. Industry potential, industry sales and the company's share, price levels and demand elasticity assumptions must be considered at least intuitively. Because of the critical importance of these forecasts in the planning process, management usually reviews them before the corresponding functional and departmental plans have been developed. Although this review of sales or revenues tells nothing about the corresponding net earnings, cash flow and return on investment, some bargaining about the forecast data takes place before they are approved.

(6) **Departmental plans**

These are based on the approved forecasts per (5) and are mostly expressed in financial terms with some (often separately developed) data on manpower, perhaps by major skill category; and also on facilities, such as space and capital equipment, inventories and other physical characteristics, or programs for action considered of importance in the particular planning cycle. All the protectionism of standard budgetary practices goes into effect at this stage.

(7) **Functional plans**

These are arrived at by consolidation of the departmental plans within each business function as required for the comprehensive business plan. This includes the reconciliation of departmental plans with implied or expressed functional objectives, such as lower unit cost of manufacture or lower selling expense in percent of revenue.

(8) **Financial summaries**

This involves the consolidation of the detailed departmental and functional plans into the customary financial statements. It includes a great deal of checking and questioning of the validity of all the data received for consolidation. Generally accepted accounting principles govern this preplanning audit.

Each of these major groupings of information for planning in turn consists of a substantial number of subsidiary data. Depending upon the size of the business and its organizational structure, these subsidiary data are either generated internally or taken from sources outside the company. For instance, a forecast of general economic conditions (item 1 above) could be developed by a department of economics within the company. In this case the many and different forecasts of general economic conditions developed by the government or the various business research associations like National Industrial Conference Board, McGraw-Hill, etc. furnish input to the task of generating a special forecast of general economic conditions for the company. On the other hand, if no company economist is available to do this job of evaluating different projections of general economic conditions, management either has to perform this analytical job themselves or accept one of the available outside forecasts as is.

Similar conditions prevail for the forecast of industry and company products (item 2 above). Here we may be faced with organizational structures in which product managers, market research personnel, and R&D management all have to work together in order to arrive at a mutually acceptable product strategy and related projections of business volumes.

Of course, the development of detailed plans for each department and function of the business (items 6 and 7) breaks down into a vast array of subsidiary tasks. Again, depending upon the size of the business, various levels of departmental management may become involved in development of the detailed plans, which in turn result in intermediate review and approval proceedings. Therefore, one can see the emergence of additional planning cycles, as the consolidation of these departmental sections within a function requires modification at the functional management level before the functional plan is completed and ready for incorporation into the overall divisional or corporate plan.

PLANNING—BARGAINING

With the above information in hand, the real planning and bargaining about goals to be accomplished at the corporate, divisional, functional, departmental, and operational level is ready to get under way.

(9) **Comprehensive view of the future**

This calls for the condensation of functional planning statistics and narratives into a summary package suitable for management review. It involves the careful selection of significant information from a large body of detailed data and requires considerable value judgment on the part of those who carry out this critical planning task. Therefore, it is quite important that the organizational unit charged with this responsibility be as free as possible from vested interest which might tend to introduce biased points of view. It is perhaps for this reason that many companies have assigned this job to a staff group reporting directly to top management, rather than within any of the established business functions.

(10) **Approval of a comprehensive business plan**

This is a task for top-level management. It is at this juncture that planning, decision making, and action have their closest interplay. Depending upon the projected results per (9), changes in the basic assumptions (1) through (5), the departmental plans (6) and (7), and the financial summarizations (8) are negotiated or forced in order to bring the results in line with the short- and long-range objectives of the business.

(11) **Publication of the official plan**

This requires the preparation of an internally consistent document containing approved summary data and supporting detail for publication to the various levels of management within the business. The implicit expectation is that the plan will be absorbed (read and understood) and used as a guide for action.

THE TIME BIND

The steps from key policies to approved forecasts of business volume may take some four weeks, depending upon the complexity of the business. The translation of the approved forecasts into detailed departmental and functional plans may take another eight weeks. Without any iterations, these seven steps alone may take about 12 weeks. The financial consolidation and preplanning review will take at least another week. A few days have to be given to those who prepare the comprehensive view for management.

The bargaining and evaluating of alternatives which follow, i.e. the substantive planning requiring changes in both the forecasts and the various departmental plans, may take another four to eight weeks. The maintenance of internal consistency in the ensuing maze of summary and subsidiary planning data is an absolute nightmare.

As a matter of fact, this process comes to a temporary conclusion only because someone with sufficient authority insists on a deadline for a completed plan.

If this is the reality of business planning, *a four- to six-month cycle with a strong tendency to perpetuate itself,* it seems reasonable to treat business planning as a continuous process rather than a periodic project, at the completion of which a sigh of relief is heard in the corridors of divisional and corporate headquarters.

In order to give proper attention to the subsidiary tasks, their relationship to the intermediate totals, and the consolidation of these intermediate totals into a divisional or corporate plan, as well as the various steps of review and approval, together with the flow of information between operating departments, more recently PERT (Program Evaluation and Review Technique) has been employed for scheduling and costing of the planning process. However, the PERT analysis only identifies and interrelates tasks. It does not address itself to the question of how these tasks are to be accomplished. It does not specify the logic which is to be used in the preparation of these planning data and which is so important for proper evaluation of the adequacy of such plans. Therefore, the general statement that "long-range plans shall be realistic, straightforward, and sufficiently comprehensive as to facilitate implementation" * would have to be broken down into a set of specifications with respect to content, sources, and economic logic that satisfy the stated qualifications.

---

* Typical planning policy statement in an Organization Manual.

4

The Planner's Role

Next let us take a look at the staff planner and the various schools of thought about his role in this process. Of course, every planner would cast himself first of all in a coordinating role. But beyond this, here are four suggested acting styles by which the reader may classify the planners with whom he has come in contact.

(1) *The growth addict or gap filler* is really a salesman and promoter of business planning, and in some companies he does all that can be done at least for the time being. He postulates growth objectives and identifies gaps to stimulate action, sometimes resulting in significant changes, even innovations. His approach is intuitive and impulsive. He will pay lip service to any of the fashionable analytical techniques if they are useful as sales promotion gimmicks, but he shies away from systematic application, since the required discipline would frustrate him. After a time this type of planner is likely to run out of steam.

(2) *The list maker and flow charter* proposes to put some substance and order into the planning process by specifying what to do and when, while avoiding an answer to the question of how to do it. He will present you with instructions like:

> Using estimated material costs, estimated labor, and overhead rates, compute estimated cost to sales . . .
>
> Prepare and submit expected total requirements for floor space and requirements for additional equipment, classified by type of proposed utilization . . .
>
> Prepare schedule for recruitment of personnel classified by skill and by type of requirement . . .
>
> Determine captial investment and compute return on investment and net income on sales . . .
>
> Prepare a formal financial statement to include source and application of funds, balance sheets, statement of income . . .

These planning instructions, together with a timetable or flow chart, are then sent out, preferably with a letter of transmittal signed by a powerful figure in the organization, to divisional, functional, and perhaps departmental managers, and the ball game begins. When challenged about the resulting confusion and frustration, as well as the questionable impact on decision making or action, this type of planner will refer you to the Eisenhower adage, "Plans are nothing; planning is everything." This insufficient rationale for a rather expensive way to massage ideas without follow-up tends to discredit planning in general and makes it ready for the cost reduction axe. The chief flaw in attitude and approach of the list maker and flow charter rests with his belief that in planning nothing is impossible if you don't have to do it yourself.

(3) In contrast, *The parametric thinker and model builder* is a serious do-it-yourself fellow. He will contribute to the planning process at all levels of management. He will concentrate on precise formulations of specific partial business problems. For instance, he might take five out of 100 products and do a detailed analysis of the significant parameters which describe the dynamics of these five products. If he is lucky—or clever in his selection—he can prove a reasonable fit between the parametric model and the actual time series of pertinent data such as sales volume, manpower requirements, manufacturing workloads, and cost. After he has proven the conceptual validity of such partial analysis, he claims with a wave of the hand that the rest is arithmetic. Which means we now need to collect the same detailed data for the other 95 products, feed them into the analytical model, and then add up the results. This approach often fails to solve the problem of covariation between the parameters of different sets of products. It also fails to face up to the logistic problem of source data, although it may have taken this planner many weeks to extract and clean up the data for his shining example.

Sometimes the parametric thinker will tackle a model of an entire business, a so-called corporate model. For practical reasons such a model must be highly aggregated, with abstract inputs for which source data can be obtained only by extensive research or statistical inference. Communications between model and decision makers become strained, often beyond repair. The chief flaw in the model builder's approach to business planning lies in his implicit belief that planning is primarily an analytical and computational problem. In other words, if he had all the data he needed, the answers would become self-evident. He presumes maximization or optimization in business environments to be as deterministic or probabilistic as in physical environments. Carried to its ultimate absurdity, this approach would replace management by a random number generator. Unfortunately this belief has many followers, some naïve, some quite sophisticated. It is further popularized by computopian science fiction.

While parametric thinking and model building can and do make important contributions in helping to solve certain partial business problems, for comprehensive business planning they do not measure up to the high-flying claims often made by their proponents.

(4) Finally, *the systems architect* tries to break away from the sequential and partial approach to business planning. He tries to represent the planning problem as a network of interrelated, simultaneous propositions. In this he does not differ from the model builder. He also tries to specify and define all the relevant decision variables. In this he does not differ from the list maker and parametric thinker. However, he recognizes that planning is primarily a bargaining process backed by more or less valid analytical argumentation (ideology of vested interests). He does not participate in the eternal search for an exhaustive set of quantifiable elements for decision making. Instead he will concentrate on specifying what can and should be quantified and on processing this data logically, consistently, quickly, and neatly. The resulting system may, of course, include formulations which would also qualify as analytical models, but they are subroutines attached on a "where feasible" basis.

By designing a system or a network of systems to take over the mundane clerical work involved in planning, this type of planner hopes to give the managers more time to deal with matters involving value judgments, motivations, agreements, and commitments.

Of course, there are no final answers and perfect solutions. Critics are accusing the systems architect of believing that, "Data is nothing, data processing is everything." Nevertheless, I submit that, in the long run, the business planner's most significant contribution to management lies in the creation, maintenance, and continued improvement of a system through which plans can be developed, analyzed, and updated.

The subsequent sections of this book describe the architecture of such a system. In reviewing and judging its merits, the reader is asked to keep in mind that the objective of the system is to assist management in the difficult task of generating goals for the entire business and in a way that achievements can be tracked and measured.

It is well to point out again that not all aspects of the decision-making process are quantifiable. Also, no system can possibly cover all the quantifiable elements. However, there is a need for something between the manual or computerized budgeting and accounting system and the "back-of-the-envelope" processing of planning data.

An illustration of the continuous problem of arriving at an acceptable set of primary planning assumptions follows. It describes in logbook form the events during 12 working days in an effort to quantify a minor revision in forecast. These events are typical for any planning system which is structured and governed by budgetary thinking. Most of the participants in these events would be in agreement that planning and budgeting deal with different managerial problems and require separate systems. But the boundaries of functional organizations and the lack of management's interest in procedural questions makes the systems architect's role in introducing a new and different approach quite challenging.

Long-Range Planning—Logbook

Reference: Submission of Primary Input Data (Volumes and Prices) Long-Range Plan from 4/18 to 5/3 (12 working days).

Participants:

Mr. A—Mgr. Long-Range Planning
Mr. B—Mgr. Market Research
Mr. C—Mgr. Sales Records
Mr. D—Mgr. Market Requirements
Mr. E—Long-Range Planning Representative (Sales)
Mr. F—Long-Range Planning Representative (Manufacturing)
Mr. G—Mgr. Market Planning Product Line Y
Mr. H—Market Research Analyst, Product Line Y
Mr. I—Profit Planning Manager
Mr. J—Assistant to Mgr. Market Planning Product Line Y
Mr. K—Long-Range Planning Representative (Financial)
Mr. L—Financial Planning Representative
Mr. M—Assistant General Manager
Mr. N—Manager Financial Planning

4/18	12:00 Noon	Mr. A requests from Mr. B new forecasts in keeping with the latest thinking concerning the pending revision of the current Budget. Mr. B completes his sales forecast by 5:00 P.M. that day. Messrs. C and D were then to provide billings and production demand in keeping with the new forecast.
4/19	5:00 P.M.	Billings and production demand have not yet been furnished. Mr. A phones Mr. C who advises that the data is now available, whereupon Mr. E goes to Mr. C's office for the information. However, Mr. E finds it to be incomplete in that product billings were not given for two out of the required eight years. Mr. C advises that he will insert this data and provide the completed forecasts first thing Monday morning.
4/22	3:00 P.M.	Mr. C returns the forecast with sales and billing information and Mr. F forwards this data to Mr. D in order that he may develop the production demand.
4/23	5:00 P.M.	Production demand given to Mr. F who reviews it and discovers four major inconsistencies.
4/24	9:30 A.M.	Mr. F returns the sales and billing forecast and the production demand schedule to Mr. D and poses questions concerning above inconsistencies.

| 4/24 | 2:00 P.M. | Forecast and production demand have not yet been completed. Mr. E asks Mr. D about status. He advises that he was trying to get necessary information from Mr. G. Mr. E phones Mr. G, but is unable to reach him. Leaves word for Mr. G to return call. |

4/24   4:00 P.M.   Mr. C advises that the sales and billing forecasts for two months of current year are to be changed and provides the new data. However, the long-range years now require updating in keeping with the new current-year assumptions. It also appears that some average prices require updating inasmuch as a review of sales for the current year indicates the following: rental price X should be $... (1.3 percent) lower; purchase price X about $... (.8 percent) lower; rental price Y should be approximately $... (1.1 percent) lower while the purchase price of Y should be some $... (2.2 percent) higher. Mr. E requests new average price assumptions from Mr. B but it isn't clear at this point as to who should provide this input. Mr. B advises that at a recent meeting, it was decided that Financial Planning would establish average prices on product X based on forecast by market section which he would provide. He assumes the same approach would be used on product line Y. In keeping with this approach, he will have Mr. H forecast line Y by model numbers which will enable Financial to address themselves to the question of how different models with their attachments will affect the average price computations.

4/24   5:15 P.M.   Mr. D returns production demand and sales billing forecasts. He has received rationale from Mr. G concerning Mr. F's questions of inconsistencies.
However, the question of production demand for product Z is still unresolved.

4/25   2:00 P.M.   Mr. E receives forecast for product Z for long-range years, however, is still waiting for average prices of product Y.

4/25   5:00 P.M   Mr. H has computed an average price assumption for product Y which differs by $... (about 8 percent) from the price furnished by Mr. L.

4/26   9:30 A.M.   Mr. B advises Financial will develop average price for Y equipment from forecast showing marketed mix of attachments. Mr. H and Mr. I to confer to develop these prices.

4/26   3:15 P.M.   Messrs. A, K, E, and I in discussion re:
derivation of average prices on Y equipment—concept of using managerial judgment for estimate in the long-range years. Mr. I advises Financial would not approve. He will continue with Mr. H to obtain detailed projections.

4/26   4:45 P.M.   Received average prices for product Y for all plan years (problem of production demand still to be resolved). Mr. F advises Mr. J that data on sales of attachments are available from Mr. H.

4/29   9:30 A.M.   Mr. F delivered forecasts to Mr. J for production demand of Y equipment. This was returned to Mr. F at 3:30 P.M. the same day. However, there are inconsistencies. Mr. F points out to Mr. J and reminds him that he had requested these be looked at. Mr. J will review with Mr. G and advise.

4/29   4:30 P.M.   Forecast for entire product line comes off computer, but shows error for last year. Mr. E. and Mr. K review the input data to determine the cause of the error and discover that two minor subsidiary revenue-producing activities are incorrectly entered. Mr. E questioned Mr. C concerning these items and is advised that with all the rush he simply had forgotten to make the corrections. As Mr. E and Mr. K compare corrected forecast with budget data prepared and distributed by Financial Planning dated April 23, they discover that the proposed revision of budget shows a change in gross income from the original budget. Since it had been decided to develop a long-range plan that dovetailed with the budget, the question arises how to adjust for this recent budget change. Mr. E and Mr. K looking at composition of revenue. Will determine first thing in A.M. how Financial proposes to handle this.

4/30   9:30 A.M.   Mr. K obtained data from Mr. L re product line revenue and volumes. Mr. E and Mr. K reviewing discover differences in three line items.

4/30   10:30 A.M.   Mr. E and Mr. K questioned Mr. C re these differences. Upon investigation Mr. C advised billings had been given in error. However, this does not answer the whole question as to the difference in the data which Divisional Planning and Financial Planning are using. Mr. C contacts Mr. L and it turns out that Financial was using incorrect data also. Question now is how will Financial handle this problem. The Controller will have to resolve. Further questions raised by Mr. E. and Mr. K concerned average prices for two items (major products). Continued question—What to do about average price assumptions in long-range years?

4/30   12:00 Noon   Mr. A setting up 4:00 P.M. meeting with Messrs. C, B, L, E, and M to discuss the question of average prices for the next five years.
Mr. L advises Mr. A that last year's price for product X given to Mr. K that morning was in error. The correct price should be $. . . (3.1 percent) lower. The other prices will be discussed at the 4:00 P.M. meeting.

4/30   4:00 P.M.   Meeting in Mr. A's office with parties indicated above. Decision was made to extend product Y prices through the long-range years as it was the consensus that the price would go no lower than that. Concerning product Z price, Market Research will give Mr. L sales by market sector and he will compute a composite of current list prices. That price will be extended for long-range years on the assumption that the product mix will shift, which will increase the average price by approximately 10 percent over the next five years. Similarly, the product X price will show a small advance as proportionately a greater percentage will be sold to commercial no-discount users. Mr. L will advise when he has developed the new price assumptions.

5/1   9:00 A.M.   Mr. C advises the forecast should be changed for three major items. This data was communicated to Mr. L together with sales by market sector for use in his price calculations.

5/1   1:00 P.M.   New prices furnished by Mr. L to Mr. E. Mr. E, Mr. L, and Mr. B agree on prices for long-range years in keeping with the decisions made in the 4:00 P.M. meeting of yesterday. Forecast is now ready for processing as soon as computer time is available.

5/1	3:00 P.M.	Computer available. First view run and copy furnished to Mr. M (Assistant General Manager).
5/1	5:30 P.M.	Mr. C advises he received phone call from Mr. M: current year billings for product Z to be changed upward. Mr. C inquired about the following years and was told that Mr. M would advise the first thing in the morning, whereupon Mr. C will furnish the data to Long-Range Planning.
5/2	9:30 A.M.	Mr. C in closed door meeting, unable to reach in person or by phone. Waiting for new input data. Mr. A tried to reach Mr. M but was unable to get him.
5/2	11:00 A.M.	Current year data available but no data for future of product Z. Mr. C has phone call in to Mr. M at Washington, D. C. waiting an answer.
5/2	2:30 P.M.	Mr. C finally reaches Mr. M in Washington. Was told to keep forecast Z as in first view. Complete forecast now available for run of second view.
5/2	4:00 P.M.	View two completed. All primary inputs now OK.
5/3	3:00 P.M.	Preliminary analysis of view two highlighting operational changes per revised forecasts. Completed and delivered to Messrs. A, N, and I for review.

OPERATIONS RESEARCH

Linear programming, multiple regression analysis, queuing and game theory, and other O. R. techniques are often mentioned as important tools for business planning. Should O. R. capabilities be considered as an integral part of a planning data system? The writer's answer is a skeptical maybe, but certainly not in the initial stages of development. Here are some of the reasons:

(1) O. R. techniques require large volumes of suitably organized data. Such are usually not available. The development of a planning data system should not be deferred pending the availability of an O. R. data base.

(2) There is sufficient doubt in the validity of making projections on the basis of past trends only. Most businessmen remember various examples to support this doubt, some having led to costly, erroneous decisions.

(3) Optimization models restrict managers and planners from participating in the planning process. Unless they have the ability to inject their opinions and managerial judgment in a way that would be meaningful to them, they will not identify with the plan, approve of it, and feel committed to it.

Operations research usually deals with physical reality, such as petroleum refining, warehouse locating, machine loading, etc. The planned goals of a business organization represent an emotional reality, much of which is beyond the reach of quantification suitable for operations research techniques.

In the process of setting planned goals which are capable of achievement, the emphasis lies on judgment and evaluation about what is possible, not by mathematical proof, but in the minds of those who are responsible for the action.

It would appear that operations research thinking needs to be applied first of all in structuring the transaction data system so that it becomes a more fruitful field for O. R. techniques. Then, better insight into the dynamics of current and past operations will, no doubt, lead to better judgment in the setting of achievable goals for the future.

GAMING

Instead of the eternal search for economic truth, more might be gained by expanding on the game playing aspects of originating and achieving planned goals.

The American Management Association and others have been able to arouse considerable interest in the use of management games for training purposes. In our terminology these games simulate conditions at the industry level (planning for whom!). The participants are not given the logic specifications which relate company data to industry data, nor are they allowed to make their own explicit assumptions about the factors and coefficients which determine the computations of industry data from company inputs. If these programs were expanded to accept alternate assumptions about the industry as well as the companies, they would approach an industry planning system. Each management team within the industry could then play its own game independently at the industry level and test various assumptions and their probable meaning for their own company. Of course, we must remember that management games were designed to study management behavior in the decision environment, not to facilitate industry planning, i.e. decision making itself.

As to systems which facilitate business planning, I am confident that considerable interest can be elicited when managers are given the opportunity to play their own game of business planning by computer. Such a system for business gaming by level of management within a medium or large-scale organization seems to be the most appropriate vehicle for improving the decision-making process about planned goals and their achievability . . . provided:

(a)   the planning logic makes managerial sense
(b)   the system is put to work by managers.

Proviso (a) is the assignment of the planner. He determines the system's quality and workmanship. Proviso (b) is the manager's job. He determines the future of the business. This is his ultimate responsibility which cannot be delegated.

5

Generating Planning Data

The previous chapters described the process through which management originates planned goals in terms of what to do. This conceptual outline of the task at hand must now be translated into operational terms, i.e. into specifications of how to do it, of jobs that have to be carried out in order to make this process meaningful and workable.

Obviously, the job of originating planned goals, in other words, the job of developing a plan, is a formidable effort in generating information. The problem of generating information is closely related to the problem of processing information, but it seems important to maintain the distinction between the two. While data-processing methods and technology are a constraining factor in the process of generating planning data, there are a number of distinct characteristics which warrant a separate discussion of the data-generating problem. Irrespective of the data-processing methods employed, there are three identifiable stages in the development or generation of planning data.

HISTORY AND STATUS

There is no need to add here to the ample literature on accounting and control systems. It is important, however, to understand the characteristics of the data in these systems. All information on the state of affairs of a business, so-called actual data about current and past events, is made up of transaction data. This data is generated as a by-product of operations. As invoices are sent out, as orders are received, as payroll checks are issued, records of the respective transactions are produced and recorded in suitably organized files. Thousands of data originators in hundreds of locations are busy at this task every day. These files then furnish the data base for extensive analysis and consolidation in the traditional control reports to management. In fact, the annual report of a corporation represents the highest level of aggregated transaction data.

Some of this analytical work on the transaction data files may have relevance for planning purposes. In a sense, it may be identified as the first step in creating suitable planning data for use in establishing goals for the future. However, more often than not, there are flaws: the information in the transaction data file may not be relevant, may be incomplete, may be hard to get at, etc. Usually there is quite some work to be done in retrieval, analysis, cleaning up, and filling in to make transaction data suitable for planning purposes. This work requires imagination, interpretation, judgment, and analytical intelligence. While modern mathematical methods, such as statistical inference or multiple regression analysis are available as aids to the planner, their application is by no means an automatic or routine job.

Many specialists in information technology fail to see this point. They continue to proceed on the assumption that planning data could be entered into or generated within a transaction data system and thereafter be processed in the same way as regular transaction data. Perhaps the fundamental difference between transaction and planning data will become more apparent when we proceed to the next stage.

FORECASTING

After we have generated a suitable planning data base—either transferred from a supposedly automatic retrieval and analysis procedure within the transaction data system or specifically entered as primary planning data from a combination of mechanical and manual procedures under human control—we enter the second stage. We now want to project into the future. The moment we leave the comparatively sound and reliable footing of transaction data, of information about actual events whose authenticity can be audited, we enter the area of conjectural information whose soundness and reliability is always subject to question.

In making projections there are really only two methods available: extrapolation of trends and projection of ratios.

TREND EXTRAPOLATION

A great many sophisticated methods for the extrapolation of time series have been developed in the past 30 years, especially in connection with business cycle analysis. From the point of view of originating planned goals within a given business organization, the use of these sophisticated techniques is often irrelevant. Whether the extrapolation of a time series is accomplished by using a straight edge with data plotted on linear graph paper or by using multiple regression analysis and high order mathematical curve fitting may have some relevance to the professional on the job, but acceptance of the resulting forecast as a planned goal is, in the end, a decision subject to managerial judgment.

RATIO PROJECTION

Here we deal with the perpetuation of meaningful relationships between different time series. This technique is usually employed as a test of reasonableness for the extrapolation of time series, or, in model building, as a means of deriving subsidiary time series. In the latter context these structural relationships are referred to as parameters or coefficients of correlation. In everyday business language the projected consistency of such ratios is based on reasoning like this: in the last three years, marketing expense has been around 17 percent of gross income; therefore we will assume that for the next five years marketing expense will continue to be 17 percent of gross income. Of course, nonlinear relationships, recognizing fixed and variable portions of marketing expense may be taken into consideration, thus lowering the percentage to gross income when gross income expands and, vice versa, raising the percentage when gross income contracts. Again the degree of sophistication in determining the structural framework, as well as the parameters or ratios themselves, can only be effective to the degree that management accepts the so-calculated forecasts as planned goals to be accomplished.

Both extrapolation and projection suffer from a methodological flaw. Almost by definition, such forecasts run counter to the objectives and goals that an aggressive management is really interested in. They are based on the implicit assumption that the causal system will remain stable during the time periods forecast. They represent the historic periods from which the factors have been derived.

In contrast, an aggressive management is interested in changing the causal system. At best, management might become convinced that these sophisticated forecasting methods furnish an indication of the boundaries for action, of certain constraints, or a picture of what might happen if the organization were left to its own momentum.

In reality, however, the task of originating planned goals for action within the organization does require a further stage, and this is the most important and significant stage in the planning-bargaining process.

SIMULATION

The term "simulation" as it is meant here is the broad area of answering "what if" questions. It involves the testing of changes in the causal system, such as the change in factors which govern the extrapolation of time series or the projection of ratios. It is in this area where management judgment, motivation, speculation, and risk taking enter the scene and are first expressed as a game-playing proposition.

Unfortunately the rules of this game are not deterministic, a fact which is not always well understood by the players. Simulation of physical systems, such as a refinery, an airplane in flight, a warehouse distribution network, or a shipping line is deterministic. The physical simulation model is capable of verification. In contrast, the business decision model is not. At best, a simulation exercise in business may produce believable information, but it can never be proven right by subsequent real events. A rather important reason for this nondeterministic character of business simulation models may be the fact that the players are not only players, but also actors. Their influence on the outcome of the simulated proposition is significant and meaningful.

This characteristic of business simulations is the key for a proper appreciation of how management originates and achieves planned goals. It also plays a decisive role in shaping the structure of a planning data system.

The popular management games which are offered as educational tools for management development avoid the open-ended character of real business decisions in two ways: First: they restrict the number of players; second, they produce results via a set of sufficiently complicated economic rules. No player is supposed to be able to understand, much less to affect these rules. Hence, they provide a deterministic feedback mechanism. Everybody who has played the management game more than once will have experienced an urge to decipher the mechanism rather than play the game. It is human nature, especially when the human is conditioned to scientific inquiry, not to take any deterministic situation, however complex, for granted and to explore the causality of it.

At this point the reader should search his mind and heart as to what he believes to be the state of reality in business and economic affairs: is it deterministic, hence predictable, or not—and to what degree? This is a philosophical point, but it has important implications for planned goals and what they mean to management.

Rather than expanding on the philosophy, it is suggested that for the present, the degree of predictability in business is so low as to make deterministic approaches unrealistic and misleading.

The insatiable appetite of management for "what if" speculations when working on the establishment of "achievable," "realistic," and "challenging" goals supports this suggestion. As a matter of fact, this type of information is the most typical of the planning data which have to be entered and processed in a planning data system. The most peculiar characteristic of this planning data is its viability, its continual change, both in terms of the logic with which the data is used and the actual numbers themselves.

Two types of "what if" questions may be identified, each dealing with a different kind of uncertainty.

First there is doubt about the correctness of a given set of agreed upon plans: are they realistic, achievable, challenging etc.? In an attempt to overcome this doubt, management often plunges into tremendous amounts of details. However, even with all the t's crossed and i's dotted the doubt cannot be eradicated. It is the very nature of goal setting that their achievement remain uncertain, because the future is uncertain.

Second, there is doubt about the direction embodied in a given set of plans: is it the best among possible options, will achievement be in keeping with the long-run success of the organization, have all significant forces and factors been properly considered and weighed?

This second type of uncertainty is more bothersome and cannot be compensated for by plunging into detail. Even a perfectly laid plan, correct in the sense of achievability, may be leading an organization into troubled waters. A management team dedicated to pragmatism in solving problems will have a great deal of conceptual difficulties with this second type of uncertainty. As Gunnar Myrdal[1] points out: "American management is by its past successes with pragmatic approaches rather uneasy, if not inept, in its reaction to this planning issue. The origination of planned goals requires involvement in both aspects of uncertainty: the development of credible alternatives and the conscious selection of one as a plan for action. This is true not only with regard to the substance of a plan, but also the procedure through which the plan is being developed."

SELECTION

In the maze of potential information for planning, the number of possible combinations is practically unlimited. Therefore, some selection must take place—and the selection of relevant planning logic and data is a tricky business. In fact development of an information system for processing planning data is nothing more than specifying and defining its own information structure and content. Unfortunately,

---

[1] Gunnar Myrdal, *Challenge to Affluence*, Random House, Inc., 1963, 4th printing, Chapter 6: Long-Range Economic Planning.

the structure and self-perpetuating content of a transaction data system is not suitable for the planning data environment.

A transaction data system relies on a steady stream of input data generated as a by-product of operations. Once data are entered in the system, they do not change. Therefore, the logic to be used in analysis and consolidation of transaction data may be easily varied. The information flow proceeds in only one direction: from the transaction record detail to the next higher level aggregation, and from there upwards to higher levels of consolidation, until finally summary data similar to a corporation's annual report are reached. The audit trail flows complete and uninterrupted "from the bottom up."

A planning data system must accept inputs at different levels of aggregation. Consolidation logic has only limited application. At one time, summary data have to be exploded into subsidiary detail and at another time subsidiary data have to be re-aggregated in order to test their validity at the summary level. In addition, most of the input data are subject to negotiation between different levels of management, as well as between different managers at the same level.

DATA BANKS

Many systems engineers, when approaching a business planning system, tend to concentrate on setting up general data files with ingenious coding schemes to handle any and all possible document generation, data retrieval, and analysis, including interesting graphic displays on CRT terminals. The implied assumption is that once the planning data are under wraps, the job is done. This, as we pointed out above, is quite understandable because it is true for transaction data systems, in which the basic data are not subject to change.

In transaction data systems, the main problems are suitable classification or coding structures, indexing of immense data banks, and speed of information retrieval either for the purpose of summarization and display or in response to random inquiries. The major objective is to represent "what is."

Conversely, in planning, the major objective is to represent "what if." Therefore, it becomes entirely acceptable for a higher-level manager to make changes in the summarized data which are submitted by lower levels in the organization for his approval. Everybody is fully aware that the data submitted do not represent transaction records, but quantified opinions, expectations, or promises. These are subject to change for two reasons: first, because underlying conditions change and necessitate a reappraisal of expectations; and second, because even without such external justifications for a change, the management at higher levels in the organization has the responsibility of imparting its own expectations and commitments upon lower management. Planning systems must handle information "from the top down *and* from the bottom up."

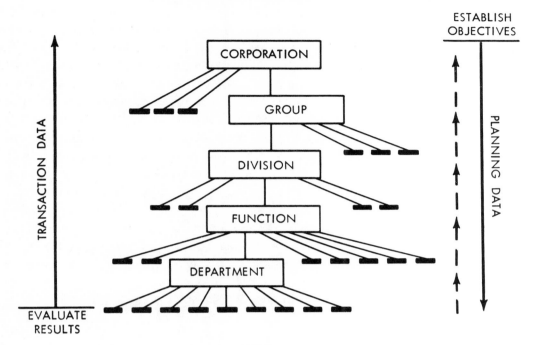

Figure 2

What we are looking for in an ideal planning system is the capability of translating summary business objectives into detailed performance requirements. However, because of the infinite numbers of permutations of alternatives on the way from a summary business objective to a detailed performance measurement, it is not feasible to design a planning system which proceeds all the way from top to bottom. But it is feasible to design several layers of systems for planning (and control) which provide linkage between various levels of management. Each link would be a self-contained system which translates business objectives from one level of management to the next, in terms which are meaningful to both. It is for this reason that the architect of a business planning system must consider to whom in the management hierarchy the system is to be of service.

In a planning data system, the critical issue is the definition of the procedures or logic which govern the generation of data and the documents which are to be prepared. Only in this context does it become necessary to settle what data about the future should be generated in support of a rational planning process.

SYSTEMS NETWORK

In order to reduce the job of structuring a planning data system to manageable size, it is necessary to treat it as a network, rather than a fully integrated structure. The network approach is also helpful because it allows each management team within the organization to participate in the development of the system and express its own point of view as to what planning data are important and relevant to its span of control. It stands to reason that the point of view, as to what needs to be planned for, changes with the level of management responsibility. The lead time between plan and action lengthens on the way up in the management hierarchy. Hence, each subsystem within the network has to be tailored to the needs of the user, the management for whom the subsystem is to be of service in generating planned goals for the future and negotiating for their acceptance with other management teams, subordinate, equal, or superior.

The network approach also provides a solution to the problem of keeping the size of each subsystem's data bank within manageable bounds. Since planning data are not available as a by-product of some external process but have to be generated within the system, the information content of the system must be tailored to the ability of the management team in keeping this information up to date.

Instead of thousands of transaction data originators at many locations, only a few trusted members of each management team are involved in generating planning data. This is not a process of collecting information but of creating, as it were, managerial intelligence.

In summary, the system's architect in structuring the planning data systems network must keep in mind that the real issue is not planning data as such but planning data for whom and how much.

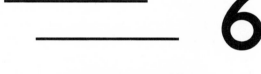

6

Processing Planning Data

It stands to reason that the methods used for processing planning data constitute a constraining influence with respect to both the availability of planning data and its quality. The question of availability refers to quantity in the sense of how much, planning information can be made available and to timeliness in the sense of how quickly and how often can this data be made available. The question of quality refers to data content in terms of relevance of data to the decision-making process and to sophistication in generating data meaningful to management.

Several stages of development might be identified as follows:

      (1)   People plus calculators and typewriters
      (2)   People plus random use of computers
      (3)   People plus coordinated use of computers

41

The last stage in turn depends on:

(a)   a user-oriented, accessible machine
(b)   a suitable programming language.

Let us discuss each stage of development in order to understand more clearly that in processing planning data, as in many other communication processes, to quote Professor MacLuhan, "The medium is the message." Let us also acknowledge from the start that in all stages of development people, be it the managers themselves or their staff assistants for planning, are the first and foremost element in the planning data processing effort.

PAPER, PENCIL, AND CALCULATORS

It is unfortunately completely safe to say that American industry and government, including corporations and agencies generally admired for their sophistication, rely in the process of originating and agreeing upon managerial goals or objectives almost entirely on manual methods. Besides pencil, paper, and mechanical calculators, slide rules and printed forms, including 14-column accounting pads, used in the origination of data, the communications process—so vital for the understanding and subsequent achievement of agreed upon goals—relies almost entirely on typewritten documents. In addition, there is an almost unbelievable lack of structure and consistency in the handling of planning data. This contrast is especially apparent when one compares the situation with respect to planning data to the situation with respect to transaction data. Even a manual bookkeeping system is usually based on a carefully thought out chart of accounts, a general ledger and subsidiary ledgers, as well as data definitions and rules for data entry, auditable source documents, and report generating logic.

When management approaches the problem of originating and deciding on planned goals, it wants to deal only with substance and forget about procedures. As a result, every study in this vast and complicated field of business planning is faced with an unresolved procedural problem. As a result, the same question asked of different staff people requires the clarification of procedures not once but as many times as the question is asked. As a result, even the same staff people, depending upon how quickly an answer is sought, operate under different procedural rules and logic formulations.

RANDOM USE OF COMPUTERS

Most companies large enough to require a formal business planning process employ computers for a variety of operational jobs, such as payroll, order entry, billing, sales analysis, inventory control, production scheduling, general accounting, etc. In all these the computer offers the ability to accept a large volume of data, store it for future use, remember complicated rules of procedure, and produce documents at high printing speeds.

It is only natural that the people engaged in originating and processing planning data would look to the computer for some help in their arduous and repetitive data-processing task. They are strengthened in this belief that the computer might be of help by salesmen of computer manufacturers and management science and operations research personnel, both inside and outside the organization in question. Articles in popular and more or less scientific business magazines are full of the same messages to management: *let the computer help you in running the business; this will make you a better manager and will give you a competitive edge.*

Occasionally, misgivings and warnings are voiced, mainly to state that there is more to this job of originating and achieving planned goals than mathematics and computer sciences, but immediately the entire community of computer addicts and related vested interests unite in silencing or discrediting the voice of caution. In the context of what is being done by management science in the area of assisting management in the development of realistic business plans by the random use of computers, criticism and caution is well justified. In practice, what happens is this. Under the influence of this barrage of propaganda, the man who has a need for computational services or who is pressed for time finally succumbs and appeals to the system's engineering or computer services department for help. He gets scheduled for an interview with some systems analysts three weeks later. In this and following meetings the manager, or assistant for planning, or business and financial analyst is faced with a formidable communications problem when he tries to explain to the systems analyst and computer expert what he needs, or what he thinks he needs.

Of course, before one can make use of a computer in planning, one must define the procedures which are to be reproduced and the documents which are to be prepared. At the same time, one must settle what data about the future should be estimated to support a reasonable planning process.

The systems engineer, on the one hand, is interested in developing a system which will solve the problem once and for all. The planner, on the other hand, is interested first in the solution of a specific computational problem. More often than not, the result of these encounters is a system engineer's proposal for an extensive study of the situation followed by a large-scale effort to build an integrated system, and the planner returning to his daily chore of answering management questions making use of the only flexible technology available to him: pencil, paper, and slide rule.

Even under ideal conditions where the systems analyst attempts to translate the planner's specifications into a specific computer programming effort, which usually takes several weeks—the results are not encouraging for either party. It would be rather unusual for a planner to have worked out his specifications so completely and explicitly that the translation into computer executable language can proceed without a hitch. More often than not, there are many unanswered questions and areas of misunderstanding requiring extensive contact between planner and programmer in an effort to come to a complete meeting of the minds. In practice this process often breaks down after a few months of frustration for both sides. At best a program is produced and applied a few times, only for the planner to find out that it doesn't quite suit his purpose, and he returns to his traditional method of generating planning data. By the same token, the systems analyst is unhappy because his program is not being put to use and collects dust on the systems department shelves.

Examples of this kind of random use of computers has produced in every company perhaps hundreds of programs, some trivial, some rather sophisticated. Most of them, however, are not being used for the purpose for which they were written and are fast becoming outdated and completely useless.

COORDINATED USE OF COMPUTERS

The coordinated use of computers should not be confused with the concept of integrated data processing. Instead, it is the logical continuation or evolution of the random use of computers in the field of generating and processing data. Integrated data processing is usually oriented toward transaction data, although planning data are often thrown in as a bonus in order to interest top management in approving the rather expensive and long-range commitment to integrated data processing.

The coordinated use of computers in planning is an attempt to overcome the linguistic barrier between the planner and the computer and to provide an architectural framework within which randomly developed procedures can be brought together and made to interact. In this fashion the coordinated use of computers is an evolutionary stage towards the creation of a network of planning data systems which is discussed in more detail in the next chapters.

As I had mentioned earlier, the success of reaching the stage of coordinated computer usage in processing planning data depends on two ingredients: computer accessibility and a suitable language.

Access to a computer means during the day (so-called prime time) not at 2 A.M. and with maximum possible ease for the planner.

A suitable language means a way of addressing the computer and a discipline to do so that fits the purpose. Again, such a language must be simple enough for planners to learn quickly, and it must enable them to write their own procedures for direct execution on the computer. At the same time, this language must be so designed that it enforces through its use a sufficient amount of discipline and uniformity for coordination to become feasible later on. The requirements for discipline are especially stringent in the area of data organization and report formats. For this reason, generalized high level computer languages such as FORTRAN, COBOL, ALGOL, PL/1, or simulators and report generators are not applicable. They give the user too much freedom and flexibility and, therefore, require for specific application too much work on the part of the user in translating his own problems into a computer-executable procedure.

What is needed, then, is a language specifically tailored to the needs of processing planning data which is not too flexible nor too restricted but nevertheless is easy to learn, quick to write, and readily executable on a computer. This is a rather tall list of specifications to meet. In addition, since the processing needs for planning data will be different in each company, division, subsidiary, profit center, or department, it is unlikely that one could develop a general language for all levels of planning. However, the structure of such a planning language could have general validity and could be used as an outline for the development of a specific planning language by any business or other planning unit.

We have used the word "language" here in the broadest sense of the term. A word of clarification is in order. Actually, this so-called planning language would not be a language in its own right. It is more in the nature of a dialect or jargon; in other words, it is a special application of a general language. Therefore, it is appropriate to give this planning dialect a name which does not include the term "language." In this book we will use the term "planning systems generator," abbreviated as "PSG." Incidentally, this is the name under which the IBM planning dialect is known in the IBM Corporation. A complete description of the structure and processing characteristics of PSG will be given in the chapter on computer usage.

Since we have made the distinction between a planning systems generator and a computer language, let us further clarify that such a PSG may be based on any of the available high-level computer languages mentioned above or on machine language directly.

A NETWORK OF PLANNING DATA SYSTEMS

If the effort in bringing about the coordinated use of computers through the use of a coordinating planning dialect has met with some success there should be after, say, one year some 50 to 100 planning procedures in existence and in use at corporate headquarters, at division headquarters, and in functional departments. Most of these procedures would be satisfying just one planning unit, but some of them might be used by several planning units at different levels in the organization. For example, a revenue projection program for the product line of one division might be used by the corporate staff to project the revenue for a new product under consideration which may be coming out of research and has not yet been assigned to an operating division.

At some point it will become necessary to arrange for the consolidation of a number of these randomized programs into a subsystem. This should be done in keeping with the general organizational structure of the corporation. For example, a cluster of such programs might become a divisional subsystem, another cluster a functional subsystem, and another cluster a corporate subsystem. In each organizational center someone would have to be assigned the responsibility for the administration and maintenance of each subsystem. This does not mean programming services. It simply means housekeeping, i.e. the storage of program source decks, the adding of appropriate transfer instructions for common data series between programs within the same subsystem, and the interface between these programs—the users and the respective computer operations. All these are essentially administrative duties directed at the efficient processing of planning data. It might be called a planning data service operation. However, under no circumstances must this planning data service be con-

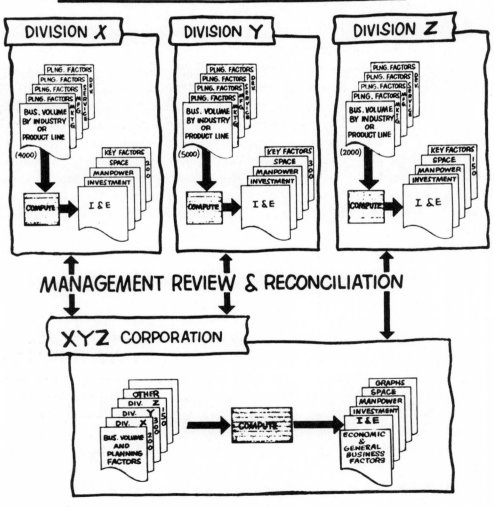

Figure 3

fused with the process of originating and achieving planned goals. The planning data service which provides for an orderly and efficient operation of a subsystem is only a processor of data. The origination and commitment to the data as meaningful objectives to be achieved is the sole responsibility of line management either directly or through their assistants for planning.

Considerable experience will have to be gained in working out the kinks and over-laps within each of the subsystems at the functional, divisional, and corporate levels before any attempt should be made to integrate this network of subsystems into one planning system for the entire company. As a matter of fact, the writer is quite doubtful whether or not such an attempt should ever be made. The amount of discipline and coordination required to translate a cluster of programs written in a common planning systems generator may already stretch the limit of feasible regimentation of people. A centralized planning data system would certainly require discipline and coordination several orders of magnitude greater than a network of loosely joined planning data subsystems.

It appears to be more in keeping with the reality of the planning-bargaining process to stay with the network characteristics and visualize the interaction between the sub-systems as one requiring managerial interpretation, judgment, and commitment, something which cannot be generated by a computer.

A network of planning data systems also gives each subsystem the freedom to incorporate within it programs which take a different view of the same business and decision-making problem which is being addressed by another subsystem. Since the process of generating and achieving planned goals is inseparable from subjective considerations and individual scales of value of the people affected, this kind of overlap or duplication is healthy and helpful in the planning-bargaining process.

TRANSACTION VERSUS PLANNING DATA

Figure 4 illustrates the problem of scope or size of these two statistical universes. The bandwidth for transaction data is very large indeed. The processing of transaction data has been vastly improved through the use of computers in the past dozen years. The information available in today's transaction data systems has been expanded beyond expectations. However, the summary reports which reach management display as always only a limited number of significant variables relevant to the span of control and responsibility of the respective management level. The reason for this is simply that the span of attention of the human mind has not increased and is not likely to increase in the future. Hence, the computer has merely added a vast amount of detail source data which back up the summary reports, and as a result management has the ability to request additional information almost without limitation. The designers of management information systems are particularly interested in expanding the ability and speed of response to such random inquiries on the part of management. Let us not forget, however, that these systems deal with unchangeable transaction data.

PLANNING - - - HOW MUCH?

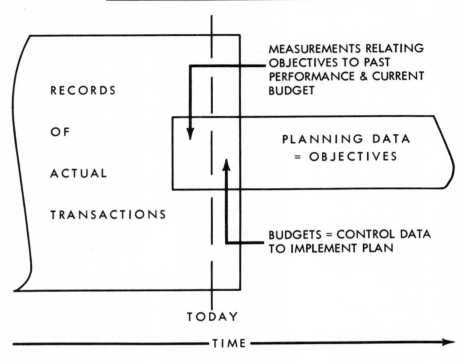

Figure 4

It would be sheer nonsense if we were to carry the bandwidth of transaction data on an estimated basis, say, for five years into the future. What then is the bandwidth or information density for planning data? The answer to this question is the key problem facing the planning systems architect. Transaction data are generated by the entire organization—thousands of people, most of them not managers but regular employees carrying out procedural instructions established by the architects of the transaction data system.

In contrast, planning data are generated or at least ultimately accepted by management making up tens, at most hundreds of people—managers at various levels of the organization. In doing so, what procedural instructions are these managers carrying out, and who are the architects of the planning data system? Except for the need of testing the logic of planning data generation on the corresponding transaction data for perhaps the past two to three years (more compatible history is usually not available anyhow), the planning data system and the transaction data system are separate entities and should be controlled by separate programming structures and preferably also by separate systems personnel.

7

Computer Usage
in Planning

Since transaction data bank methods are not applicable for the processing of planning data, what then is the recommended approach to the use of the computer in planning?

Let us first deal with the problem of planning data banks. The plural is used advisedly. As we shall see, it is considered unlikely that a single, central data bank for planning will succeed in the foreseeable future.

PLANNING DATA BANKS

Every planning data bank should be dimensioned, at least conceptually, before systems implementation, i.e. programming begins. This is a complex problem in-

49

volving substantive and procedural questions. In a way the structuring of a planning data bank is equivalent to the development of the planning process itself. Since the writer believes that in this problem the medium (computerized information technology) has a significant bearing on the message (planning process within the management system), we will concentrate on the medium first.

A planning data bank in principle will have to be visualized as a three-dimensional array.

One dimension deals with the number of subsets for business planning, such as product lines, technologies, market sectors, etc. In practice, planning often requires taking several different cuts at the spectrum of business activities. Therefore, it is necessary that the planning system be flexible enough so that a variety of subsets can be processed through it. The second dimension deals with the number of decision variables for each business subset which should be taken into account. The third dimension is time.

PLANNING DATA BANK

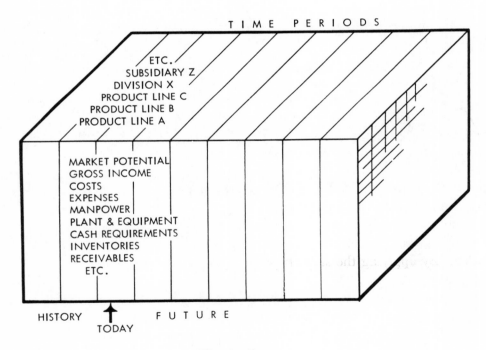

Figure 5

The more variables, subsets, and time periods called for in the planning system, the more difficult becomes the search for and maintenance of appropriate input values. Planning data are not generated as the by-product of current operations but require the exercise of human intelligence, both in terms of understanding what this data means and in terms of identification with this data as an expression of expected results of pending action. It is for this reason that the planning data bank may not exceed the capability of its users to comprehend and maintain. It is extremely important that the planning systems' architect understands this issue and keeps count of the data cells in this planning data bank, especially with respect to the ultimate planned period, for which the generation of meaningful data will be most tenuous.

SCOPE AND DATA STRUCTURE

The problem of the size of the planning data bank, the question of "planning how much," is independent of the question of "planning for whom." Regardless of which level or area of responsibility in the vast and diversified hierarchy of management a planning data system is to be of service, the problem of scope and data structure must be resolved within the practical limitation of data availability and upkeep in each case. In other words, each subsystem is a self-contained universe with its own data bank, and planning logic is tailored to its specific environment.

Let us examine the dimensions of a representative system. Figure 6 shows the scope and data structure for nine interrelated modules with a total of 267 gross input lines. However, of these, 56 are redundant. This duplication of certain planning data is inevitable because each module is developed and can be operated independently. The net data structure and planning logic is based on 211 line items. For example, the Profit and Loss Summary specifies 11 lines of input. Of these ten are transferable, three from Administration, one from Gross Profit, two from Service, one from Marketing, two from Engineering, and one from Product Plan & Forecast. This leaves one net data line which is the Corporate Tax Rate, not heretofore used in the system. In turn, the P & L Summary sends one line (After Tax Net Income) to Investment. Of course, this P & L Summary program may be used independently with its own complete set of 11 input data lines.

All input data lines represent decision variables such as the key quantities and performance ratios to which a manager pays most attention when reviewing current operations. By applying the same business logic to the evaluation of the future and the measuring of current operations, the system operates with time series of internally consistent data. For the historic years, this data is derived from actual transaction records; for the future years it represents objectives which are used to calculate the implied activity levels required to accomplish these objectives. In this systematic approach to the processing of planning data, no claim is made that the objectives of the future are an extrapolation of past measurements. They are merely displayed together to assist the manager in setting attainable objectives for his part of the organization. It is the manager himself who establishes the objectives either at the time of input into the system or by approving the output of implied activity levels.

BUSINESS PLANNING SYSTEM
SCOPE & DATA STRUCTURE

NUMBER OF LINE ITEMS

GROSS INPUTS	TRANSFERS BY SECTION									TRANSFER TOTALS	NET INPUTS
13									PRODUCT PLAN & FORECAST		13
14									ENGINEERING		14
30	6								MARKETING	6	24
52	2								SERVICE	2	50
52	2	2							MANUFACTURING	4	48
9	2			1	1				GROSS PROFIT	4	5
52	2		4	6	3	3			ADMINISTRATION	18	34
11	1	2	1	2		1	3		PROFIT & LOSS	10	1
34	2		1	1	4	3		1	INVESTMENT	12	22
267	17	4	6	10	8	7	3	1	TOTALS	56	211

Figure 6

SUBSETS AND TIME PERIODS

Given certain limitations in the print capabilities of computers, eight years appears as good a time dimension as any. It permits the inclusion of two past years, the current year, plus five years into the future. For example, 1969 being the current year, these eight years would cover the period from 1967 through 1974. Of course, any other eight years may be processed, all in the past or all in the future. Since the system operates with its own data bank, the definition of what is to be the first year is under the user's control.

As to the subsetting of the business, the system must provide for complete freedom of choice, e.g. the entry of data by product line, major manufacturing operation, sales group, etc.

Figure 7 illustrates the interplay between variables and subsets. While the system specifies 211 net variables, actually 1,104 lines of source data are involved. Take manufacturing: if we deal with 24 products, eight product families, 13 burden centers, eight space areas, and, luckily, only one plant location, we add up to 296 line items representing the dynamics of manufacturing operations, though the data structure and logic specifies only 48 decision variables.

BUSINESS PLANNING SYSTEM
SOURCE DATA REQUIREMENTS

| | LINE ITEMS WITH 9 QUANTITIES EACH | | | |
	BY SUBSET	OTHER	TOTAL	STRUCTURAL LOGIC *
PRODUCT PLAN & FORECAST				
20 Products	9	4	184	13
ENGINEERING				
5 Programs	10	4	54	14
MARKETING				
5 Product Lines	14	2	72	10
2 Sales Groups	14	–	28	14
SERVICE				
6 Product Types	25	27	177	50
MANUFACTURING				
24 Products	6	–	144	6
8 Product Classes	10	–	80	8
13 Burden Centers	2	7	33	9
8 Space Areas	2	2	18	4
1 Plant Location	–	21	21	21
ADMINISTRATION				
5 Product Lines	3	35	50	25
General & Other Charges		14	14	9
FINANCE				
5 Product Lines & Total				
Gross Profit	6	3	33	5
P & L	11	11	66	1
Investment	24	10	130	22
GRAND TOTAL			1104	211

* Excluding Transferable Line Items

Figure 7

The planning data bank to be visualized in this sample system would consist of a total of 9,936 data cells, i.e. 1,104 cross sections for nine time periods. The cross section also defines the data requirements for the ultimate planning period.

Incidentally, if the system's output data is to cover eight time periods, it is usually advisable to allow for one more, i.e. nine time periods of input data. Otherwise growth rates can be neither applied nor derived for the first output period, and the same planning logic cannot be applied across all eight output years.

HARDWARE

As long as the processing of planning data relies on people and calculators or on people and the random use of computers, the traditional approach through the functionally specialized departments of an organization poses no problem. However, when one reaches the stage of processing planning data in the mode of people plus the coordinated use of computers as a first milestone towards a network of planning data systems, some basic organizational questions arise and have to be resolved. We will discuss these more fully in the chapter on Socioeconomic Problems. In the current chapter we will in the meantime deal with the technical questions of computer usage. In order to develop and operate a system for the processing of planning data by people through the coordinated use of computers one needs of course computers and programs. In computer jargon these two needs, which are inseparable and really comprise only two aspects of the reality of computer usage, are generally referred to as "hardware" and "software." Let us first discuss the hardware question.

Most companies who are in need of a computerized system for processing planning data do have computers in the house which are usually overloaded with work on the transaction data system, and therefore may be available for developmental work on planning data systems on the third shift—that is between midnight and 8 A.M.

While demands for computer time in development and later in operation of planning data systems is not high, it differs in nature from the operational workloads for transaction data systems which are regular, repetitive, and therefore lend themselves to scheduling. In contrast the workload in the development and operation of planning data systems is irregular, nonrepetitive and rather difficult to schedule. In the heat of a decision-making process over, say, the revision of a plan for a division, the demands on the planning data system would have a very high priority, because top management is personally involved in the decision making and may require quite a bit of computer time. Then again for weeks on end computer usage may be very low, caused merely by the introduction of new planning logic or the refinement of existing planning procedures.

Nevertheless, it is probably best to begin the development of planning data systems on computer equipment already available in the house. It would be rather difficult to justify initially, separate and fully dedicated computing equipment for the development and operation of planning data systems, management science services, and other so-called exotic computer application.

In this context it might be illustrative that the first planning data system for one of the IBM divisions was developed on an IBM 1401 computer with 16K memory and five tape drives. This kind of equipment would today be classified as rather low powered. This lack of power did present some problems especially with respect to programming, but it should be significant to point out that nevertheless this level of computing power was sufficient to develop and operate a divisional planning data system for almost five years from 1962 through 1966. The cycle time for this divisional system in its entirety including many functional modules ranged from 30 to 45 minutes. Individual modules cycled in less than ten minutes. The total computer time requirements for the developmental and operational workload connected with the system ranged between 15 and 20 hours per month.

Of course, ideally, the development and operation of a network of planning data systems should be accomplished on a dedicated network of computer hardware with as much power as possible. For example, in 1966 the IBM Corporation's planning data systems were converted to operate through an installation in Poughkeepsie consisting of a directly coupled IBM 7044 and IBM 7094 II, with several disk files and many tape units to which were connected IBM 1974 terminals at each divisional and corporate headquarters location. The connections were mostly voice grade telephone lines. The IBM 1974 terminal consists of a card reader/punch unit, a 150 lines a minute printer, and a control unit with 4K memory. The rather slow speed printer imposes a desirable discipline on the designer of planning data displays and prevents the production of reams and reams of undigested data rather than informational intelligence.

Figure 8 gives a schematic diagram of this hardware setup. It should be pointed out that this falls into the category of teleprocessing arrangements. Each job entered into the system waits in line for processing under the control of an internal priority scheduling program. Since the cycle time of each job is rather short (due to the high computational power of the IBM 7094 II), there is no need to go into the expensive program interrupt and associated routines for so-called time sharing. Teleprocessing merely permits remote entry to a high power, central computer. It makes computing power available to the user at his terminal which would not otherwise be available to him and allows access to a joint library of planning logic procedures. It also facilitates the transmittal of planning data from one terminal to another, that is from one division to corporate headquarters or from one division to another and vice versa.

While the advantages of access to high power are a strong recommendation for installation of central computer facilities with remote entry, it is access to a joint library of planning procedures, easy exchange of programs, and transmittal of planning data which are of prime importance in the development, maintenance, and operation of a fully coordinated network comprising a planning data system. These important considerations make this type of hardware configuration almost mandatory. This line of reasoning will become more obvious when we proceed to the discussion of software.

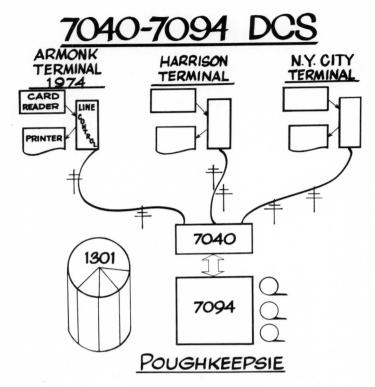

Figure 8

For the noncomputer-oriented reader it should be added that all major computer manufacturers offer second and third generation equipment with the above described operational characteristics.

SOFTWARE

In order to make use of a computer one must have a program. To many financial analysts, line managers, business planners, and especially to top level management (not excluding the management of computer manufacturers) programming is considered a special trade. It certainly is not yet considered a skill requirement for holding a position involving business decisions, business judgment, and economic analysis. Much has been written about the problems of computer programming and it is not the purpose of this book to add to this literature. However, since development of a network of planning data systems involves coordinated use of computers, the problem of programming must be solved at least within this context.

Programming means talking to a computer. It is a language problem. The linguistic skills required to talk to a computer are inversely proportional to the computer's power. This means the programming has to be most clever with a computer of least power, and conversely the more powerful a computer at our disposal the less sophistication is needed in its programming. The use of so-called high level computer languages such as Fortran, Algol, and Cobol has greatly increased the number of people who dare talk to a computer. But these high level languages still do not fulfill the requirements of a language which accomplishes the development of a coordinated system. Furthermore, the use of these languages continues to represent a special skill which must be learned and maintained and remains outside the skill requirements of those people who are involved in the origination and achievement of planned goals.

As long as we separate the programming of the system and its operation from the user of the data which the system is processing we are faced with the following two dilemmas:

(1)   The user's thinking is not truly represented in the programmer's program, or

(2)   The programmer's program is not acceptable to the user.

Only when the user, the manager himself, or his trusted assistant for planning writes his own program will this two-pronged dilemma be eliminated. The foregoing discussion of the language problem connected with development of a network of planning data systems clearly indicates the need for a special language, a dialect, as it were, which does two things: (a) it incorporates a sufficient amount of structures so that procedures written in it become modules in a coordinated system; and (b) it is simple enough for nonprogrammers to learn and use to express themselves in computer executable instructions. In principle, such a planning dialect may be written in any of the legitimate computer languages. It should therefore not be considered an additional computer language but a specific application of existing computer languages. This statement is meant for those who like the writer are disturbed by the current babylonian confusion in computer languages.

PROGRAMMING

Let me re-emphasize that the key issues in planning data systems are: (1) definition of planning documentation, (2) definition of planning logic, and (3) availability of source data. This is true for any planning system—manual, unit record equipment, or computer-operated.

The manual system is slow, but, as it relies on the human hand and brain, extremely flexible. Any mechanized planning system requires prethinking, or, if you like, planning of planning. Someone has to sit down and write "planning specifications," get them approved by management, and publish and maintain them. This is a big and difficult job. The writer suggests that this is the main job for the planning staff.

If the planning data system is to make use of computers, then the planning specifications must be written in a language which a computer understands. Once the system is in operation, someone, perhaps a special department, has to be given responsibility for planning data service. This includes the maintenance of source data in machine-readable form (cards, tape, or disk), preparation of computer output, and its distribution. Appropriate security measures have to be established for access to source data, for authorized changes in source data, as well as authority to request output displays from the system.

Some of us are intrigued about the possibilities of displaying data on cathode ray tubes in managers' offices or planning committee meeting rooms with touch keyboard entry of alternate assumptions and almost immediate feedback of the resulting change in summary statistics and graphs. But these things are a matter of human adaptability to the challenges of advanced data-processing technology. In the meantime, most companies have more computer power available than they need to accomplish a substantially improved job for business planning. However, we must first define what this job for business planning consists of, and that is the real issue.

With manual systems there is no programming, so they say. This is, of course, a semantic fallacy. The financial analyst who sets up a 14-column worksheet is programming the job he is about to do. As he fills in line item descriptions and headings, he defines the logic he will use and the source data he will need to work with, in keeping with his knowledge of their availability. When a computer is to be used, the programming is generally viewed as a separate job. This is not necessarily so.

The computer language or dialect for planning can and should follow the user's familiar approach. It must be specifically designed and must make it easy to translate the manual program (columnar worksheets, calculations, plus typing of good looking planning data displays) into a program executable on a computer. It must also include sufficient coordinative structure; otherwise the resulting programs will continue to represent random use of computers. Therefore, general purpose computer languages are not suitable. Recognition of the need for this type of a problem-oriented computer dialect, tailored to the data-processing needs of business planning, has been one of the most significant advances in planning systems development.

Since this computer dialect closely reflects the management jargon and idiosyncrasies of the user, a general solution is not possible. Just as in spoken language, a dialect is the creation of a local environment; the notion of one planning dialect for all types of business and corporate organizations is a contradiction in terms.

However, there are a great many characteristics or features of such a planning dialect which can be generalized. Therefore, it is worthwhile to learn more about one such dialect as a basis for the development of one's own.

THE LANGUAGE OF PLANNING LOGIC

Without an established method to specify planning logic, many alternatives exist. One may describe the inputs, computational formulations, and outputs in extensive narrative form, using full-fledged English. On a high-speed line printer the length of a descriptive term is only a space problem. It takes no more time to print "MAN-POWER" than "MPW." However, the definition of computational logic in extensive English becomes very involved and difficult to understand. The obvious answer is to use symbolic abbreviations in the logic while using full-fledged English in the input/output displays. But this creates new problems of understanding.

First of all, the number of mnemonically intelligible symbols is limited. Hence, if looking up of symbolic reference tables becomes necessary why not use numeric codes and make the planning documents themselves serve both as a display of descriptions with data and a glossary of terms. Therefore, one might adopt a method of defining computational logic by numbering the input variables and output lines and showing the connecting logic directly in suitable listings. This simplifies the logic review and eliminates the need for mnemonic symbols altogether.

An example may illustrate this: If manpower (MPW) is, say, a function of workload (WLD) and productivity (PRY), we end up with a statement looking like this: MPW = WLD/PRY. Unless the reviewer remembers what MPW, WLD, and PRY stand for, he must look up the definitions of these symbols in a glossary of symbolic terms.

In the numeric method, all logic is expressed by relating line numbers of input to line numbers of output. Where this relationship becomes too involved, it is possible to introduce intermediate lines without calling on them in the print specifications. In the above example assuming WORKLOAD appears as input line 5 (A5) and PRODUCTIVITY as input line 7 (A7), while MANPOWER is assigned output line 12 (B12) the formulation would read B12 = A5/A7. This offers an additional advantage. In order to prepare esthetically pleasing hard copy the same data may be labeled by different descriptors, such as:

FORM 1	GROSS INCOME	
	DIVISION X	A11
	DIVISION Y	A21
	GROSS PROFIT	
	DIVISION X	A13
	DIVISION Y	A23
FORM 2	DIVISION X	
	GROSS INCOME	A11
	GROSS PROFIT	A13
	DIVISION Y	
	GROSS INCOME	A21
	GROSS PROFIT	A23

If the descriptors are to serve the function of data identifiers as well, they would have to be complete in each case, such as:

GROSS INCOME DIVISION X
GROSS INCOME DIVISION Y
etc.

It stands to reason that the separation of descriptors and identifiers of data provides for complete flexibility in the design of eye-appealing displays, free from the gobbledegook of supposedly mnemonic hieroglyphics.

From this method of specifying planning logic as a means of instructing a computer programmer, the planner is rather close to addressing the computer directly. This small but significant step was later taken through the Planning Systems Generator approach.

PLANNING SYSTEMS GENERATOR

In the IBM Corporation a planning-oriented language was developed under the name Planning Systems Generator, abbreviated PSG. It is a carefully thought out housekeeping structure written in Fortran IV. The use of PSG facilitates the development of planning data systems by providing the planner or analyst with a coordinated discipline for:

data entry and storage with easy updating
report generation in final reproducible formats
iterative processing of subsets and summaries
access to a number of typical planning logic functions
simple rules for specifying his own planning logic

PSG makes available three data matrices, called A, B, and C.

The A matrix for source data
The B matrix for computed results
The C matrix for accumulation of subset data

Each matrix has nine columns and 400 lines. Column 1 is used for prior data, columns two to nine for the regular eight yearly planning periods.

PSG also makes available two data files, one for the storage of source data, the other for the storage of transfer data. PSG reads source data into the A matrix first from the source data file (historic planning data), then from source data cards, and finally from the transfer data file. The last data read has priority.

Logic specifications, as written by the PSG user, control the entry of data into the B or C matrix or the transfer data file.

Print specifications, as written by the PSG user, control the printing of data lines from the A, B, or C matrix together with appropriate headings, descriptions, foot-notes, etc.

PSG makes available several print formats, such as *

> input worksheet with nine data columns
> single column display with eight single data columns
> double column display with eight double data columns
> index chart for up to eight line items of data

A set of logic and print specifications pertaining to a group of planning documents (display forms and input worksheets) becomes a planning procedure. Each PSG procedure may have as many as nine sets of planning documents under separate copy control. One of these must be input worksheets.

PSG provides space for 100 planning procedures, each of which may be iterated with up to 100 subsets of source data. Data lines in the A, B, or C matrix of one procedure may be entered into the transfer data file for automatic pickup by another procedure.

Matrix A and B are reset with each procedure iteration (change in subset number). The C matrix and the transfer file are reset with each new system iteration (change in view number).

Writing a planning specification in the language of PSG means writing an executable program. The use of two-dimensional data matrices which the user may visualize to be images of columnar worksheets, eliminates the need for symbolic notations without limiting the use of mathematical logic. This facilitates understanding, since, as we all know, most businessmen dislike being confronted with mathematical symbolics. How sophisticated a logic one employs depends on the state of the art in the organization. A planning procedure with simple logic in operation is many times more useful than one with advanced logic in the talking stage.

There are many other features. The developers of this language built on many years of experience in planning systems work. The vocabulary of PSG incorporates the typical needs experienced in the divisional and corporate planning process.

A planning dialect like PSG can be taught to an experienced business planner or financial analyst in one week. He need have no experience in programming whatsoever. After that he will require some assistance on more complicated logic problems and occasional help in debugging, but otherwise he is able to write his own planning specifications in computer-executable language, with not much more effort than the setting up of traditional multicolumn account worksheets for hand calculating.

Exhibits 7-1 and 7-2 show a listing of the complete print and logic specifications as

---

* For examples see Chapters 8 and 9.

P S G   PROGRAM LIBRARY LISTING

```
D E S C R I P T I O N S        TERM   *  L O G I C   S T A T E M E N T      *  SEQ.
    CARD COLUMNS 1 - 31        32-37              41 - 79                        NO.

)PROGRAM 91                                                                      1
                                      IF SUBSET NE 0 THEN GO TO $LABEL1          2
        SUMMARY SUBSET                COPY (C,B)                                 3
                                      GO TO $LABEL2                              4
        DETAIL SUBSETS                $LABEL1                                    5
)FORM 1, DOUBLE COLUMNS (AMT,O/O), HEADING FORM 91-1 // PROFIT + LOSS SUMMARY    6
GROSS INCOME                                                                     7
    PRODUCTS                          B1=EXTEND(2,FILL(2,GRO(3,A1,A2))),B2       8
    SERVICE                           B3=EXTEND(2,FILL(2,GRO(3,A3,A4))),B4       9
        TOTAL                         B5=B1+B2 , B6                             10
                                                                               11
GROSS PROFIT                                                                    12
    PRODUCTS                          B11=A11+A12*B1/100 , B12                  13
    SERVICE                           B13=A13+A14*B3/100 , B14                  14
        TOTAL                         B15=B11+B12 , B16                         15
                                                                               16
EXPENSES                                                                        17
    MARKETING                         B21=A21+A22*B5/100,B22                    18
    PRODUCT MGMT                      B23=A23+A24*B5/100,B24                    19
    ADMINISTRATION                    B25=A25+A26*B5/100,B26                    20
                                                                               21
    ENGINEERING                       B27=A27+A28*B5/100,B28                    22
    GENERAL                           B29=A29+A30*B5/100,B30                    23
    OTHER CHARGES *)                  B31=A31+A32*B5/100,B32                    24
                                                                               25
NET BEFORE TAX                        B41=B15-B39 , B42                         26
                                                                               27
NET AFTER TAX                         B45=B41-B43 , B46                         28
                                                                               29
)HEADING /PERCENT CHANGE OVER PRIOR YEAR/                                       30
)HEADING DOUBLE COLUMNS (YGR,CGR)                                               31
GROSS INCOME                                                                    32
    PRODUCTS                          B101 , B102                               33
    SERVICE                           B103 , B104                               34
        TOTAL                         B105 , B106                               35
                                                                               36
GROSS PROFIT                                                                    37
    PRODUCTS                          B111 , B112                               38
    SERVICE                           B113 , B114                               39
        TOTAL                         B115 , B116                               40
                                                                               41
EXPENSE                                                                         42
    MARKETING                         B121 , B122                               43
    PRODUCT MGMT                      B123 , B124                               44
    ADMINISTRATION                    B125 , B126                               45
                                                                               46
    ENGINEERING                       B127 , B128                               47
    GENERAL                           B129 , B130                               48
    OTHER CHARGES *)                  B131 , B132                               49
                                                                               50
NET BEFORE TAX                        B141 , B142                               51
                                                                               52
NET AFTER TAX                         B145 , B146                               53
                                                                               54
*) NET OF OTHER INCOME                                                          55
```

Exhibit 7-1

written by the PSG user to produce the Profit and Loss Summary and Input Worksheet per Exhibits 7-3 and 7-4. The PSG program involves the keypunching of 103
cards (including 14 blank cards for line spacing). The PSG master program, plus
these 103 cards would be executed either with original source data cards (up to 22)
or change data cards for a given set of historic planning data. Under routine opera-

```
                    P S G   PROGRAM  LIBRARY  LISTING

    D E S C R I P T I O N S        TERM    *  L O G I C   S T A T E M E N T      *   SEQ.
        CARD COLUMNS 1 - 31        32-37              41 - 79                          NO.

    )END FORM, END PAGE                                                                56
                                                                                       57
            TOTAL EXPENSES                     B39=B21+B23+B25+B27+B29+B31             58
            INCOME TAX                         B43=A51+A52*B42/100                     59
                                           DO L = 1 TO 45 BY 2                         60
                ACCUMULATE DETAIL DATA           C(L)=C(L)+B(L)                        61
                                                 END                                   62
        FOR DETAIL AND SUMMARY             $LABEL2                                     63
                                           DO L = 1 TO 5 BY 2                          64
        INCOME DISTRIBUTION                  B(L+1)=PCT(B(L),B5)                       65
        GROSS MARGINS                        B(L+11)=PCT(B(L+10),B(L))                 66
                                             END                                       67
                                           DO L = 21 TO 45 BY 2                        68
        EXPENSE RATIOS                       B(L+1)=PCT(B(L),B5)                       69
                                             END                                       70
                                           DO L = 1 TO 45 BY 2                         71
        YEARLY GROWTH RATES                  B(L+100)=YGR(B(L))                        72
        COMPOUND GROWTH RATES                B(L+101)=CGR(B(L),0,0)                    73
                                             END                                       74
                                                                                       75
    )FORM 9, WORKSHEET, HEADING FORM 91-9 // P + L INPUT WORKSHEET                     76
    GROSS INCOME                                                                       77
        PRODUCTS, AMOUNT              M $    A1                                        78
            OR GROWTH RATE            O/O    A2                                        79
        SERVICE, AMOUNT              M $    A3                                        80
            OR GROWTH RATE            O/O    A4                                        81
    GROSS PROFIT                                                                       82
        PRODUCTS, AMOUNT              M $    A11                                       83
            AND INCOME RATIO          O/O    A12                                       84
        SERVICE, AMOUNT              M $    A13                                       85
            AND INCOME RATIO          O/O    A14                                       86
    EXPENSES                                                                           87
        MARKETING, AMOUNT            M $    A21                                       88
            AND INCOME RATIO          O/O    A22                                       89
        PRODUCT MANAGEMENT, AMOUNT    M $    A23                                       90
            AND INCOME RATIO          O/O    A24                                       91
        ADMINISTRATION, AMOUNT        M $    A25                                       92
            AND INCOME RATIO          O/O    A26                                       93
        ENGINEERING, AMOUNT          M $    A27                                       94
            AND INCOME RATIO          O/O    A28                                       95
        GENERAL, AMOUNT              M $    A29                                       96
            AND INCOME RATIO          O/O    A30                                       97
        OTHER CHARGES LESS OTHER INC. M $    A31                                       98
            AND INCOME RATIO          O/O    A32                                       99
    INCOME TAX, AMOUNT                M $    A51                                      100
            AND TAX RATE              O/O    A52                                      101
    )END FORM, END PAGE                                                              102
    )END PROGRAM 91                                                                  103
```

Exhibit 7-2

tion, the PSG master deck, PSG program decks, and historic planning data decks would all be stored in the computer's random access memory for easy recall by appropriate control cards in the actual execution deck. In this way the planner or analyst needs to submit a minimum of PSG control and data cards to execute either one or several modules within a planning data subsystem or an entire subsystem with complete linkage of all modules. In all cases the PSG master program would maintain discipline, coordinate the data files and transfers, and provide for an auditable documentation of the assumptions which generated the resulting planning data.

WHO KNOWS WHAT'S IN THE FUTURE

TOTAL COMPANY

| FORM 91-1 | | | | | | | | | | | | | | | | PROFIT + LOSS SUMMARY |

SUBSET 0

DESCRIPTION	1984 AMT	1984 O/O	1985 AMT	1985 O/O	1986 AMT	1986 O/O	1987 AMT	1987 O/O	1988 AMT	1988 O/O	1989 AMT	1989 O/O	1990 AMT	1990 O/O	1991 AMT	1991 O/O
GROSS INCOME																
PRODUCTS	110.0	90.2	120.0	89.6	132.0	89.6	125.4	89.6	137.9	89.6	145.3	89.1	152.6	88.7	160.0	88.2
SERVICE	12.0	9.8	14.0	10.4	15.4	10.4	14.6	10.4	16.1	10.4	17.7	10.9	19.5	11.3	21.4	11.8
TOTAL	122.0	100.0	134.0	100.0	147.4	100.0	140.0	100.0	154.0	100.0	163.0	100.0	172.1	100.0	181.4	100.0
GROSS PROFIT																
PRODUCTS	56.0	50.9	62.0	51.7	66.0	50.0	62.7	50.0	69.0	50.0	72.6	50.0	76.3	50.0	80.0	50.0
SERVICE	7.0	58.3	8.0	57.1	9.0	58.4	8.0	54.7	9.0	55.9	10.0	56.5	11.0	56.5	12.0	56.0
TOTAL	63.0	51.6	70.0	52.2	75.0	50.9	70.7	50.5	78.0	50.6	82.6	50.7	87.3	50.7	92.0	50.7
EXPENSES																
MARKETING	18.5	15.2	21.0	15.7	23.7	16.1	23.0	16.4	24.4	15.8	25.3	15.5	26.2	15.2	27.1	15.0
PRODUCT MGMT	2.3	1.9	2.6	1.9	2.9	2.0	2.6	1.9	2.9	1.9	3.2	2.0	3.5	2.0	3.8	2.1
ADMINISTRATION	6.2	5.1	7.4	5.5	8.7	5.9	8.4	6.0	9.2	6.0	9.8	6.0	10.3	6.0	10.9	6.0
ENGINEERING	8.8	7.2	9.6	7.2	10.4	7.1	9.6	6.9	10.4	6.8	11.2	6.9	12.0	7.0	12.8	7.1
GENERAL	1.0	.8	1.0	.7	1.0	.7	1.0	.7	1.0	.6	1.0	.6	1.0	.6	1.0	.6
OTHER CHARGES *)	2.2	1.8	2.4	1.8	2.6	1.8	2.4	1.7	2.6	1.7	2.8	1.7	3.0	1.7	3.2	1.8
NET BEFORE TAX	24.0	19.7	26.0	19.4	25.7	17.4	23.7	16.9	27.4	17.8	29.4	18.0	31.3	18.2	33.2	18.3
NET AFTER TAX	12.0	9.8	13.0	9.7	12.8	8.7	11.8	8.5	13.7	8.9	14.7	9.0	15.6	9.1	16.6	9.1

PERCENT CHANGE OVER PRIOR YEAR

DESCRIPTION	1984 YGR	1984 CGR	1985 YGR	1985 CGR	1986 YGR	1986 CGR	1987 YGR	1987 CGR	1988 YGR	1988 CGR	1989 YGR	1989 CGR	1990 YGR	1990 CGR	1991 YGR	1991 CGR
GROSS INCOME																
PRODUCTS	10.0	10.0	9.1	9.5	10.0	9.7	-5.0	5.8	10.0	6.6	5.3	6.4	5.1	6.2	4.8	6.1
SERVICE	20.0	20.0	16.7	18.3	10.0	15.5	-5.0	10.0	10.0	10.0	10.0	10.0	10.0	10.0	10.0	10.0
TOTAL	10.9	10.9	9.8	10.4	10.0	10.2	-5.0	6.2	10.0	7.0	5.8	6.8	5.6	6.6	5.4	6.5
GROSS PROFIT																
PRODUCTS	12.0	12.0	10.7	11.4	6.5	9.7	-5.0	5.8	10.0	6.6	5.3	6.4	5.1	6.2	4.8	6.1
SERVICE	16.7	16.7	14.3	15.5	12.5	14.5	-11.1	7.5	12.5	8.4	11.1	8.9	10.0	9.0	9.1	9.1
TOTAL	12.5	12.5	11.1	11.8	7.1	10.2	-5.7	6.0	10.3	6.8	6.0	6.7	5.7	6.6	5.4	6.4
EXPENSE																
MARKETING	15.6	15.6	13.5	14.6	13.0	14.1	-3.1	9.5	6.1	8.8	3.7	7.9	3.6	7.3	3.5	6.8
PRODUCT MGMT	15.0	15.0	13.0	14.0	11.5	13.2	-10.3	6.8	11.5	7.7	10.3	8.1	9.4	8.3	8.6	8.4
ADMINISTRATION	24.0	24.0	19.4	21.7	17.5	20.3	-3.4	13.9	10.0	13.1	5.8	11.8	5.6	10.9	5.4	10.2
ENGINEERING	10.0	10.0	9.1	9.5	8.3	9.1	-7.7	4.7	8.3	5.4	7.7	5.8	7.1	6.0	6.7	6.1
GENERAL																
OTHER CHARGES *)	10.0	10.0	9.1	9.5	8.3	9.1	-7.7	4.7	8.3	5.4	7.7	5.8	7.1	6.0	6.7	6.1
NET BEFORE TAX	9.1	9.1	8.3	8.7	-1.3	5.3	-7.7	1.9	15.7	4.5	7.1	4.9	6.5	5.2	6.0	5.3
NET AFTER TAX	9.1	9.1	8.3	8.7	-1.3	5.3	-7.7	1.9	15.7	4.5	7.1	4.9	6.5	5.2	6.0	5.3

*) NET OF OTHER INCOME

PSG - PLANNING SYSTEMS GENERATOR   - COMPANY CONFIDENTIAL -   ANY DATE

Exhibit 7-3

FORM 91-9   SUBSET 1   TOTAL COMPANY   P + L INPUT WORKSHEET

CODE	DESCRIPTION	TERM	PRIOR 18-24	1984 25-31	1985 32-38	1986 39-45	1987 46-52	1988 53-59	1989 60-66	1990 67-73	1991 74-80
	GROSS INCOME										
9100001	PRODUCTS, AMOUNT	M $	100.0	110.0	120.0	.	.	.	.	.	160.0
9101002	OR GROWTH RATE	O/O	.	.	.	10.0	-5.0	10.0	.	.	.
9100003	SERVICE, AMOUNT	M $	10.0	12.0	14.0	.	.	10.0	.	.	.
9101004	OR GROWTH RATE	O/O	.	.	.	10.0	-5.0	10.0	.	.	.
	GROSS PROFIT										
9100011	PRODUCTS, AMOUNT	M $	50.0	56.0	62.0	.	.	.	.	.	.
9101012	AND INCOME RATIO	O/O	.	.	.	50.0	50.0	50.0	50.0	50.0	50.0
9100013	SERVICE, AMOUNT	M $	6.0	7.0	8.0	9.0	8.0	9.0	10.0	11.0	12.0
9101014	AND INCOME RATIO	O/O	.	.	.	.	.	.	.	.	.
	EXPENSES										
9100021	MARKETING, AMOUNT	M $	16.0	18.5	21.0	9.0	9.0	9.0	9.0	9.0	9.0
9101022	AND INCOME RATIO	O/O	.	.	.	10.0	10.0	10.0	10.0	10.0	10.0
9100023	PRODUCT MANAGEMENT, AMOUNT	M $	2.0	2.3	2.6	2.9	2.6	2.9	3.2	3.5	3.8
9101024	AND INCOME RATIO	O/O	.	.	.	.	.	.	.	.	.
9100025	ADMINISTRATION, AMOUNT	M $	5.0	6.2	7.4	.	.	.	.	.	.
9101026	AND INCOME RATIO	O/O	.	.	.	5.9	6.0	6.0	6.0	6.0	6.0
9100027	ENGINEERING, AMOUNT	M $	8.0	8.8	9.6	10.4	9.6	10.4	11.2	12.0	12.8
9101028	AND INCOME RATIO	O/O	.	.	.	.	.	.	.	.	.
9100029	GENERAL, AMOUNT	M $	1.0	1.0	1.0	1.0	1.0	1.0	1.0	1.0	1.0
9101030	AND INCOME RATIO	O/O	.	.	.	.	.	.	.	.	.
9100031	OTHER CHARGES LESS OTHER INCOME	M $	2.0	2.2	2.4	2.6	2.4	2.6	2.8	3.0	3.2
9101032	AND INCOME RATIO	O/O	.	.	.	.	.	.	.	.	.
9100051	INCOME TAX, AMOUNT	M $	11.0	12.0	13.0	.	.	.	.	.	.
9100052	AND TAX RATE	O/O	.	.	.	50.0	50.0	50.0	50.0	50.0	50.0

PSG - PLANNING SYSTEMS GENERATOR   - COMPANY CONFIDENTIAL -   ANY DATE

Exhibit 7-4

8

Corporate Planning Data

Up to now we have developed a thesis that the task of originating and accomplishing planned goals requires that management has available an efficient network of planning data systems through which these goals and their underlying assumptions can be developed, evaluated, documented, and updated.

Let us now take a closer look at the dimensions of that subsystem within this network which would serve the corporate management. The task of establishing corporate goals does not consist of just adding up the subgoals submitted by divisional management, but it requires a separate and distinct effort on the part of corporate management. This effort consists of the development of an independent corporate view for each of the component divisions that make up the corporation. Of course, this view must be based on assumptions and logic which is defensible first of all within the corporate management group, usually consisting of the corporate line management and a corporate staff competent in the various business functions, such as manufacturing, engineering, marketing, legal, personnel, etc., and secondly acceptable to divisional management. As we have discussed in previous chapters, a need for this independent point of view on the part of corporate management is essential for a smooth functioning of the ensuing bargaining process between divisional and corporate management about the finally agreed upon planned goals. If corporate management does not possess this independent point of view, the bargaining will degenerate into a more or less emotional probing and bluffing game.

THE XYZ COMPANY

The following illustration material will be based on a fictitious corporation which we shall call the XYZ Company. This corporation is engaged in the manufacture, marketing, and service of some durable consumer or producer's goods (durable, as otherwise there would be no need for service). The corporation's business is conveniently organized into three separate divisions called X, Y, and Z. Each of these three divisions handles a number of product lines and is fully integrated with its own manufacturing, marketing, and service functions. In addition, the corporation is considering entry into some new product line which is, for the time being, called "special products." The company is also active outside of the United States. These business activities are lumped together under foreign operations.

INCOME ANALYSIS

The sample display in Exhibit 8-1 shows a cross-sectional analysis of divisional gross income, gross profit, net before and net after tax, for the entire XYZ Corporation. The reader is asked to study this document carefully, because it is a typical summary display of corporate planning data which top-level executives like to refer to when they think about their business or when they talk to their associates and division general managers about the future of the company.

Before we deal with the question of how this data is generated let us take a look at what this document tells about the company. This type of display of planning data, called a double column display, shows first of all two years of actual data, 1967 and 1968. For 1969, it shows the approved operating budget. For the ensuing five years, it shows what we might call the strategic plan which expresses management's expectations about the future.

The line items of information consist of gross income, gross profit, and net profit before tax, as well as the respective margins for each of the three product lines; gross income and net before tax for special products; and gross income, gross profit, and net before and after tax for foreign operations. For the total corporation, in addition to gross income and net before and after tax, the expenditures for research, development, and corporate headquarters administration, which had been allocated to the divisions, are recapped in total for easy review.

FORM 08-1   SUBSET 0   TOTAL CORPORATION   INCOME ANALYSIS

DESCRIPTION	1967 AMT	1967 O/O	1968 AMT	1968 O/O	1969 AMT	1969 O/O	1970 AMT	1970 O/O	1971 AMT	1971 O/O	1972 AMT	1972 O/O	1973 AMT	1973 O/O	1974 AMT	1974 O/O
DIVISION X																
GROSS INCOME	120.1	5.4	130.9	9.0	142.2	8.6	182.4	28.3	221.7	21.5	261.0	17.7	309.7	18.7	353.1	16.7
GROSS PROFIT	59.6	8.4	67.3	12.9	68.3	1.5	89.8	31.5	111.3	23.9	130.9	17.6	155.0	18.4	176.4	16.8
NET BEFORE TAX	18.6	3.9	20.3	9.1	8.7	-57.1	22.6	159.8	31.4	38.9	38.4	22.3	48.3	25.8	57.1	17.4
GROSS MARGIN	49.6		51.4		48.0		49.2		50.2		50.2		50.0		50.0	
NETBT MARGIN	15.5		15.5		6.1		12.4		14.2		14.7		15.6		16.2	
DIVISION Y																
GROSS INCOME	84.1	5.1	90.4	7.5	90.7	.3	90.1	-.7	98.1	8.9	101.1	3.0	104.1	3.0	109.5	3.8
GROSS PROFIT	27.7	7.7	42.1	11.7	41.6	-1.2	40.6	-2.3	45.0	10.8	46.2	2.7	47.4	2.6	50.1	4.1
NET BEFORE TAX	13.0	8.3	14.6	12.3	8.3	-43.2	13.2	59.5	15.5	16.8	15.8	1.8	16.7	5.8	18.1	4.9
GROSS MARGIN	44.8		46.6		45.9		45.1		45.9		45.7		45.6		45.8	
NETBT MARGIN	15.5		16.2		9.2		14.7		15.8		15.6		16.0		16.6	
DIVISION Z																
GROSS INCOME	36.0	5.9	40.5	12.5	39.7	-2.0	42.4	6.9	44.4	4.7	47.7	7.4	50.7	6.4	54.8	6.2
GROSS PROFIT	21.9	9.5	25.2	15.2	24.7	-1.9	26.1	5.5	27.8	6.8	29.5	6.0	31.6	7.0	34.3	6.6
NET BEFORE TAX	8.9	11.1	10.4	17.2	9.5	-8.5	10.0	5.2	11.3	12.6	12.2	7.7	13.7	12.7	15.1	7.9
GROSS MARGIN	60.8		62.3		62.3		61.5		62.7		61.9		62.2		62.6	
NETBT MARGIN	24.7		25.7		24.0		23.6		25.4		25.5		27.0		27.6	
SPECIAL PRODUCTS																
GROSS INCOME			10.0		11.0	10.0	12.1	10.0	13.3	10.0	14.6	10.0	16.1	10.0	17.7	10.0
NET BEFORE TAX	-2.0		-1.0	-50.0	.1	NA	-.2	120.0	.8	230.0	1.5	83.3	2.1	43.0	2.7	NA
NETBT MARGIN			-10.0		1.0		2.0		6.0		10.0		13.0		15.0	
FOREIGN OPERATIONS																
GROSS INCOME	42.0	5.0	44.0	4.8	46.2	5.0	48.5	5.0	50.9	5.0	53.5	5.0	56.2	5.0	59.0	5.0
GROSS PROFIT	21.0	5.0	22.0	4.8	23.1	5.0	24.3	5.0	25.5	5.0	26.7	5.0	28.1	5.0	29.5	5.0
NET BEFORE TAX	8.4	5.0	8.8	4.8	9.2	5.0	9.7	5.0	10.2	5.0	10.7	5.0	11.2	5.0	11.8	5.0
NET AFTER TAX	4.2	5.0	4.4	4.8	4.6	5.0	4.9	5.0	5.1	5.0	5.3	5.0	5.6	5.0	5.9	5.0
GROSS MARGIN	50.0		50.0		50.0		50.0		50.0		50.0		50.0		50.0	
NETBT MARGIN	20.0		20.0		20.0		20.0		20.0		20.0		20.0		20.0	
NETAT MARGIN	10.0		10.0		10.0		10.0		10.0		10.0		10.0		10.0	
TOTAL CORPORATION																
GROSS INCOME	282.2	5.3	315.8	11.9	329.8	4.4	375.5	13.9	428.4	14.1	477.9	11.5	536.8	12.3	594.1	11.2
NET BEFORE TAX	46.9	2.2	53.1	13.3	35.9	-32.5	55.5	55.5	69.1	23.9	78.5	13.5	92.0	17.2	104.8	12.2
NET AFTER TAX	24.2	5.5	27.4	13.3	17.4	-36.6	27.0	55.0	33.4	23.8	37.9	13.4	44.4	17.2	50.5	11.1
RESEARCH	4.0	-2.4	3.8	-5.0	3.6	-5.3	3.6	-.0	3.1	-14.4	3.6	17.2	3.9	9.1	4.2	.7
DEVELOPMENT	10.9	9.0	11.5	5.5	12.5	8.7	13.5	8.2	14.9	9.8	15.6	5.3	17.3	10.5	19.4	8.6
CHQ ADMIN.	13.4	9.8	15.2	13.4	17.8	17.1	19.7	10.7	23.3	18.4	26.8	15.0	30.6	14.1	35.0	14.7
O/O OF GROSS INCOME																
NET BEFORE TAX	16.6		16.8		10.9		14.9		16.1		16.4		17.1		17.6	
NET AFTER TAX	8.6		8.7		5.3		7.2		7.8		7.9		8.3		8.5	
RESEARCH	1.42		1.20		1.09		.96		.72		.76		.73		.71	
DEVELOPMENT	3.86		3.64		3.79		3.60		3.47		3.27		3.22		3.26	
CHQ ADMIN''ION	4.75		4.81		5.40		5.25		5.44		5.61		5.70		5.89	

NOTE - O/O COLUMN SHOWS YEARLY GROWTH RATE, EXCEPT FOR LAST YEAR, WHERE IT SHOWS COMPOUND GROWTH RATE OVER FIRST YEAR.

PSG - PLANNING SYSTEMS GENERATOR   - COMPANY CONFIDENTIAL -

12/16/68

Exhibit 8-1

As to the double columns for each year, the left side shows millions of dollars and the right side percentage change over prior year, except for the last percentage column where a compound growth rate of the last year over the first year is shown (see footnote on the document itself).

This type of document is probably more interesting from the point of view of what information is not shown, rather than from what is shown. In this lies one of the challenges for the designer of a planning data system. The number of line items and columns to be shown on such a document is restricted by the printing capabilities of the computer. On the other hand, the computer makes possible the selection of line items at random without the need for subtotals to follow individual amounts and grand totals to follow subtotals, as is the practice with electric accounting machines and tabulating equipment. For example, subtotals for all domestic products, though easily computed, are not shown because of lack of space on the page.

One of the guiding principles in the development of planning data systems postulates that we first design the displays to management—the output documents of the system. These formats must be well thought out pages of as much as possible familiar content. They play a key role because they define not only the output of the system, but also the minimum input and data bank requirements. As a linguist might point out jokingly, the word "information" has the term "format" embedded in it. This is especially applicable to planning information. In planning data systems we are simultaneously displaying and creating information, whereas in transaction data systems we are only displaying information which has been created by other means.

INDEX CHARTS

In addition to the type of summary income statistics in Exhibit 8-1, another popular type of display for top level management is a graphic index chart as shown in Exhibits 8-2, 8-3, and 8-4. Such index charts may be called out to compare any two or more time series contained in the planning data bank. The index chart 8-3 shows a comparison of net before tax across all divisional operations. Incidentally, a standard computer printer will not draw lines between the points charted. The lines have to be drawn by hand. Those familiar with data-processing equipment may suggest that these charts be prepared on a plotter. This is, of course, possible, but requires the scheduling of different data-processing equipment. In practice the use of only one output device, i.e. a printer, and the manual drawing of the lines, will be faster. Another suggestion may be offered by those familiar with cathode ray tube displays for both the statistical data and the graphs. Here we are faced with limitations in the character grid of the display unit. For example, an IBM 2250 handles 72 by 54 characters while a printed page handles 131 by 54 characters. The design of a planning data system around a 72 by 54 character display capability imposes rather severe limitations. At best, the CRT display may be called into action as a subsidiary

SUBSET   0

TOTAL CORPORATION

COMPARISON OF GROSS INCOME

DESCRIPTION	TERM	REF.	1967	1968	1969	1970	1971	1972	1973	1974
TOTAL CORPORATION	M $	1	282.2	315.8	329.8	375.5	428.4	477.9	536.8	594.1
DIVISION X	M $	2	120.1	130.9	142.2	182.4	221.7	261.0	309.7	353.1
DIVISION Y	M $	3	84.1	90.4	90.7	90.1	98.1	101.1	104.1	109.5
DIVISION Z	M $	4	36.0	40.5	39.7	42.4	44.4	47.7	50.7	54.8
FOREIGN OPERATIONS	M $	5	42.0	44.0	46.2	48.5	50.9	53.5	56.2	59.0

- COMPANY CONFIDENTIAL -

PSG - PLANNING SYSTEMS GENERATOR   12/16/68

Exhibit 8-2

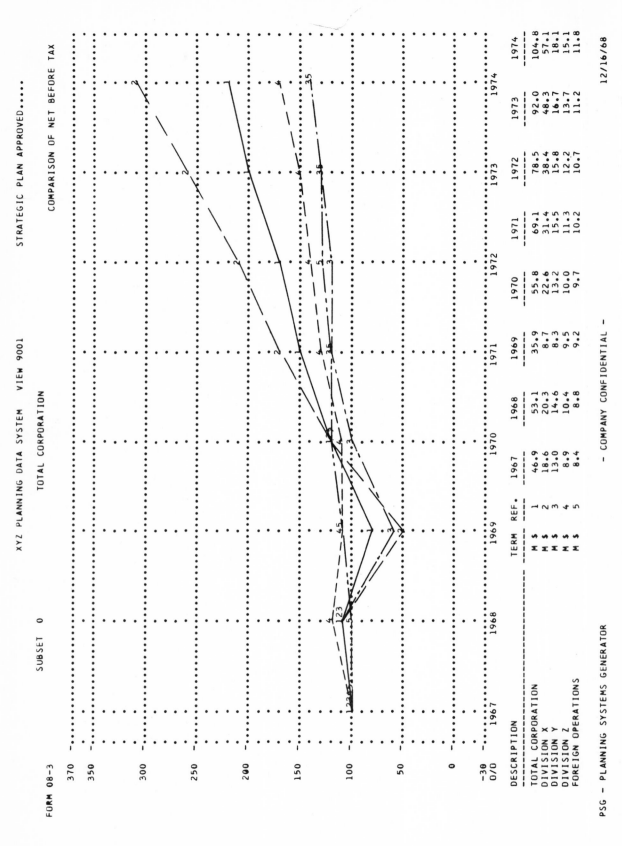

FORM 08-3

SUBSET   0

XYZ PLANNING DATA SYSTEM   VIEW 9001

STRATEGIC PLAN APPROVED.....

TOTAL CORPORATION

COMPARISON OF NET BEFORE TAX

DESCRIPTION	TERM	REF.	1967	1968	1969	1970	1971	1972	1973	1974
TOTAL CORPORATION	M $	1	46.9	53.1	35.9	55.8	69.1	78.5	92.0	104.8
DIVISION X	M $	2	18.6	20.3	8.7	22.6	31.4	38.4	48.3	57.1
DIVISION Y	M $	3	13.0	14.6	8.3	13.2	15.5	15.8	16.7	18.1
DIVISION Z	M $	4	8.9	10.4	9.5	10.0	11.3	12.2	13.7	15.1
FOREIGN OPERATIONS	M $	5	8.4	8.8	9.2	9.7	10.2	10.7	11.2	11.8

- COMPANY CONFIDENTIAL -

12/16/68

PSG - PLANNING SYSTEMS GENERATOR

Exhibit 8-3

XYZ PLANNING DATA SYSTEM   VIEW 9001   STRATEGIC PLAN APPROVED.....

SUBSET 0   TOTAL CORPORATION   ANALYSIS OF SUPPORT OPERATIONS

DESCRIPTION	TERM	REF.	1967	1968	1969	1970	1971	1972	1973	1974
CORP.PRETAX NET	M $	1	46.9	53.1	35.9	55.8	69.1	78.5	92.0	104.8
RESEARCH	M $	2	4.0	3.8	3.6	3.6	3.1	3.6	3.9	4.2
DEVELOPMENT	M $	3	10.9	11.5	12.5	13.5	14.9	15.6	17.3	19.4
CHQ ADMINISTRATION	M $	4	13.4	15.2	17.8	19.7	23.3	26.8	30.6	35.0

PSG - PLANNING SYSTEMS GENERATOR   - COMPANY CONFIDENTIAL -   12/16/68

Exhibit 8-4

output device for interrogation into procedural logic, data bank review and updating, etc. As such it would be of more utility to the system's designer than to the system's user. However, these are secondary questions connected with data-processing technology and will in time be solved. The development of a planning data system is not to be mistaken for an effort to advance the state of the art in data processing. It is an effort to advance the state of the art in business planning. For this purpose, current computer capabilities are far in excess of what is currently being done in the way of assisting management in the task of setting goals.

WORKSHEETS

We must now proceed to deal with the question of source data. In the beginning, the income analysis and index charts would be a self-contained module (or procedure) within the corporate planning data system. The following Exhibits 8-5 and 8-6 show the worksheets for the entry or generation of data required in these displays. These worksheets serve two functions:

(1) They serve as a display and hence an audit trail for the data which were used as entered or contained in the planning data bank.

(2) They serve as a key punch form for the entry of data into the data bank or for the entry of changes. The reader's attention is drawn to the card column instructions indicated as part of the column headings.

For each line item of output data required in the display usually several input data options are specified. Most typically the amount called for itself or some planning factor, a growth rate or a ratio to gross income, may be used to enter or generate data in the planning data bank. The purpose of these input options is rather obvious. Even such highly aggregated planning data as specified in a one-page corporate income analysis are often subjected to manipulations on the basis of rather crude relationships. While the management scientist and operation's researcher may wince, it is nevertheless true that, more often than not, planned goals are established, agreed upon, and acted upon by corporate and divisional management on the basis of rather basic economic analysis. Hence, the planning logic specifications behind this income analysis procedure do provide the planner with the ability to distinguish between fixed amounts and variable ratios. Furthermore each year is treated separately in keeping with the fact that the nature of fixed and variable proportions changes with time and, while speaking of 1969, most cost and expenses may be considered fixed— this would be less true for 1970 and less and less so the farther out we go into the future. This type of optional treatment of decision variables will do more for management's understanding of economics than the assumption of constant fixed charges across all future years built into many a model based on regression analysis. Fallacious

FORM 08-9   SUBSET   0

TOTAL CORPORATION

CODE	DESCRIPTION	TERM	PRIOR	1967	1968	1969	1970	1971	1972	1973	1974
COL.1-7			18-24	25-31	32-38	39-45	46-52	53-59	60-66	67-73	74-80
	DIVISION X										
0800011	GROSS INCOME AMOUNT	M $ T	114.0	120.1	130.9	142.2	182.4	221.7	261.0	309.7	353.1
0800012	OR GROWTH RATE	0/0 T	0.	0.	0.	0.	0.	0.	0.	0.	0.
0800013	GROSS PROFIT AMOUNT	M $ T	55.0	59.6	67.3	68.3	89.8	111.3	130.9	155.0	176.4
0800014	GROSS INCOME RATIO	0/0 T	0.	0.	0.	0.	0.	0.	0.	0.	0.
0800015	NET BEFORE TAX AMOUNT	M $ T	17.9	18.6	20.3	8.7	22.6	31.4	38.4	48.3	57.1
0800016	GROSS INCOME RATIO	0/0 T	0.	0.	0.	0.	0.	0.	0.	0.	0.
	DIVISION Y										
0800021	GROSS INCOME AMOUNT	M $ T	80.0	84.1	90.4	90.7	90.1	98.1	101.1	104.1	109.5
0800022	OR GROWTH RATE	0/0 T	0.	0.	0.	0.	0.	0.	0.	0.	0.
0800023	GROSS PROFIT AMOUNT	M $ T	35.0	37.7	42.1	41.6	40.6	45.0	46.2	47.4	50.1
0800024	GROSS INCOME RATIO	0/0 T	0.	0.	0.	0.	0.	0.	0.	0.	0.
0800025	NET BEFORE TAX AMOUNT	M $ T	12.0	13.0	14.6	8.3	13.2	15.5	15.8	16.7	18.1
0800026	GROSS INCOME RATIO	0/0 T	0.	0.	0.	0.	0.	0.	0.	0.	0.
	DIVISION Z										
0800031	GROSS INCOME AMOUNT	M $ T	34.0	36.0	40.5	39.7	42.4	44.4	47.7	50.7	54.8
0800032	OR GROWTH RATE	0/0 T	0.	0.	0.	0.	0.	0.	0.	0.	0.
0800033	GROSS PROFIT AMOUNT	M $ T	20.0	21.9	25.2	24.7	26.1	27.8	29.5	31.6	34.3
0800034	GROSS INCOME RATIO	0/0 T	0.	0.	0.	0.	0.	0.	0.	0.	0.
0800035	NET BEFORE TAX AMOUNT	M $ T	8.0	8.9	10.4	9.5	10.0	11.3	12.2	13.7	15.1
0800036	GROSS INCOME RATIO	0/0 T	0.	0.	0.	0.	0.	0.	0.	0.	0.

NOTE - INPUT DATA SPECIFIED AS AN AMOUNT AND AS A RATIO ARE COMPLEMENTS UNLESS THE RATIO IS PREFACED BY 'OR.'

PSG - PLANNING SYSTEMS GENERATOR

- COMPANY CONFIDENTIAL -

12/16/68

Exhibit 8-5

TOTAL CORPORATION

FORM 08-9   SUBSET O

CODE	DESCRIPTION	TERM	PRIOR	1967	1968	1969	1970	1971	1972	1973	1974
COL.1-7			18-24	25-31	32-38	39-45	46-52	53-59	60-66	67-73	74-80
	SPECIAL PRODUCTS										
0800061	GROSS INCOME AMOUNT	M $	.	.	10.0	.	.	.	.	.	.
0800062	OR GROWTH RATE	0/0	.	.		10.0	10.0	10.0	10.0	10.0	10.0
0800065	NET BEFORE TAX AMOUNT	M $	.	-2.0	-1.0	.	.	.	.	.	.
0800066	GROSS INCOME RATIO	0/0	.	.		1.0	2.0	6.0	10.0	13.0	15.0
	FOREIGN OPERATIONS										
0800071	GROSS INCOME AMOUNT	M $	40.0	42.0	44.0	.	.	.	.	.	.
0800072	OR GROWTH RATE	0/0	.	.		5.0	5.0	5.0	5.0	5.0	5.0
0800073	GROSS PROFIT AMOUNT	M $	20.0	.	.	.	.	.	.	.	.
0800074	GROSS INCOME RATIO	0/0	.	50.0	50.0	50.0	50.0	50.0	50.0	50.0	50.0
0800075	NET BEFORE TAX AMOUNT	M $	8.0	.	.	.	.	.	.	.	.
0800076	GROSS INCOME RATIO	0/0	.	20.0	20.0	20.0	20.0	20.0	20.0	20.0	20.0
	SUPPORT OPERATIONS										
0800143	RESEARCH AMOUNT	M $ T	4.1	4.0	3.8	3.6	3.6	3.1	3.6	3.9	4.2
0800144	GROSS INCOME RATIO	0/0 T	0.	0.	0.	0.	0.	0.	0.	0.	0.
0800141	DEVELOPMENT AMOUNT	M $ T	10.0	10.9	11.5	12.5	13.5	14.9	15.6	17.3	19.4
0800142	GROSS INCOME RATIO	0/0 T	0.	0.	0.	0.	0.	0.	0.	0.	0.
0800145	CHQ ADMINISTRATION AMOUNT	M $ T	12.2	13.4	15.2	17.8	19.7	23.3	26.8	30.6	35.0
0800146	GROSS INCOME RATIO	0/0 T	0.	0.	0.	0.	0.	0.	0.	0.	0.
	INCOME TAXES										
0800198	TAX RATE, DOMESTIC	0/0 T	50.00	48.00	48.00	52.00	52.00	52.00	52.00	52.00	52.00
0800199	FOREIGN	0/0	50.00	50.00	50.00	50.00	50.00	50.00	50.00	50.00	50.00

NOTE - INPUT DATA SPECIFIED AS AN AMOUNT AND AS A RATIO ARE COMPLEMENTS UNLESS THE RATIO IS PREFACED BY 'OR.'

- COMPANY CONFIDENTIAL -

PSG - PLANNING SYSTEMS GENERATOR

12/16/68

Exhibit 8-6

reasoning, especially when implicit, is extremely dangerous in the corporate decision-making process.

A corporate planning data system would certainly not be worth the name "subsystem within a network of planning data systems" if it consisted of only one procedure. In this connection, the reader's attention is drawn to the fact that on the input worksheets for the income analysis a "T" appears between the term column and the first data column. This "T" notifies the planner that the data on this line has not been entered through input cards per this worksheet but was transferred from another procedure within the system.

DIVISIONAL MODULES

It stands to reason that the planning logic, consisting of two input options for each line item of planning data to be generated, would not furnish corporate management with a sufficient rationale to back up a meaningful bargaining position in its discussions with divisional management. Therefore, the corporate planning data system must contain modules which more dynamically represent a division's operating environment. These divisional modules are still rather aggregate and will not compare with the power and planning logic contained in the divisional subsystem which is at the disposal of divisional management. However, these divisional modules should be sufficiently detailed to allow for the development of reasonable independent judgment about the future of any division within the corporation. Let's take a look at the typical planning documents produced by a divisional procedure within a corporate planning data system, as follows:

Exhibit 8-7	Income and Expense Summary
Exhibit 8-8	Source and Application of Funds
Exhibit 8-9	Balance Sheet
Exhibit 8-10	Year-End Manpower
Exhibit 8-11	Space, Buildings and Land

The reader is asked to study these documents at leisure. He will find that in the divisional module a substantial amount of information, both in physical and fiscal (financial) terms, is presented. Among other things, gross income and gross profit are broken down by major sources, such as products, service, and supplies. Expenses are detailed by seven subsidiary accounts. Percentages to gross income, as well as rates of change for the major items are displayed. In addition, there is some information on business volume assumptions relating the division's sales to general market data. Since all descriptors are spelled out, these planning documents are self-explanatory to anyone familiar with accounting terminology and related analytical

XYZ PLANNING DATA SYSTEM   VIEW 9001

STRATEGIC PLAN APPROVED.....

DIVISION Y

INCOME AND EXPENSE SUMMARY

FORM 03-1   SUBSET 2

DESCRIPTION	1967 M$	1967 O/O	1968 M$	1968 O/O	1969 M$	1969 O/O	1970 M$	1970 O/O	1971 M$	1971 O/O	1972 M$	1972 O/O	1973 M$	1973 O/O	1974 M$	1974 O/O
BUSINESS VOLUME																
MARKET ESTIMATE	1040.0		1081.6		1124.9		1173.6		1222.4		1271.2		1320.0		1373.4	
SALES POTENTIAL	90.0		93.6		97.3		105.0		107.5		109.9		112.3		119.4	
O/O REPLACEMENT	5.0		5.0		5.0		5.0		5.0		5.0		5.0		5.0	
XYZ POSITION	230.0		240.0		249.8		258.2		268.9		279.7		290.4		302.1	
REMOVALS	11.0		11.5		12.0		12.5		12.9		13.4		14.0		14.5	
SHIPMENTS	21.0		21.5		21.8		20.9		23.6		24.2		24.7		26.3	
O/O XYZ POSITION	22.1		22.2		22.2		22.0		22.0		22.0		22.0		22.0	
XYZ REMOVALS	5.0		5.0		5.0		5.0		5.0		5.0		5.0		5.0	
XYZ SHIPMENTS	23.3		23.0		22.4		19.9		22.0		22.0		22.0		22.0	
GROSS INCOME																
PRODUCTS	45.8	54.5	48.2	53.3	48.4	53.4	46.3	51.4	52.5	53.5	53.7	53.1	54.9	52.7	58.3	53.3
SERVICE	37.2	44.2	41.0	45.4	41.4	45.6	42.9	47.6	44.6	45.5	46.4	45.9	48.2	46.3	50.2	45.8
SUPPLIES																
OTHER	1.1	1.3	1.2	1.3	.9	1.0	.9	1.0	1.0	1.0	1.0	1.0	1.0	.9	1.0	.9
TOTAL	84.1	100.0	90.4	100.0	90.7	100.0	90.1	100.0	98.1	100.0	101.1	100.0	104.1	100.0	109.5	100.0
GROSS PROFIT																
PRODUCTS	26.4	57.6	30.2	62.7	30.3	62.6	29.0	62.6	32.9	62.6	33.6	62.6	34.3	62.6	36.5	62.6
SERVICE	10.6	28.5	11.1	27.1	10.7	25.8	11.1	25.8	11.5	25.8	12.0	25.8	12.4	25.8	12.9	25.8
SUPPLIES																
OTHER	.7	63.6	.8	66.7	.6	66.7	.6	65.0	.6	65.0	.6	65.0	.6	65.0	.7	65.0
TOTAL	37.7	44.8	42.1	46.6	41.6	45.9	40.6	45.1	45.0	45.9	46.2	45.7	47.4	45.6	50.1	45.8
EXPENSES																
RESEARCH	1.0	1.2	1.0	1.1	1.0	1.1	.9	1.0	1.0	1.0	1.0	1.0	1.0	1.0	1.1	1.0
DEVELOPMENT	3.6	4.3	3.6	4.0	3.9	4.3	3.6	4.0	3.9	4.0	4.0	4.0	4.3	4.1	4.6	4.2
FIELD SALES	10.7	12.7	11.6	12.8	14.4	15.9	10.5	11.7	12.1	12.3	12.1	12.0	12.5	12.0	12.7	11.6
MKTG.SUPPORT	.9	1.1	1.1	1.2	1.3	1.4	1.2	1.3	1.3	1.3	1.2	1.2	1.2	1.1	1.2	1.1
ADMINISTRATION	3.1	3.7	3.4	3.8	3.5	3.9	3.6	4.0	3.7	3.8	3.6	3.6	3.5	3.4	3.5	3.2
OTHER	.7	.8	1.5	1.7	3.3	3.6	1.9	2.1	1.3	1.8	1.8	1.8	1.4	1.4	1.4	1.3
APPORTIONMENTS	4.7	5.6	5.3	5.9	5.9	6.5	5.7	6.3	6.3	6.4	6.7	6.6	6.9	6.6	7.4	6.8
TOTAL	24.7	29.4	27.5	30.4	33.3	36.7	27.4	30.4	29.5	30.1	30.5	30.1	30.8	29.6	32.0	29.2
NET BEFORE TAX	13.0	15.5	14.6	16.2	8.3	9.2	13.2	14.7	15.5	15.8	15.8	15.6	16.7	16.0	18.1	16.6
NET AFTER TAX	6.8	8.0	7.6	8.4	4.0	4.4	6.4	7.1	7.4	7.6	7.6	7.5	8.0	7.7	8.7	8.0
EARNINGS/SHARE	2.25		2.53		1.33		2.12		2.48		2.52		2.67		2.90	

RATES OF CHANGE (O/O)

DESCRIPTION	1967	1968	1969	1970	1971	1972	1973	1974
MARKET ESTIMATE	4.0	4.0	4.0	4.3	4.2	4.0	3.8	4.0
XYZ POSITION	4.5	4.3	4.1	3.3	4.2	4.0	3.8	4.0
GROSS INCOME	5.1	7.5	.3	-.7	8.9	3.0	3.0	5.2
GROSS PROFIT	7.7	11.7	-1.2	-2.3	10.8	2.7	2.6	5.7
TOTAL EXPENSES	7.4	11.3	21.1	-17.8	7.8	3.1	1.0	3.9
NET BEFORE TAX	8.3	12.3	-43.2	59.5	16.8	1.8	5.8	8.9
NET AFTER TAX	12.7	12.3	-47.5	59.5	16.8	1.8	5.8	8.9

PSG - PLANNING SYSTEMS GENERATOR

- COMPANY CONFIDENTIAL -

12/16/68

Exhibit 8-7

STRATEGIC PLAN APPROVED.....

DIVISION Y

SOURCE AND APPLICATION OF FUNDS

FORM 03-2   SUBSET 2

DESCRIPTION	TERM	1967	1968	1969	1970	1971	1972	1973	1974
NET CURRENT ASSETS 1-1	M $	40.0	41.1	45.1	45.8	29.8	31.3	34.8	38.3
NET EARNINGS	M $	6.8	7.6	4.0	6.4	7.4	7.6	8.0	8.7
DEPRECIATION ETC.	M $	3.4	4.6	3.3	3.6	3.9	4.1	4.2	4.3
FUNDS FROM OPERATIONS	M $	10.2	12.2	7.3	10.0	11.3	11.7	12.2	13.0
SALE OF STOCK	M $								
LONG TERM DEBT INCURRED	M $								
MISCELLANEOUS	M $								
TOTAL FUNDS PROVIDED	M $	10.2	12.2	7.3	10.0	11.3	11.7	12.2	13.0
TOTAL FUNDS AVAILABLE	M $	50.2	53.2	52.3	55.8	41.1	43.0	47.0	51.4
LAND AND BUILDINGS	M $	-.0	.0	.1	2.2	1.1	.1	.2	.4
EQUIPMENT	M $	4.4	3.3	3.4	2.2	4.3	3.5	3.6	4.0
TOTAL INVESTMENTS	M $	4.3	3.3	3.5	2.2	5.3	3.6	3.9	4.4
LONG TERM DEBT REPAID	M $								
CASH DIVIDEND	M $	4.8	4.8	3.0	3.8	4.5	4.5	4.8	5.2
TOTAL FUNDS APPLIED	M $	9.1	8.1	6.5	26.0	9.8	8.1	8.7	9.6
NET CURRENT ASSETS 12-31	M $	41.1	45.1	45.8	29.8	31.3	34.8	38.3	41.8
ANALYTICAL RATIOS									
PLANT AND EQUIPMENT/TOTAL	0/0	47.5	41.1	53.9	8.5	54.4	44.2	44.6	45.6
EARNINGS PER SHARE	$	2.25	2.53	1.33	2.12	2.48	2.52	2.67	2.90
CASH DIVIDEND PAYOUT	0/0	71.0	63.2	75.3	60.0	60.0	60.0	60.0	60.0
RATES OF CHANGE									
FUNDS FROM OPERATIONS	0/0		19.3	-40.2	36.9	13.4	3.5	4.2	7.1
TOTAL FUNDS PROVIDED	0/0		19.3	-40.2	36.9	13.4	3.5	4.2	7.1
INVESTMENTS	0/0		-22.9	5.0	-37.0	140.6	-32.4	7.4	13.1
TOTAL FUNDS APPLIED	0/0		-10.9	-20.1	299.8	-62.4	-16.8	6.5	10.8
NET CURRENT ASSETS 12-31	0/0	2.6	9.8	1.7	-35.1	5.1	11.4	10.1	9.0
MANPOWER - CHANGES IN HEADCOUNT									
MANUFACTURING	MEN	14	-78	-94	-84	15	-43	-36	-9
ENGINEERING	MEN	17	3	15	-19	17	6	11	17
MARKETING	MEN	19	26	97	-180	67	-1	15	11
SERVICE	MEN	28	16	25	-223	-80	-70	-61	-46
ADMINISTRATION	MEN	3	3	-8	2	-1	-6	-6	-4
TOTAL NET CHANGE	MEN	81	-30	35	-503	18	-113	-77	-32
TOTAL ON BOARD 12-31	MEN	4337	4307	4342	3838	3856	3743	3667	3635
INCREASE OVER PRIOR YEAR	0/0	1.9	-.7	.8	-11.6	.5	-2.9	-2.0	-.9

PSG - PLANNING SYSTEMS GENERATOR

- COMPANY CONFIDENTIAL -

12/16/68

Exhibit 8-8

STRATEGIC PLAN APPROVED.....

DIVISION Y

BALANCE SHEET

FORM 03-3   SUBSET 2

DESCRIPTION	TERM	1967	1968	1969	1970	1971	1972	1973	1974
ASSETS									
CASH	M $	16.2	18.6	19.5	8.0	8.0	9.9	11.7	13.2
MARKETABLE SECURITIES	M $	7.0	8.0	8.4	3.4	3.4	4.2	5.0	5.7
NOTES AND ACCTS. RECEIVABLE	M $	16.3	17.5	17.6	17.5	19.0	19.6	20.2	21.3
INVENTORIES	M $	27.6	28.7	29.7	29.5	31.8	32.8	33.8	35.5
PREPAYMENTS	M $	2.1	2.3	2.3	1.5	1.6	1.7	1.9	2.1
CURRENT ASSETS	M $	69.2	75.0	77.5	59.9	63.8	68.3	72.7	77.7
OTHER INVESTMENTS	M $								
LAND	M $	5.0	5.0	5.0	5.0	6.0	6.0	6.0	6.0
BUILDINGS	M $	6.1	6.1	6.2	6.2	6.2	6.4	6.6	7.0
NET LAND AND BUILDINGS	M $	5.6	5.1	4.7	4.2	4.7	4.3	4.1	3.9
FACTORY AND OFFICE EQUIPMENT	M $	19.4	22.7	26.1	28.3	32.6	36.1	39.7	43.6
NET FACTORY AND OFFICE	M $	10.6	10.1	10.9	10.2	11.3	11.4	11.6	11.9
PATENTS AND GOOD WILL	M $	1.8	1.6	1.4	1.2	1.0	.8	.6	.4
TOTAL ASSETS	M $	87.2	91.8	94.5	75.5	80.9	84.9	88.9	94.0
LIABILITIES AND EQUITY									
INCOME TAXES	M $	1.6	1.8	1.1	1.7	2.0	2.0	2.2	2.4
ACCTS. PAYABLE AND ACCRUALS	M $	26.6	28.2	30.6	28.5	30.5	31.5	32.2	33.6
LOANS PAYABLE	M $								
CURRENT LIABILITIES	M $	28.1	30.0	31.7	30.2	32.5	33.5	34.4	35.9
DEFERRALS AND RESERVES	M $	20.0	20.0	20.0					
LONG TERM DEBT	M $								
TOTAL LIABILITIES	M $	48.1	50.0	51.7	30.2	32.5	33.5	34.4	35.9
EQUITY CAPITAL	M $	39.0	41.8	42.8	45.4	48.3	51.4	54.6	58.0
NUMBER OF SHARES OUTSTANDING	K	3000	3000	3000	3000	3000	3000	3000	3000
ANALYTICAL RATIOS									
CURR. ASSETS/CURR. LIAB.	0/0	246.0	250.5	244.7	198.6	196.1	203.9	211.5	216.3
CURRENT/TOTAL ASSETS	0/0	79.4	81.7	82.0	79.3	78.9	80.5	81.8	82.7
CURR. LIAB./TOTAL ASSETS	0/0	32.3	32.6	33.5	39.9	40.2	39.5	38.7	38.2
EQUITY PER SHARE	$	13.02	13.95	14.28	15.12	16.11	17.12	18.19	19.35
RETURN ON CAPITAL	0/0	11.4	12.3	6.3	14.0	15.4	14.7	14.7	15.0
CAPITAL TURNOVER RATIO	X	1.42	1.46	1.44	1.99	2.03	1.97	1.91	1.89
EARNINGS PER SHARE	$	2.25	2.53	1.33	2.12	2.48	2.52	2.67	2.90
RATES OF CHANGE									
CURRENT ASSETS	0/0	1.7	8.5	3.3	-22.7	6.5	7.1	6.4	6.9
NET LAND AND BUILDINGS	0/0	-8.8	-8.8	-7.9	-10.8	13.4	-8.0	-6.4	-3.0
NET FACTORY AND OFFICE	0/0	18.3	-5.0	8.1	-6.3	10.7	.5	1.5	3.1
CURRENT LIABILITIES	0/0	.4	6.5	5.8	-4.7	7.9	2.9	2.6	4.5
EQUITY CAPITAL	0/0	8.5	7.1	2.4	5.9	6.5	6.3	6.2	6.4

- COMPANY CONFIDENTIAL -

PSG - PLANNING SYSTEMS GENERATOR

12/16/68

Exhibit 8-9

FORM 03-4   SUBSET 2

DIVISION Y   YEAR-END MANPOWER

DESCRIPTION	TERM	1967	1968	1969	1970	1971	1972	1973	1974
MANUFACTURING									
DIRECT	MEN	437	398	351	309	317	295	277	273
INDIRECT	MEN	437	398	351	309	317	295	277	273
TOTAL	MEN	874	796	702	618	633	590	555	545
GROWTH RATE	O/O	1.6	-8.9	-11.8	-11.9	2.4	-6.8	-6.1	-1.7
NEW HIRES	MEN	126	21	35	-53	46	-13	-8	18
HIRING RATE	O/O	14.4	2.6	5.0	-8.5	7.3	-2.2	-1.5	3.3
COST FACTOR PER MAN	K $	22.2	22.6	25.8	28.0	31.0	34.0	37.0	40.0
ENGINEERING									
PROFESSIONAL	MEN	131	133	143	131	142	146	154	165
SUPPORT	MEN	66	67	72	65	71	73	77	83
TOTAL	MEN	197	200	215	196	213	220	231	248
GROWTH RATE	O/O	9.2	1.5	7.5	-8.7	8.9	3.0	5.0	7.3
NEW HIRES	MEN	20	7	19	-15	22	11	16	22
HIRING RATE	O/O	10.4	3.5	9.0	-7.6	10.2	5.0	6.8	8.8
COST FACTOR PER MAN	K $	23.4	23.1	22.8	23.0	23.0	23.0	23.0	23.0
MARKETING									
FIELD	MEN	516	542	639	467	531	530	544	555
SUPPORT	MEN	29	29	29	21	24	24	24	25
TOTAL	MEN	545	571	668	488	555	554	569	580
GROWTH RATE	O/O	3.6	4.8	17.0	-27.0	13.8	-.2	2.7	2.0
NEW HIRES	MEN	63	66	137	-156	95	27	43	40
HIRING RATE	O/O	11.5	11.6	20.5	-31.9	17.1	4.8	7.6	7.0
COST FACTOR PER MAN	K $	21.3	22.2	23.5	24.0	24.0	24.0	24.0	24.0
SERVICE									
FIELD	MEN	2628	2644	2600	2352	2275	2208	2150	2105
SUPPORT	MEN			69	94	91	88	86	84
TOTAL	MEN	2628	2644	2669	2446	2366	2296	2236	2189
GROWTH RATE	O/O	1.1	.6	.9	-8.3	-3.3	-2.9	-2.7	-2.1
NEW HIRES	MEN	265	241	239	-27	109	114	118	129
HIRING RATE	O/O	10.1	9.1	8.9	-1.1	4.6	5.0	5.3	5.9
COST FACTOR PER MAN	K $	10.1	11.3	11.5	13.0	14.0	15.0	16.0	17.0
ADMINISTRATION									
PROFESSIONAL	MEN	93	96	88	90	89	83	77	73
SUPPORT	MEN								
TOTAL	MEN	93	96	88	90	89	83	77	73
GROWTH RATE	O/O	3.3	3.2	-8.3	2.3	-1.5	-6.8	-7.0	-5.1
NEW HIRES	MEN	4	4	-7	3	-5	-5	-5	-3
HIRING RATE	O/O	4.2	4.1	-8.1	3.3	-.5	-6.3	-6.5	-4.4
COST FACTOR PER MAN	K $	33.3	35.4	39.8	40.0	42.0	44.0	46.0	48.0
TOTAL BUSINESS									
ON BOARD	MEN	4337	4307	4342	3838	3856	3743	3667	3635
GROWTH RATE	O/O	1.9	-.7	.8	-11.6	.5	-2.9	-2.0	-.9
NEW HIRES	MEN	477	339	423	-247	272	133	164	206
HIRING RATE	O/O	11.0	7.9	9.7	-6.4	7.0	3.6	4.5	5.7

PSG - PLANNING SYSTEMS GENERATOR

- COMPANY CONFIDENTIAL -

Exhibit 8-10

12/16/68

XYZ PLANNING DATA SYSTEM   VIEW 9001

FORM 03-5   SUBSET 2

DIVISION Y

STRATEGIC PLAN APPROVED......

SPACE, BUILDINGS + LAND

DESCRIPTION	TERM	1967	1968	1969	1970	1971	1972	1973	1974
SPACE FORECAST									
PLANTS	KSQFT	159	145	128	113	115	107	101	99
WAREHOUSES	KSQFT	24	22	19	17	17	16	15	15
LABORATORIES	KSQFT	57	58	62	57	62	64	67	72
OFFICES	KSQFT	327	331	343	302	301	293	288	284
TOTAL	KSQFT	567	556	552	489	495	481	471	470
OCCUPANCY FACTORS/MAN									
MANUFACTURING	SQFT	260	260	260	260	260	260	260	260
MFG. EXTRA SHIFT RATIO	O/O	30.0	30.0	30.0	30.0	30.0	30.0	30.0	30.0
MFG. WAREHOUSING	O/O	15.0	15.0	15.0	15.0	15.0	15.0	15.0	15.0
ENGINEERING	SQFT	290	290	290	290	290	290	290	290
OTHER	SQFT	100	100	100	100	100	100	100	100
SPACE AVAILABILITY REVIEW									
PLANTS OWNED	KSQFT	128	128	128	128	128	128	128	128
LEASED	KSQFT	32	32	32	32	32	32	32	32
VARIANCE	KSQFT	-1	-15	-32	-47	-45	-53	-59	-61
WAREHOUSES OWNED	KSQFT	4	4	4	4	4	4	4	4
LEASED	KSQFT	16	16	16	16	16	16	16	16
VARIANCE	KSQFT	4	2	-1	-3	-3	-4	-5	-5
LABORATORIES OWNED	KSQFT	60	60	60	60	60	60	60	60
LEASED	KSQFT								
VARIANCE	KSQFT	-3	-2	2	-3	2	4	7	12
OFFICES OWNED	KSQFT	33	33	33	33	33	33	33	33
LEASED	KSQFT	297	297	297	297	297	297	297	297
VARIANCE	KSQFT	-3	1	13	-28	-29	-37	-42	-46
TOTAL OWNED	KSQFT	225	225	225	225	225	225	225	225
LEASED	KSQFT	345	345	345	345	345	345	345	345
REQUIRED (+)	KSQFT	4	3	15		2	4	7	12
BUILDINGS PLANNED AND REQUIRED									
PLANTS	KSQFT	-2.0							
WAREHOUSES	KSQFT	.8	.3						
LABORATORIES	KSQFT			2.2		1.8	3.7	6.9	11.8
OFFICES	KSQFT		.1	1.3					
TOTAL (GROSS)	KSQFT	-1.2	.5	3.5		1.8	3.7	6.9	11.8
NET INVESTMENT IN BUILDINGS									
PLANTS	M $	-.0							
WAREHOUSES	M $	.0	.0						
LABORATORIES	M $			.0		.1	.1	.2	.4
OFFICES	M $		.0	.1					
TOTAL	M $	-.0	.0	.1		.1	.1	.2	.4
LAND HOLDINGS									
AREA ON HAND YEAR-END	ACRES	1000.9	1000.9	1000.9	1000.9	1500.9	1500.9	1500.9	1500.9
PURCHASES	ACRES					500.0			
NET INVESTMENT	M $					1.0			

PSG - PLANNING SYSTEMS GENERATOR

12/16/68

- COMPANY CONFIDENTIAL -

Exhibit 8-11

ratios. The planning logic which governs the generation of these many different lines of information proceeds as follows:

Market potential = f (market growth, share of market).

Sales = f (company position, removal patterns, share of potential).

Gross income = f (delivery time lag, installed equipment, supply requirements).

Gross profit = f (fixed cost, amount, marginal cost ratio).

Expenses = f (fixed amount, variable ratio).

Manpower = f (fixed amount, output cost factor).

Space = f (fixed amount, occupancy factors).

Investment in new buildings = f (space requirements, available space, building costs).

Working capital = f (income, cost and expense).

A study of the seven pages of input options to this divisional module within a corporate system (Exhibits 8-12 to 8-18) will give the reader a good insight into the logic embodied in this planning procedure. A complete listing of the PSG program specifications for this divisional module is given in the appendix.

CORPORATE PLANNING DATA BANK

Since throughout this book we have emphasized the need for keeping count of the dimensions of the data bank implied in the planning procedures written within each subsystem of the network, we have to pause and take account of the corporate planning data subsystem so far described. The procedure for income analysis specifies 36 lines of input options (324 data cells). The divisional module procedure specifies 142 lines (1,278 data cells). However, the divisional module is used three times for divisions X, Y, and Z. Similar planning data support must be envisioned for the special products and foreign operations modules, the latter perhaps in turn subdivided by several major lines of business making for a total of at least ten subsets. Hence, the data bank for this still rather stylized corporate planning data system already reaches some 1,450 lines (13,000 data cells). If we continue with the assumption that firm data are available only for the first three columns covering the prior period and the first two years, about 8,700 data cells within this bank are subject to intelligent monitoring and potentially frequent change.

It is easy to visualize that a further refinement of the corporate planning data system will explode this data bank to a size which quickly becomes unmanageable. Only extreme restraint and self-discipline will prevent the proliferation of the corporate system by the adding of procedures which cover functional dynamics by product category, plant location, marketing territory, etc. This type of detail must

XYZ PLANNING DATA SYSTEM   VIEW 9001

STRATEGIC PLAN APPROVED......

FORM 03-9   SUBSET 2

DIVISION Y

INPUT WORKSHEET 1 OF 7

CODE	DESCRIPTION	TERM	PRIOR	1967	1968	1969	1970	1971	1972	1973	1974
COL.1-7			18-24	25-31	32-38	39-45	46-52	53-59	60-66	67-73	74-80
	BUSINESS VOLUME ASSUMPTIONS										
0302201	MARKET, AMOUNT	M $	1000.0	.	.	.	.	.	.	1320.0	.
0302202	OR GROWTH RATE	0/0	.	4.0	4.0	4.0	.	.	.	.	.
0302203	REPLACEMENT AMOUNT	M $	.	.	.	.	.	.	.	.	.
0302204	FACTOR	0/0	.	5.0	5.0	5.0	5.0	5.0	5.0	5.0	5.0
0302205	XYZ POSITION, AMOUNT	M $	220.0	230.0	240.0	.	.	.	.	.	.
0302206	OR GROWTH RATE	0/0	.	.	.	4.1	.	.	.	.	4.0
0302207	OR SHARE OF MARKET	0/0	.	.	.	.	22.0	22.0	22.0	22.0	22.0
0302209	XYZ REMOVALS, AMOUNT	M $	.	.	.	.	.	.	.	.	.
0302210	FACTOR	0/0	.	5.0	5.0	5.0	5.0	5.0	5.0	5.0	5.0
	GROSS INCOME										
0302001	PRODUCTS, AMOUNT	M $	43.0	45.8	48.2	48.4	.	.	.	.	.
0302002	OR SHIPMENT FACTOR	0/0	.	.	.	.	222.0	222.0	222.0	222.0	222.0
0302003	SERVICE, AMOUNT	M $	36.0	37.2	41.0	41.4	.	.	.	.	.
0302004	OR POSITION FACTOR	0/0	.	.	.	.	16.6	16.6	16.6	16.6	16.6
0302005	SUPPLIES, AMOUNT	M $	.	.	.	.	.	.	.	.	.
0302006	OR POSITION FACTOR	0/0	.	.	.	.	.	.	.	.	.
0302007	OTHER, AMOUNT	M $	1.0	1.1	1.2	.9	.	.	.	.	.
0302008	OR SHARE OF TOTAL INCOME	0/0	.	.	.	.	1.0	1.0	1.0	1.0	1.0

NOTE - INPUT DATA SPECIFIED AS AN AMOUNT AND AS A RATIO ARE COMPLEMENTS UNLESS THE RATIO IS PREFACED BY 'OR.'

PSG - PLANNING SYSTEMS GENERATOR

- COMPANY CONFIDENTIAL -

12/16/68

Exhibit 8-12

FORM 03-9   SUBSET 2   DIVISION Y

CODE	DESCRIPTION	TERM	PRIOR 18-24	1967 25-31	1968 32-38	1969 39-45	1970 46-52	1971 53-59	1972 60-66	1973 67-73	1974 74-80
COL.1-7	GROSS PROFIT										
0302011	PRODUCTS, AMOUNT	M $	24.4	26.4	30.2	30.3	.	.	.	.	.
0302012	GROSS INCOME RATIO	O/O	.	.	.	.	62.6	62.6	62.6	62.6	62.6
0302013	SERVICE, AMOUNT	M $	10.0	10.6	11.1	10.7	.	.	.	.	.
0302014	GROSS INCOME RATIO	O/O	.	.	.	.	25.8	25.8	25.8	25.8	25.8
0302015	SUPPLIES, AMOUNT	M $	.	.	.	.	.	.	.	.	.
0302016	GROSS INCOME RATIO	O/O	.	.	.	.	.	.	.	.	.
0302017	OTHER, AMOUNT	M $	.6	.7	.8	.6	.	.	.	.	.
0302018	GROSS INCOME RATIO	O/O	.	.	.	.	65.0	65.0	65.0	65.0	65.0
	EXPENSES										
0302025	RESEARCH, AMOUNT	M $	1.0	1.0	1.0	1.0	.	.	.	.	.
0302026	GROSS INCOME RATIO	O/O	.	.	.	.	1.0	1.0	1.0	1.0	1.0
0302027	DEVELOPMENT, AMOUNT	M $	3.0	3.6	3.6	3.9	.	.	.	.	.
0302028	GROSS INCOME RATIO	O/O	.	.	.	.	4.0	4.0	4.0	4.1	4.2
0302029	FIELD SALES, AMOUNT	M $	10.0	10.7	11.6	14.4	.	.	.	.	.
0302030	GROSS INCOME RATIO	O/O	.	.	.	.	11.7	12.3	12.0	12.0	11.6
0302031	MKTG.SUPPORT, AMOUNT	M $	.7	.9	1.1	1.3	.	.	.	.	.
0302032	FIELD SALES RATIO	O/O	.	.	.	.	11.1	10.4	9.6	9.3	9.6
0302033	ADMINISTRATION, AMOUNT	M $	2.8	3.1	3.4	3.5	.	.	.	.	.
0302034	GROSS INCOME RATIO	O/O	.	.	.	.	4.0	3.8	3.6	3.4	3.2
0302035	OTHER EXP.OR INC.AMOUNT	M $	1.4	.7	1.5	3.3	1.9	1.3	1.8	1.4	1.4
0302036	GROSS INCOME RATIO	O/O	.	.	.	.	.	.	.	.	.
0302037	APPORTIONMENTS, AMOUNT	M $	4.1	4.7	5.3	5.9	6.3	6.4	6.6	6.6	6.8
0302038	GROSS INCOME RATIO	O/O	.	.	.	.	.	.	.	.	.
0302045	CORPORATE TAX RATE	O/O	50.0	48.0	48.0	52.0	52.0	52.0	52.0	52.0	52.0
0302046	OR TAX AMOUNT	M $	.	.	.	.	.	.	.	.	.

PSG - PLANNING SYSTEMS GENERATOR

- COMPANY CONFIDENTIAL -

12/16/68

Exhibit 8-13

FORM 03-9
SUBSET 2

CODE	DESCRIPTION	TERM	PRIOR	1967	1968	1969	1970	1971	1972	1973	1974
COL.1-7			18-24	25-31	32-38	39-45	46-52	53-59	60-66	67-73	74-80
	CHANGE IN FIXED ASSETS										
0302050	EQUIPMENT, AMOUNT	M $	15.0	4.0	4.0	4.0	4.0	4.0	4.0	4.0	4.0
0302051	MANUFACTURING PER MAN	K $	.	10.0	10.0	10.0	10.0	10.0	10.0	10.0	10.0
0302052	ENGINEERING PER MAN	K $	.	8.0	8.0	8.0	8.0	8.0	8.0	8.0	8.0
0302053	OTHER PER MAN	K $	.	2.0	2.0	2.0	2.0	2.0	2.0	2.0	2.0
0302054	PATENTS AND GOODWILL	M $	3.0	.	.	.	.	.	.	.	.
	WORKING CAPITAL FACTORS										
0302101	CURRENT ASSETS (PRIOR ONLY)	M $	68.0	.	.	.	.	.	.	.	.
0302102	CURRENT LIABILITIES (PRIOR ONLY)	M $	28.0	.	.	.	.	.	.	.	.
0302091	A/R AMOUNT	M $	.	.	.	.	.	.	.	.	.
0302092	OF GROSS INCOME - PRODUCTS	O/O	.	19.0	19.0	19.0	19.0	19.0	19.0	19.0	19.0
0302093	SERVICE	O/O	.	20.0	20.0	20.0	20.0	20.0	20.0	20.0	20.0
0302094	SUPPLIES	O/O	.	25.0	25.0	25.0	25.0	25.0	25.0	25.0	25.0
0302095	OTHER	O/O	.	15.0	15.0	15.0	15.0	15.0	15.0	15.0	15.0
0302096	SECURITIES/DISPOSABLE FUNDS (CO)	O/O	.	30.0	30.0	30.0	30.0	30.0	30.0	30.0	30.0
0302097	PREPAYMENTS/NET CURRENT ASSETS (CO)	O/O	.	5.0	5.0	5.0	5.0	5.0	5.0	5.0	5.0
0302098	SUNDRY ASSETS	M $	.	.	.	.	.	.	.	.	.
0302099	INCOME TAXES PAYABLE/TAXES DUE (CO)	O/O	.	25.0	25.0	25.0	25.0	25.0	25.0	25.0	25.0
0302105	A/P AND ACCRUALS, AMOUNT	M $	.	.	.	.	.	.	.	.	.
0302106	COST + EXPENSE FACTOR	O/O	.	40.0	40.0	40.0	40.0	40.0	40.0	40.0	40.0
0302107	LOANS PAYABLE	M $	.	.	.	.	.	.	.	.	.
0302109	DEFERRALS AND RESERVES, AMOUNT	M $	.	.	.	.	.	.	.	.	.
0302110	MANPOWER FACTOR	$	.	200.	200.	200.	200.	220.	220.	220.	220.

NOTE - INPUT DATA SPECIFIED AS AN AMOUNT AND AS A RATIO ARE COMPLEMENTS UNLESS THE RATIO IS PREFACED BY 'OR.'

- COMPANY CONFIDENTIAL -

PSG - PLANNING SYSTEMS GENERATOR   12/16/68

Exhibit 8-14

DIVISION Y

SUBSET 2

FORM 03-9

CODE	DESCRIPTION	TERM	PRIOR 18-24	1967 25-31	1968 32-38	1969 39-45	1970 46-52	1971 53-59	1972 60-66	1973 67-73	1974 74-80
COL.1-7	DEPRECIATION FACTORS										
0302061	BUILDINGS, AMOUNT	M $	5.0	.5	.5	.5	.5	.5	.5	.5	.5
0302062	BOOKLIFE	YRS	.	20.0	20.0	20.0	20.0	20.0	20.0	20.0	20.0
0302063	EQUIPMENT, AMOUNT	M $	6.0	2.0	2.0	.	.	.	.	.	.
0302064	BOOKLIFE	YRS	.	5.0	5.0	5.0	5.0	5.0	5.0	5.0	5.0
0302065	PATENTS AND GOODWILL, AMOUNT	M $	1.0	.2	.2	.2	.2	.2	.2	.2	.2
0302066	BOOKLIFE	YRS	.	15.0	15.0	15.0	15.0	15.0	15.0	15.0	15.0
0302067	OTHER NON-CASH, AMOUNT	M $	.	.	.	.	.	.	.	.	.
	OTHER FUNDING AND INVESTMENTS										
0302103	EQUITY CAPITAL (PRIOR ONLY)	M $	36.0	.	.	.	.	.	.	.	.
0302074	SALE OF CAPITAL STOCK (CO)	M $	.	.	.	.	.	.	.	.	.
0302073	NUMBER OF SHARES ISSUED	K	3000.	.	.	.	.	.	.	.	.
0302075	INCREASE IN LONG TERM DEBT- (CO)	M $	20.0	.	.	.	.	.	.	.	.
0302076	REDUCTION IN LONG TERM DEBT (CO)	M $	.	.	.	.	20.0	.	.	.	.
0302077	MISCELLANEOUS	M $	.	.	.	.	.	.	.	.	.
	INVENTORIES										
0302081	PARTS, AMOUNT	M $	14.0	.	.	.	.	.	.	.	.
0302082	POSITION FACTOR	0/0	.	6.0	6.0	6.0	6.0	6.0	6.0	6.0	6.0
0302083	WORK IN PROCESS, AMOUNT	M $	6.0	.	.	.	.	.	.	.	.
0302084	SHIPMENT FACTOR	0/0	.	50.0	50.0	50.0	50.0	50.0	50.0	50.0	50.0
0302085	OTHER INVENTORIES, AMOUNT	M $	.	.	.	.	.	.	.	.	.
0302086	COST + EXPENSE FACTOR	0/0	.	5.0	5.0	5.0	5.0	5.0	5.0	5.0	5.0

NOTE - INPUT DATA SPECIFIED AS AN AMOUNT AND AS A RATIO ARE COMPLEMENTS UNLESS THE RATIO IS PREFACED BY 'OR.'

PSG - PLANNING SYSTEMS GENERATOR

- COMPANY CONFIDENTIAL -

12/16/68

Exhibit 8-15

FORM 03-9   SUBSET 2

DIVISION Y

CODE	DESCRIPTION	TERM	PRIOR	1967	1968	1969	1970	1971	1972	1973	1974
COL.1-7			18-24	25-31	32-38	39-45	46-52	53-59	60-66	67-73	74-80
	DIVIDEND POLICY										
0302078	CASH DIVIDEND, AMOUNT/SHARE (CO)	$	.	1.60	1.60	1.00	.	.	.	.	.
0302079	OR PAYOUT/NET EARNINGS (CO)	O/O	.	.	.	.	60.0	60.0	60.0	60.0	60.0
	YEAR-END MANPOWER										
0302140	MANUFACTURING COST/MAN	K $	.	.	.	.	28.0	31.0	34.0	37.0	40.0
0302141	DIRECT	MEN	430.	437.	398.	351.	.	.	.	.	.
0302143	INDIRECT	MEN	430.	437.	398.	351.	.	.	.	.	.
0302144	RATIO	O/O	.	.	.	.	100.0	100.0	100.0	100.0	100.0
0302148	ATTRITION	MEN	.	112.	99.	129.	.	.	.	.	.
0302149	RATIO	O/O	.	.	.	.	5.0	5.0	5.0	5.0	5.0
0302150	ENGINEERING COST/MAN	K $	.	.	.	.	23.0	23.0	23.0	23.0	23.0
0302151	PROFESSIONAL	MEN	180.	131.	133.	143.	.	.	.	.	.
0302153	SUPPORT	MEN	.	.	.	.	.	.	.	.	.
0302154	RATIO	O/O	.	50.0	50.0	50.0	50.0	50.0	50.0	50.0	50.0
0302158	ATTRITION	MEN	.	.	.	.	.	.	.	.	.
0302159	RATIO	O/O	.	2.0	2.0	2.0	2.0	2.0	2.0	2.0	2.0
0302160	MARKETING COST/MAN	K $	.	.	.	.	24.0	24.0	24.0	24.0	24.0
0302161	FIELD	MEN	500.	516.	542.	639.	.	.	.	.	.
0302163	SUPPORT	MEN	26.	29.	29.	29.	.	.	.	.	.
0302164	RATIO	O/O	.	.	.	.	4.5	4.5	4.5	4.5	4.5
0302168	ATTRITION	MEN	.	.	.	.	.	.	.	.	.
0302169	RATIO	O/O	.	8.0	7.0	6.0	5.0	5.0	5.0	5.0	5.0

NOTE - INPUT DATA SPECIFIED AS AN AMOUNT AND AS A RATIO ARE COMPLEMENTS UNLESS THE RATIO IS PREFACED BY 'OR.'

- COMPANY CONFIDENTIAL -

PSG - PLANNING SYSTEMS GENERATOR   12/16/68

Exhibit 8-16

FORM 03-9   SUBSET 2   DIVISION Y   INPUT WORKSHEET 6 OF 7

CODE	DESCRIPTION	TERM	PRIOR	1967	1968	1969	1970	1971	1972	1973	1974
COL.1-7			18-24	25-31	32-38	39-45	46-52	53-59	60-66	67-73	74-80
	YEAR-END MANPOWER CONTINUED										
0302170	SERVICE COST/MAN	K $	.	.	.	.	13.0	14.0	15.0	16.0	17.0
0302171	FIELD	MEN	2600.	2628.	2644.	2600.	.	.	.	.	.
0302173	SUPPORT	MEN	.	.	.	69.	.	.	.	.	.
0302174	RATIO	O/O	.	.	.	.	4.0	4.0	4.0	4.0	4.0
0302178	ATTRITION	MEN	.	.	.	.	.	.	.	.	.
0302179	RATIO	O/O	.	9.0	8.5	8.0	8.0	8.0	8.0	8.0	8.0
0302180	ADMINISTRATION COST/MAN	K $	.	.	.	.	40.0	42.0	44.0	46.0	48.0
0302181	PROFESSIONAL	MEN	90.	93.	96.	88.	.	.	.	.	.
0302183	SUPPORT	MEN	.	.	.	.	.	.	.	.	.
0302184	RATIO	O/O	.	.	.	.	.	.	.	.	.
0302188	ATTRITION	MEN	.	.	.	.	.	.	.	.	.
0302189	RATIO	O/O	.	1.0	1.0	1.0	1.0	1.0	1.0	1.0	1.0
	SPACE FORECAST										
0302221	MANUFACTURING, AMT.	KSQFT	.	.	.	.	.	.	.	.	.
0302222	PER MAN	SQFT	.	260.	260.	260.	260.	260.	260.	260.	260.
0302220	EXTRA SHIFT RATIO	O/O	.	30.0	30.0	30.0	30.0	30.0	30.0	30.0	30.0
0302223	WAREHOUSING, AMT.	KSQFT	.	.	.	.	.	.	.	.	.
0302224	TO MFG. SPACE	O/O	.	15.0	15.0	15.0	15.0	15.0	15.0	15.0	15.0
0302225	ENGINEERING, AMT.	KSQFT	.	.	.	.	.	.	.	.	.
0302226	PER MAN	SQFT	.	290.	290.	290.	290.	290.	290.	290.	290.
0302227	OTHER, AMT.	KSQFT	.	.	.	.	.	.	.	.	.
0302228	PER MAN	SQFT	.	100.	100.	100.	100.	100.	100.	100.	100.

NOTE - INPUT DATA SPECIFIED AS AN AMOUNT AND AS A RATIO ARE COMPLEMENTS UNLESS THE RATIO IS PREFACED BY 'OR.'

PSG - PLANNING SYSTEMS GENERATOR

- COMPANY CONFIDENTIAL -

12/16/68

Exhibit 8-17

DIVISION Y

FORM 03-9   SUBSET 2

CODE	DESCRIPTION	TERM	PRIOR	1967	1968	1969	1970	1971	1972	1973	1974
COL.1-7			18-24	25-31	32-38	39-45	46-52	53-59	60-66	67-73	74-80
	SPACE AVAILABLE										
0302231	PLANTS, TOTAL	KSQFT	160.	160.	160.	160.	160.	160.	160.	160.	160.
0302232	OWNED, AMT.	KSQFT	130.	.	.	.	.	.	.	.	.
0302233	RATIO	O/O	.	80.0	80.0	80.0	80.0	80.0	80.0	80.0	80.0
0302235	WAREHOUSES, TOTAL	KSQFT	20.	20.	20.	20.	20.	20.	20.	20.	20.
0302236	OWNED, AMT.	KSQFT	4.	.	.	.	.	.	.	.	.
0302237	RATIO	O/O	.	.	20.0	20.0	20.0	20.0	20.0	20.0	20.0
0302239	LABORATORIES, TOTAL	KSQFT	60.	60.	60.	60.	60.	60.	60.	60.	60.
0302240	OWNED, AMT.	KSQFT	60.	.	.	.	.	.	.	.	.
0302241	RATIO	O/O	.	100.0	100.0	100.0	100.0	100.0	100.0	100.0	100.0
0302243	OFFICES, TOTAL	KSQFT	330.	330.	330.	330.	330.	330.	330.	330.	330.
0302244	OWNED, AMT.	KSQFT	33.	.	.	.	.	.	.	.	.
0302245	RATIO	O/O	.	10.0	10.0	10.0	10.0	10.0	10.0	10.0	10.0
	BUILDING COST PER SQFT										
0302261	PLANTS	$	25.00	25.00	25.00	25.00	25.00	25.00	25.00	25.00	25.00
0302262	WAREHOUSES	$	20.00	20.00	20.00	20.00	20.00	20.00	20.00	20.00	20.00
0302263	LABORATORIES	$	35.00	35.00	35.00	35.00	35.00	35.00	35.00	35.00	35.00
0302264	OFFICES	$	20.00	20.00	20.00	20.00	20.00	20.00	20.00	20.00	20.00
	LAND PURCHASES (CO)										
0302266	ACREAGE	UTS	1000.0	.	.	.	.	500.0	.	.	.
0302267	SQ. FOOTAGE	KUTS	40.	.	.	.	.	.	.	.	.
	LAND ACQUISITION COST (CO)										
0302268	PER ACRE	$	1000.	.	.	.	.	2000.	.	.	.
0302269	PER SQ. FOOT	$	100.00	.	.	.	.	.	.	.	.

NOTE - INPUT DATA SPECIFIED AS AN AMOUNT AND AS A RATIO ARE COMPLEMENTS UNLESS THE RATIO IS PREFACED BY 'UR'

PSG - PLANNING SYSTEMS GENERATOR

- COMPANY CONFIDENTIAL -

12/16/68

Exhibit 8-18

be kept out of the corporate system and relegated to the divisional subsystems. Since the latter do not deal with the consolidation of different divisions into a comprehensive view at the corporate level, they are at liberty to deal with subsets at the functional level when preparing a comprehensive view for the division.

9

Divisional Planning Data

While the corporate planning data system is designed to deal with inter-divisional resource allocations and the analysis of divisional plans for consistency and credibility, a divisional planning data system is more properly concerned with business planning as such. A functionally integrated company would be concerned with a system at this business level only. The process of originating achievable planned goals in a divisional organization requires resolution of two substantive business issues:

1. Making assumptions about the economy, technology, markets, products (own and competitive), and applications (uses and sales). These refer primarily to the external business environment. While some progress has been made in systematizing the making of these assumptions, particularly in the area of market research, technology life cycle analysis, etc., it is essentially managerial judgment which determines the specific market or product strategy to be incorporated in a business plan.

93

2. Estimating the scale of future operations, such as engineering, manufacturing, marketing, administration, and financing. These deal with workloads, manpower, space, expenses, investments, and cash requirements. They refer primarily to the organization's internal environment, and are dependent not only upon the external assumptions but also upon management's intent to improve operational effectiveness.

Since the managerial judgment which determines the outward strategy is in turn influenced by the respective operational results, there exists a feedback loop between the external and internal environments. A system for divisional planning must make this feedback meaningful by responding to alternative assumptions in both areas.

BUSINESS PLANNING SYSTEM CONCEPT

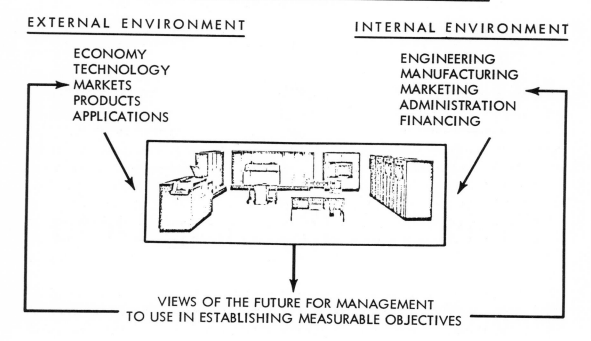

EXTERNAL ENVIRONMENT

ECONOMY
TECHNOLOGY
MARKETS
PRODUCTS
APPLICATIONS

INTERNAL ENVIRONMENT

ENGINEERING
MANUFACTURING
MARKETING
ADMINISTRATION
FINANCING

VIEWS OF THE FUTURE FOR MANAGEMENT
TO USE IN ESTABLISHING MEASURABLE OBJECTIVES

Figure 9

However, these two substantive business issues at the divisional level are not the end of the story. The task of generating planned goals at the divisional level further requires their reconciliation with divisional goals or objectives worked out by corporate management, as well as the development of a set of functional goals acceptable to line management within the division. The latter bargaining process within the division is further complicated by the fact that usually a functional corporate staff gets into the act. While the division's general management is mainly concerned with accomplishing overall objectives agreed upon with the corporate general management, the division's functional management is not only concerned with supporting the division's general objectives, but also with satisfying the constraints and directives established by the functional corporate staff. This makes for a three-way bargaining situation which requires a high degree of political sensitivity and statesmanship from the people involved. While such a process satisfies the traditional requirements for checks and balances, it does not facilitate the finding of optimal solutions for the total corporation.

In a fully developed divisional planning data system, the impact of corporate staff functions should be felt not so much as a quasi-line interference with divisional operations but as a co-authorship for the planning logic employed in the functional planning procedures. If both the functional experts on the corporate staff and the planners in the divisional line management of the respective function develop a common logic for planning, then the review and approval process needs to deal only with input assumptions (data). This separation of logic development from data processing is an important advancement in planning and is facilitated by the planning data systems network approach.

Before we proceed with the specifics of a divisional planning data system, we have to restate a number of assumptions about the nature of the divisional business and its organizational structure. We had assumed that a division within the XYZ Corporation is assigned complete business responsibility for an entire product area. Full business responsibility would include product development, manufacture, marketing, service, and administration. The reader is reminded that one of our first premises was that the XYZ Corporation is doing business in durable goods. Division X, which is now the subject of discussion, also does business in the durable goods market.

Let us further assume that the general product area assigned to division X may be grouped into, say, five product lines which for convenience sake we will call A, B, C, D, and E. These product lines represent the subsets within division X's planning data system.

Physical plant and organization structure may be quickly outlined as follows. Division X operates one large-scale plant. A one-plant operation is economically justified because the product is comparatively small and of high value per weight and cubic footage shipped, so that the benefits of large-scale, centralized manufacturing exceed the cost of long-distance shipping and warehouse operations. The marketing and service functions cover the entire United States through some 200 branch offices. To add some more realistic flavor to the example, we will assume that there are two marketing groups, one dealing with product lines A, B, C, the other dealing with product lines D and E. This additional grouping of division X's product lines is deemed necessary because of the different usage and application of these two product groups on the part of the customer and the corresponding specialized training and orientation required for sales personnel. In contrast, the technology of all five product lines being highly compatible, the service function does not require the same additional grouping. In other words, all five product lines are being serviced by one service force. The product development function operates several laboratories, one of which is located near the plant. However, laboratory location is not considered a relevant factor for the planning of product development since all work is organized by project. Some of the projects are of a general nature, such as laboratory services and maintenance; others are bordering on research. However, most are strictly product-oriented projects and as such are supported by the usual sets of planning data, including projections of expected expenditures, investments, and payoffs.

DIVISIONAL SUMMARY

The proponents of fully integrated planning supported by fully integrated management information systems would stipulate that the divisional summary data in the divisional planning system must be exactly the same as the divisional subset data in the corporate planning system. This sounds very attractive and reasonable but is highly impractical. We must keep in mind that all these subsystems are going to be in different stages of development. The entire effort in the development of planning data systems is evolutionary and cannot be prefabricated for quick on-site assembly. The development of a planning data system, in fact, is a creative process and constitutes both an expression of management's thinking about its business, and a vehicle for the introduction of new ways of thinking. Any masterminding of a divisional system by corporate staff specialists would deprive divisional management of the educational value of a do-it-yourself effort.

The argument that a corporate prefabricated package would be better (more sophisticated, more powerful) than its divisional homegrown counterpart does not hold water. The quality of a planning data system cannot be measured on some absolute scale of sophistication but only on a relative scale of utility to management in the particular managerial situation. In this context it is most important that the management in question learns to translate its own thinking about its particular situation into reproducible planning logic so that the resulting procedures become an effective means of generating planned goals to which it feels committed. The utility of simple and straightforward planning procedures, which are actively used in the planning process, is greater than that of complex and highly sophisticated procedures which are not understood by active management and, therefore, are not used in the planning process.

Of course, it would be desirable if a divisional planning system were to produce as part of its summary routines the input data required for its divisional subset within the corporate system. But this expression of a desirable feature for a divisional planning data system is not the same as the imposition of strict uniformity in display lineage and planning logic. Therefore, let us look at a divisional planning data system as an independent subsystem within a network and deal with the interaction of these subsystems at the divisional and corporate level in the chapter on sociopolitical problems.

DIVISIONAL SUMMARY DATA

Exhibits 9-1, 9-2, and 9-3 show the profit and loss summary and two charts for Division X. The P & L format which is familiar to Division X's management, differs from the corresponding I & E format for Division X as a subset in the corporate system. This is a typical phenomenon in any large-scale, decentralized organization. It is important, however, that we do not get upset about this lack of discipline and uniformity.

In order to fully appreciate the interaction between the divisional summary, its subsets, and its functional modules, we will trace a few representative line items through the respective functional procedures and input data options. But first let us take a look at some other summary data displays for Division X, such as an investment analysis (Exhibit 9-4) including balance sheet and cash flow information, and a manpower summary (Exhibit 9-5). Again the reader should not get disturbed about lack of uniformity between Division X's and the corresponding corporate displays.

SUBSET DATA BY PRODUCT LINE

In order to follow the divisional planning logic, we must first step behind the divisional totals and pull out one of the subsets, for example, product line C. The corresponding P & L and related input worksheet is shown in Exhibits 9-6 and 9-7. As usual, some dynamic input options are provided for. In addition to specific amounts of gross income, gross profit, and expenses, appropriate ratios may be entered to calculate estimated results. Of course, this P & L procedure also provides for the calculation of vertical and horizontal percentages. This is quite satisfactory for a great deal of direct data manipulation at the aggregate level by product line. Usually, however, alternatives would be introduced in the functional modules of the divisional system.

Product line C is assumed to enter the market in 1969. Let us now follow the audit trail into the supporting source data and concentrate our attention on one year, say, 1970.

MARKETING

Marketing manpower and expense (totaling 11.0M$), per Exhibit 9-8, is generated by the planning assumptions shown in Exhibits 9-9, 9-10, and 9-11. Product Gross Income of 29.7M, as well as 38.2M Retail Value of Orders, 34.4M Retail Value of

DIVISION X PLANNING DATA   VIEW 2001

STRATEGIC PLAN SUBMITTED .....

TOTAL DIVISION

PROFIT + LOSS SUMMARY

FORM 21-1

SUBSET 0

DESCRIPTION	1967 AMT	1967 O/O	1968 AMT	1968 O/O	1969 AMT	1969 O/O	1970 AMT	1970 O/O	1971 AMT	1971 O/O	1972 AMT	1972 O/O	1973 AMT	1973 O/O	1974 AMT	1974 O/O
GROSS INCOME																
PRODUCTS	76.4	63.6	82.0	62.6	92.4	65.0	126.1	69.1	155.8	70.3	186.4	71.4	219.7	70.9	247.4	70.1
SERVICE	42.0	35.0	46.9	35.8	48.7	34.3	54.4	29.8	64.5	29.1	72.7	27.9	88.1	28.5	103.1	29.2
OTHER	1.7	1.4	2.0	1.5	1.1	.8	1.9	1.0	1.4	.6	1.9	.7	1.9	.6	2.6	.7
TOTAL	120.1	100.0	130.9	100.0	142.2	100.0	182.4	100.0	221.7	100.0	261.0	100.0	309.7	100.0	353.1	100.0
GROSS PROFIT																
PRODUCTS	46.4	60.7	53.0	64.6	57.0	61.7	76.9	61.0	96.3	61.8	115.2	61.8	136.2	62.0	155.1	62.7
SERVICE	12.1	28.8	13.0	27.7	10.6	21.8	11.7	21.5	14.2	21.9	14.5	20.0	17.6	19.9	19.6	19.0
OTHER	1.1	64.7	1.3	65.0	.7	63.6	1.2	63.2	.9	64.3	1.2	63.2	1.2	63.2	1.7	65.4
TOTAL	59.6	49.6	67.3	51.4	68.3	48.0	89.8	49.2	111.4	50.2	130.9	50.2	155.0	50.0	176.4	50.0
EXPENSES																
MARKETING	18.5	15.4	20.4	15.6	28.0	19.7	31.7	17.4	40.4	18.2	47.6	18.2	55.9	18.0	62.2	17.6
PRODUCT DEVELOP	6.4	5.3	6.8	5.2	7.4	5.2	8.4	4.6	9.2	4.1	9.7	3.7	10.8	3.5	12.0	3.4
PRODUCT TEST	1.1	.9	2.0	1.5	2.4	1.7	2.6	1.4	2.6	1.2	2.7	1.0	2.8	.9	2.9	.8
ADMINISTRATION	4.6	3.8	5.0	3.8	5.5	3.9	6.9	3.8	8.4	3.8	9.8	3.8	11.7	3.8	12.9	3.7
OTHER CHARGES *)	1.2	1.0	2.9	2.2	4.9	3.4	4.0	2.2	3.5	1.6	3.5	1.3	2.7	.8	2.9	.8
APPORTIONMENTS	6.7	5.6	7.6	5.8	9.3	6.5	11.4	6.2	14.2	6.4	17.1	6.6	20.4	6.6	23.8	6.7
NET BEFORE TAX	21.1	17.6	22.6	17.3	10.8	7.6	24.8	13.6	33.0	14.9	40.5	15.5	50.7	16.4	59.7	16.9
NET AFTER TAX	11.0	9.1	11.7	9.0	5.2	3.7	11.9	6.5	15.8	7.1	19.4	7.4	24.3	7.9	28.7	8.1

PERCENT CHANGE OVER PRIOR YEAR

DESCRIPTION	1967	1968	1969	1970	1971	1972	1973	1974
GROSS INCOME								
PRODUCTS	4.7	7.3	12.7	36.5	23.6	19.6	17.9	12.6
SERVICE	5.0	11.7	3.9	11.7	18.5	12.7	21.2	17.0
OTHER	70.0	17.6	-45.0	72.7	-26.3	35.7		36.8
TOTAL	5.4	9.0	8.7	28.3	21.5	17.7	18.7	14.0
GROSS PROFIT								
PRODUCTS	6.9	14.2	-7.5	34.9	25.2	19.6	18.2	13.9
SERVICE	19.9	7.3	-18.2	10.1	21.1	2.6	21.0	11.5
OTHER	83.3	18.2	-46.2	71.4	-25.0	33.3		41.7
TOTAL	10.2	12.9	1.5	31.4	24.0	17.6	18.4	13.8
EXPENSE								
MARKETING	8.8	10.3	37.3	13.2	27.6	17.8	17.3	11.3
PRODUCT DEVELOP	16.4	6.3	8.8	13.5	9.5	5.4	11.3	11.1
PRODUCT TEST	57.1	81.8	20.0	8.3		3.8	3.7	3.6
ADMINISTRATION	21.1	8.7	10.0	25.5	21.7	16.7	19.4	10.3
OTHER CHARGES *)	-14.3	141.7	69.0	-18.4	-12.5	.0	-22.9	7.4
APPORTIONMENTS	9.8	13.4	22.4	22.6	24.6	20.4	19.3	16.7
NET BEFORE TAX	7.7	7.0	-52.1	129.1	33.2	22.7	25.2	17.8
NET AFTER TAX	12.0	7.0	-55.8	129.1	33.2	22.7	25.2	17.8

*) NET OF OTHER INCOME

PSG - PLANNING SYSTEMS GENERATOR

- COMPANY CONFIDENTIAL -

11/15/68

Exhibit 9-1

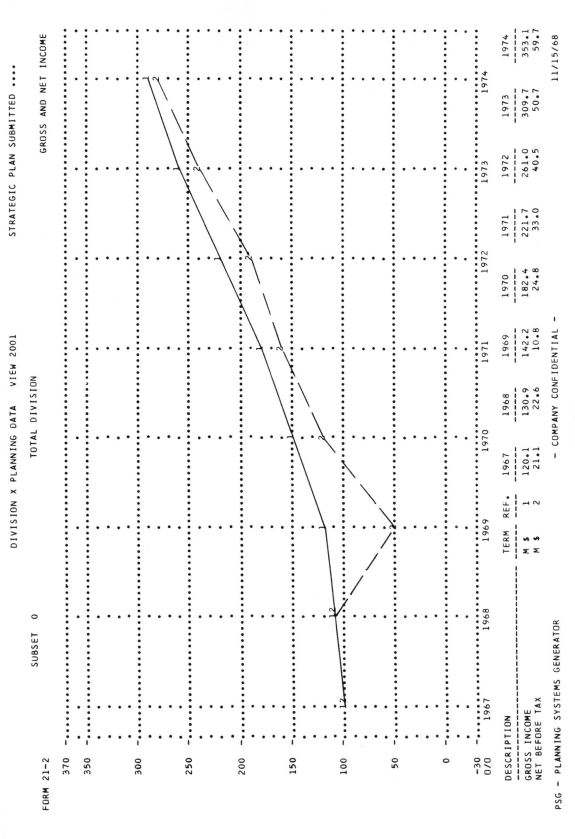

Exhibit 9-2

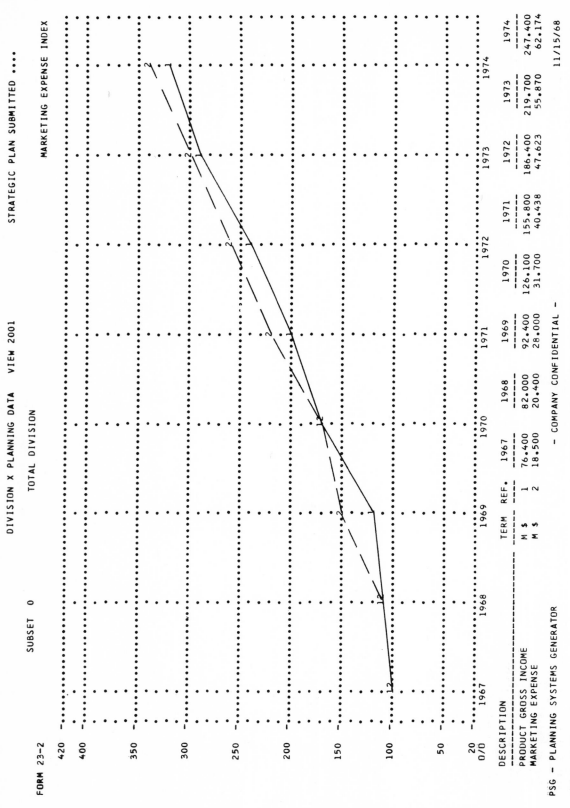

Exhibit 9-3

DIVISION X PLANNING DATA   VIEW 2001

STRATEGIC PLAN SUBMITTED ....

FORM 22-1

SUBSET 0

TOTAL DIVISION

CASH FLOW + INVESTMENT

DESCRIPTION	TERM	1967	1968	1969	1970	1971	1972	1973	1974
BALANCE SHEET									
CURRENT ASSETS									
CASH	M $	23.6	29.3	19.1	15.3	12.6	2.3	-5.6	-16.6
MARKETABLE SECURITIES	M $	10.1	12.6	8.2	6.6	5.4	1.0	75.5	85.7
NOTES + ACCTS. REC.	M $	29.8	32.5	35.2	45.2	54.6	64.0	92.3	113.5
INVENTORIES + PREPAID ITEMS	M $	37.2	39.7	43.3	51.0	61.2	74.2	162.2	182.5
TOTAL CURRENT ASSETS	M $	100.7	114.2	105.7	118.1	134.0	141.5		
FACTORIES, BLDGS, OTHER PROPERTY									
LAND AND BUILDINGS	M $	20.3	20.7	24.4	27.5	29.3	30.8	33.2	35.5
NET LAND AND BUILDINGS	M $	19.5	19.0	21.6	23.5	23.8	23.5	23.7	23.4
PLANT + EQUIPMENT	M $	34.9	38.6	44.6	53.2	59.7	66.4	73.3	81.1
NET PLANT + EQUIPMENT	M $	30.6	28.4	29.5	31.7	31.7	31.7	31.8	32.5
OTHER ASSETS	M $	2.8	2.6	2.4	2.2	2.0	1.8	1.6	1.4
TOTAL ASSETS (NET)	M $	153.6	164.2	159.2	175.6	191.6	198.5	219.3	239.8
LIABILITIES AND EQUITY									
CURRENT LIABILITIES	M $	38.2	43.3	46.4	57.8	67.2	76.0	86.7	95.2
LONG TERM INDEBTEDNESS	M $	30.0	30.0	20.0	20.0	20.0	10.0	10.0	10.0
OTHER LIABILITIES	M $	2.4	2.6	3.4	3.7	4.2	4.7	5.4	5.9
EQUITY	M $	83.1	88.2	89.4	94.0	100.2	107.8	117.2	128.7
TOTAL LIABILITIES + CAPITAL	M $	153.6	164.2	159.2	175.6	191.6	198.5	219.3	239.8
SOURCE AND APPLICATION OF FUNDS									
NET CURRENT ASSETS-BEGINNING	M $	60.0	62.6	70.8	59.3	60.3	66.8	65.5	75.5
FUNDS PROVIDED DURING YEAR									
NET EARNINGS	M $	11.0	11.8	5.2	11.9	15.8	19.4	24.3	28.7
NON-CASH ITEMS	M $	5.3	7.0	6.2	7.8	8.2	8.7	9.2	9.9
TOTAL FUNDS FROM OPERATIONS	M $	16.3	18.8	11.4	19.7	24.0	28.1	33.5	38.6
MISCELLANEOUS	M $	-.8	-.8	-.8	-.6	-.6	-.8	-.8	1.0
CORPORATE ADJUSTMENT	M $	-1.2	-1.2	-1.0	-1.1	-.7	-1.0	-1.1	-1.3
TOTAL FUNDS AVAILABLE	M $	75.9	80.9	82.0	78.5	84.2	94.8	98.7	113.9
FUNDS APPLIED DURING YEAR									
CAPITAL EXPENDITURES	M $	7.3	4.1	9.7	11.7	8.3	8.2	9.2	10.1
REDUCTION OF LONG TERM DEBT	M $			10.0			10.0		
CASH DIVIDENDS	M $	6.0	6.0	3.0	6.5	9.0	11.1	13.9	16.4
TOTAL FUNDS APPLIED DURING YEAR	M $	13.3	10.1	22.7	18.2	17.3	29.3	23.2	26.5
NET CURRENT ASSETS AT END OF YEAR	M $	62.6	70.8	59.3	60.3	66.8	65.5	75.5	87.3
RATIOS									
NET PROFIT TO GROSS INCOME	0/0	9.1	9.0	3.6	6.4	6.8	7.0	7.2	7.5
RETURN ON EQUITY	0/0	13.2	13.4	5.8	12.7	15.8	18.0	20.7	22.3
RETURN ON TOTAL ASSETS	0/0	7.2	7.2	3.3	6.8	8.2	9.8	11.1	12.0

11/15/68

- COMPANY CONFIDENTIAL -

PSG - PLANNING SYSTEMS GENERATOR

Exhibit 9-4

FORM 29-3   SUBSET 0

DIVISION X PLANNING DATA   VIEW 2001

STRATEGIC PLAN SUBMITTED ....

TOTAL DIVISION

AVERAGE MANPOWER SUMMARY

DESCRIPTION	TERM	1967	1968	1969	1970	1971	1972	1973	1974
SALES									
BRANCH OFFICES	MEN	898	964	1245	1430	1807	2122	2508	2741
DISTRICTS	MEN	78	86	112	123	144	163	181	188
HEADQUARTERS	MEN	127	156	199	217	246	274	299	299
TOTAL	MEN	1103	1206	1556	1770	2197	2559	2988	3228
CUSTOMER SERVICE									
BRANCH OFFICES	MEN	2939	3022	3229	3500	3970	4232	4770	5107
DISTRICTS	MEN	20	20	20	20	20	20	20	20
HEADQUARTERS	MEN	28	35	47	53	60	64	71	77
PLANT *	MEN	108	120	134	147	168	181	200	216
TOTAL	MEN	3095	3197	3430	3720	4218	4497	5061	5420
MANUFACTURING									
PRODUCTION	MEN	2175	2150	2629	2990	2970	3020	2982	2974
DEVELOPMENT	MEN	204	208	224	256	292	328	376	428
OTHER	MEN	217	267	266	286	310	319	339	356
TOTAL	MEN	2596	2625	3119	3532	3572	3667	3697	3758
PRODUCT MANAGEMENT + TESTING									
HEADQUARTERS	MEN	12	11	12	12	13	13	13	13
PLANT *	MEN	109	147	132	139	142	138	139	140
TOTAL	MEN	121	158	144	151	155	151	152	153
GENERAL + ADMINISTRATIVE									
ADMINISTRATION	MEN	20	22	24	26	28	30	32	34
FINANCIAL	MEN	198	220	234	269	295	315	341	357
GENERAL MANAGEMENT	MEN	22	22	22	22	23	22	22	20
TOTAL	MEN	240	264	280	317	346	367	395	411
DIVISIONAL									
GRAND TOTAL	MEN	6938	7183	8263	9204	10178	10922	11954	12614
HEADQUARTERS	MEN	407	466	538	599	665	718	778	800

PERCENT CHANGE OVER PRIOR YEAR

DESCRIPTION	TERM	1967	1968	1969	1970	1971	1972	1973	1974
SALES	0/0	12.6	9.3	29.0	13.8	24.1	16.5	16.8	8.0
CUSTOMER SERVICE	0/0	2.5	3.3	7.3	8.5	13.4	6.6	12.5	7.1
MANUFACTURING	0/0	1.4	1.1	18.8	13.2	1.1	2.7	.8	1.6
PRODUCT MANAGEMENT + TESTING	0/0	6.3	30.6	-8.9	4.9	2.6	-2.6	-.7	-.7
GENERAL + ADMINISTRATIVE	0/0	10.1	10.0	6.1	13.2	9.1	6.1	7.6	4.1
DIVISIONAL TOTAL	0/0	7.0	3.5	15.0	11.4	10.6	7.3	9.4	5.5
HEADQUARTERS TOTAL	0/0	12.6	14.5	15.5	11.3	11.0	8.0	8.4	2.8

* INCLUDED IN MANUFACTURING-OTHER

PSG - PLANNING SYSTEMS GENERATOR

- COMPANY CONFIDENTIAL -

11/15/68

Exhibit 9-5

DIVISION X PLANNING DATA   VIEW 2001

STRATEGIC PLAN SUBMITTED .....

PRODUCT LINE C

PROFIT + LOSS SUMMARY

FORM 21-1   SUBSET 3

DESCRIPTION	1967 AMT	O/O	1968 AMT	O/O	1969 AMT	O/O.	1970 AMT	O/O	1971 AMT	O/O	1972 AMT	O/O	1973 AMT	O/O	1974 AMT	O/O
GROSS INCOME																
PRODUCTS					11.7	97.5	29.7	89.5	54.1	83.8	78.5	79.2	105.6	75.5	122.0	71.9
SERVICE					.3	2.5	3.5	10.5	10.5	16.2	20.6	20.8	34.3	24.5	47.6	28.1
OTHER																
TOTAL					12.0	100.0	33.2	100.0	64.6	100.0	99.1	100.0	139.9	100.0	169.6	100.0
GROSS PROFIT																
PRODUCTS					4.5	38.5	14.9	50.2	28.8	53.2	43.4	55.3	59.7	56.5	69.1	56.6
SERVICE					.1	34.0	1.0	29.5	2.3	22.5	4.3	21.0	7.7	22.4	9.2	19.3
OTHER																
TOTAL					4.6	38.4	15.9	48.0	31.1	48.3	47.7	48.2	67.4	48.2	78.3	46.2
EXPENSES																
MARKETING	1.9		2.1		5.1	42.5	11.0	33.1	18.4	28.6	24.6	24.9	32.8	23.4	39.1	23.0
PRODUCT DEVELOP					2.3	19.2	2.6	7.8	3.0	4.6	3.2	3.2	3.7	2.6	3.9	2.3
PRODUCT TEST			.7		.9	7.5	1.0	3.0	1.0	1.5	1.2	1.2	1.3	.8	1.3	.8
ADMINISTRATION					.4	3.3	1.3	3.9	2.5	3.9	3.7	3.7	5.3	3.8	6.3	3.7
OTHER CHARGES *)	.3		1.1		1.0	8.3	.7	2.1	.5	.8	.6	.6	.7	.5	.8	.5
APPORTIONMENTS					.8	6.7	2.0	6.0	4.2	6.5	6.4	6.5	9.3	6.6	11.6	6.8
NET BEFORE TAX	-2.2		-3.9		-5.9	-49.2	-2.7	-8.0	1.5	2.3	8.0	8.1	14.3	10.2	15.3	9.0
NET AFTER TAX	-1.1		-2.0		-2.8	-23.6	-1.3	-3.9	.7	1.1	3.8	3.9	6.9	4.9	7.3	4.3

PERCENT CHANGE OVER PRIOR YEAR

DESCRIPTION	1967	1968	1969	1970	1971	1972	1973	1974
GROSS INCOME								
PRODUCTS				153.8	82.2	45.1	34.5	15.5
SERVICE				NA	198.9	96.6	67.0	38.7
OTHER								
TOTAL				176.7	94.5	53.4	41.3	21.2
GROSS PROFIT								
PRODUCTS				231.1	93.3	50.7	37.6	15.7
SERVICE				921.8	127.6	83.5	78.4	19.3
OTHER								
TOTAL				246.3	95.5	53.2	41.2	16.2
EXPENSE								
MARKETING	90.0			115.7	67.6	33.5	33.1	19.2
PRODUCT DEVELOP		10.5	9.5	13.0	15.4	6.7	15.6	5.4
PRODUCT TEST			28.6	11.1		20.0	8.3	
ADMINISTRATION				225.0	92.3	48.0	43.2	18.9
OTHER CHARGES *)	50.0	266.7	-9.1	-30.0	-28.6	20.0	16.7	14.3
APPORTIONMENTS				150.0	110.0	52.4	45.3	24.7
NET BEFORE TAX	83.3	77.3	51.3	-54.8	NA		79.3	6.9
NET AFTER TAX	90.7	77.3	39.6	-54.8	NA		79.3	6.9

*) NET OF OTHER INCOME

PSG - PLANNING SYSTEMS GENERATOR

- COMPANY CONFIDENTIAL -

11/15/68

Exhibit 9-6

DIVISION X PLANNING DATA   VIEW 2001

PRODUCT LINE C

STRATEGIC PLAN SUBMITTED ....

P + L INPUT WORKSHEET

FORM 21-9   SUBSET 3

CODE	DESCRIPTION	TERM	PRIOR	1967	1968	1969	1970	1971	1972	1973	1974
COL.1-7			18-24	25-31	32-38	39-45	46-52	53-59	60-66	67-73	74-80
	GROSS INCOME										
2103001	PRODUCTS, AMOUNT	M $ T	0.	0.	0.	11.7	29.7	54.1	78.5	105.6	122.0
2103002	OR GROWTH RATE	O/O	.	.	.	.	.	.	.	.	.
2103003	SERVICE, AMOUNT	M $ T	0.	0.	0.	.3	3.5	10.5	20.6	34.3	47.6
2103004	OR GROWTH RATE	O/O	.	.	.	.	.	.	.	.	.
2103007	OTHER, AMOUNT	M $ T	0.	0.	0.	0.	0.	0.	0.	0.	0.
2103008	OR GROWTH RATE	O/O	.	.	.	.	.	.	.	.	.
	GROSS PROFIT										
2103011	PRODUCTS, AMOUNT	M $ T	0.	0.	0.	4.5	14.9	28.8	43.4	59.7	69.1
2103012	GROSS INCOME RATIO	O/O	.	.	.	.	.	.	.	.	.
2103013	SERVICE, AMOUNT	M $ T	0.	0.	0.	.1	1.0	2.3	4.3	7.7	9.2
2103014	GROSS INCOME RATIO	O/O	.	.	.	.	.	.	.	.	.
2103017	OTHER, AMOUNT	M $ T	0.	0.	0.	0.	0.	0.	0.	0.	0.
2103018	GROSS INCOME RATIO	O/O	.	.	.	.	.	.	.	.	.
	EXPENSES										
2103021	MARKETING, AMOUNT	M $ T	0.	0.	0.	5.1	11.0	18.4	24.6	32.8	39.1
2103022	GROSS INCOME RATIO	O/O	.	.	.	.	.	.	.	.	.
2103023	PRODUCT DEVELOPMENT, AMOUNT	M $ T	1.0	1.9	2.1	2.3	2.6	3.0	3.2	3.7	3.9
2103024	GROSS INCOME RATIO	O/O	.	.	.	.	.	.	.	.	.
2103025	PRODUCT TEST, AMOUNT	M $ T	0.	0.	.7	.9	1.0	1.0	1.2	1.3	1.3
2103026	GROSS INCOME RATIO	O/O	.	.	.	.	.	.	.	.	.
2103027	GENERAL + ADMINISTRATION, AMOUNT	M $ T	0.	0.	0.	.4	1.3	2.5	3.7	5.3	6.3
2103028	GROSS INCOME RATIO	O/O	.	.	.	.	.	.	.	.	.
2103029	OTHER CHARGES LESS OTHER INCOME	M $ T	.2	.3	1.1	1.0	.7	.5	.6	.7	.8
2103030	GROSS INCOME RATIO	O/O	.	.	.	.	.	.	.	.	.
2103031	APPORTIONMENTS, AMOUNT	M $ T	0.	0.	0.	.8	2.0	4.2	6.4	9.3	11.6
2103032	GROSS INCOME RATIO	O/O	.	.	.	.	.	.	.	.	.
2103051	INCOME TAX, AMOUNT	M $									
2103052	TAX RATE	O/O	50.0	48.0	48.0	52.0	52.0	52.0	52.0	52.0	52.0

NOTE - LINE ITEMS SPECIFIED AS AN AMOUNT AND A RATIO ARE ADDED, UNLESS THE RATIO IS PREFACED BY 'OR.'

PSG - PLANNING SYSTEMS GENERATOR

- COMPANY CONFIDENTIAL -

11/15/68

Exhibit 9-7

DIVISION X PLANNING DATA   VIEW 2001

PRODUCT LINE C

STRATEGIC PLAN SUBMITTED .....

MARKETING MANPOWER + EXPENSE

FORM 23-1   SUBSET 3

DESCRIPTION	TERM	1967	1968	1969	1970	1971	1972	1973	1974
MANPOWER									
SALESMEN	MEN			153	317	477	646	860	1028
ASSISTANT SALESMEN	MEN			17	79	205	277	369	441
SUBTOTAL	MEN			170	397	682	923	1229	1469
MANAGERS	MEN			20	48	82	111	147	176
SUBTOTAL BRANCH OFFICES	MEN			191	444	763	1033	1376	1645
STUDENTS	MEN			50	80	104	94	137	117
DISTRICT OFFICES	MEN			11	27	46	62	83	99
HEADQUARTERS	MEN			15	36	61	83	110	132
TOTAL MARKETING	MEN			268	587	975	1272	1706	1992
GROWTH RATE	O/O				119.2	66.1	30.5	34.1	16.8
CHANGE AT BRANCHES	MEN			202	276	358	322	412	351
NEW HIRES	MEN			252	306	381	311	455	331
EXPENSES									
SALESMEN SALARIES	M $			2.535	5.710	9.476	12.825	17.079	20.413
PERCENT TO PGI	O/O			21.7	19.2	17.5	16.3	16.2	16.7
PERCENT TO RVS	O/O			17.6	16.6	15.5	14.9	14.9	15.3
OTHER BRANCH OFFICE	M $			1.715	3.997	6.871	9.300	12.385	14.803
TO PRODUCT GROSS INCOME	O/O			14.7	13.5	12.7	11.8	11.7	12.1
TO RETAIL VALUE SHIPMENTS	O/O			11.9	11.6	11.2	10.8	10.8	11.1
DISTRICT OFFICE	M $			.172	.400	.687	.930	1.239	1.480
TO PRODUCT GROSS INCOME	O/O			1.5	1.3	1.3	1.2	1.2	1.2
TO RETAIL VALUE SHIPMENTS	O/O			1.2	1.2	1.1	1.1	1.1	1.1
HEADQUARTERS-DEPARTMENTAL	M $			.352	.406	.381	.311	.455	.331
FUNCTIONAL									
SALES TRAINING	M $								
SALES MANAGEMENT	M $			.038	.089	.153	.207	.275	.329
SALES PROMOTION	M $			.440	.573	.870	1.050	1.337	1.719
ADVERTISING	M $								
SUBTOTAL FUNCTIONAL	M $			.831	1.068	1.404	1.568	2.067	2.379
TOTAL HEADQUARTERS	M $			.831	1.068	1.404	1.568	2.067	2.379
TO PRODUCT GROSS INCOME	O/O			7.1	3.6	2.6	2.0	2.0	1.9
TO RETAIL VALUE SHIPMENTS	O/O			5.8	3.1	2.3	1.8	1.8	1.8
PLANNING VARIANCE	M $			-.152	-.175				
PERCENT OF TOTAL	O/O			-3.0	-1.6				
TOTAL MARKETING EXPENSE	M $			5.100	11.000	18.438	24.623	32.770	39.074
TO PRODUCT GROSS INCOME	O/O			43.6	37.0	34.1	31.4	31.0	32.0
TO RETAIL VALUE SHIPMENTS	O/O			35.4	32.0	30.2	28.6	28.6	29.2

PSG - PLANNING SYSTEMS GENERATOR

- COMPANY CONFIDENTIAL -

11/15/68

Exhibit 9-8

PRODUCT LINE C

FORM 23-9   MARKETING WORKSHEET 1 OF 3

SUBSET 3

CODE	DESCRIPTION	TERM	PRIOR	1967	1968	1969	1970	1971	1972	1973	1974
COL.1-7			18-24	25-31	32-38	39-45	46-52	53-59	60-66	67-73	74-80
2303001	PRODUCT GROSS INCOME	M $ T	0.	0.	0.	11.700	29.700	54.100	78.500	105.600	122.000
	WORKLOAD PROJECTIONS										
2303002	RETAIL VALUE ORDERS	M $ T	0.	0.	0.	16.000	38.200	66.900	95.500	133.700	171.900
2303003	RETAIL VALUE SHIPMENTS	M $ T	0.	0.	0.	14.400	34.400	61.100	86.000	114.600	133.700
2303009	VALUE INSTALLED EQUIPMENT	M $ T	0.	0.	0.	14.400	48.800	109.900	171.000	285.600	419.300
	PRODUCTIVITY MEASUREMENTS/MAN										
2303026	SELLING	K $	.	.	.	285.000	300.000	315.000	330.000	345.000	360.000
2303027	INSTALLING	K $	.	.	.	150.000	160.000	170.000	180.000	190.000	200.000
2303028	COVERING	K $	.	.	.	800.000	900.000	1000.000	1100.000	1200.000	1300.000
2303029	ASSISTANCE	O/O	.	.	.	10.0	20.0	30.0	30.0	30.0	30.0
	OTHER MANPOWER FACTORS										
2303015	BRANCH MANAGERS/SALESMEN	O/O	.	10.0	11.0	12.0	12.0	12.0	12.0	12.0	12.0
2303016	DISTRICT OFFICE/FIELD	O/O	.	5.0	5.0	6.0	6.0	6.0	6.0	6.0	6.0
2303017	HEADQUARTERS/FIELD	O/O	.	8.0	8.0	8.0	8.0	8.0	8.0	8.0	8.0
2303018	ATTRITION OF FIELD FORCE	O/O	.	8.0	7.0	6.0	5.0	5.0	5.0	5.0	5.0
2303019	TRAINING PERIOD	MTHS	.	3.0	3.0	3.0	3.5	3.5	3.5	4.0	4.0
	PRIOR YEAR MANPOWER										
2303013	SALESMEN	MEN	.	.	.	.	.	.	.	.	.
2303014	BRANCH MANAGERS	MEN	.	.	.	.	.	.	.	.	.
2303011	STUDENTS	MEN	.	.	.	.	.	.	.	.	.

PSG - PLANNING SYSTEMS GENERATOR

- COMPANY CONFIDENTIAL -

11/15/68

Exhibit 9-9

FORM 23-9   SUBSET 3

PRODUCT LINE C

CODE	DESCRIPTION	TERM	PRIOR 18-24	1967 25-31	1968 32-38	1969 39-45	1970 46-52	1971 53-59	1972 60-66	1973 67-73	1974 74-80
COL. 1-7											
	EXPENSE OBJECTIVES										
	BRANCH OFFICE SALARIES/MAN										
2303021	SALESMEN	K $	•	12.000	12.000	13.000	13.000	13.000	13.000	13.000	13.000
2303024	ASSISTANT SALESMEN	K $	•	8.000	8.000	8.000	8.000	8.000	8.000	8.000	8.000
2303023	MANAGERS	K $	•	18.000	19.000	20.000	20.000	20.000	20.000	20.000	20.000
	BRANCH OFFICE EXPENSE/MAN										
2303030	TRAVEL	K $	•	•	•	•	•	•	•	•	•
2303031	TELEPHONE	K $	•	•	•	•	•	•	•	•	•
2303032	MOVING OF FIELD FORCE	O/O	•	•	•	•	•	•	•	•	•
2303033	COST PER MOVE	K $	•	•	•	•	•	•	•	•	•
2303035	DEMONSTRATORS	K $	•	•	•	•	•	•	•	•	•
2303038	ALL OTHER	K $	•	2.000	2.100	3.000	3.000	3.000	3.000	3.000	3.000
2303039	APPORTIONMENT	K $	•	5.800	6.000	6.000	6.000	6.000	6.000	6.000	6.000
2303037	SERVICE CHARGES	M $	•	•	•	•	•	•	•	•	•
	DISTRICT EXPENSE/MAN										
2303041	SALARIES	K $	•	•	•	•	•	•	•	•	•
2303042	TRAVEL	K $	•	•	•	•	•	•	•	•	•
2303043	TELEPHONE	K $	•	•	•	•	•	•	•	•	•
2303046	ADMINISTRATION	K $	•	•	•	•	•	•	•	•	•
2303047	ALL OTHER	K $	•	14.000	15.000	15.000	15.000	15.000	15.000	15.000	15.000
2303048	BRANCH OFFICE MEETINGS/FIELD	K $	•	•	•	•	•	•	•	•	•

PSG - PLANNING SYSTEMS GENERATOR

- COMPANY CONFIDENTIAL -

11/15/68

Exhibit 9-10

DIVISION X PLANNING DATA   VIEW 2001

FORM 23-9   SUBSET 3

PRODUCT LINE C   MARKETING WORKSHEET 3 OF 3

CODE	DESCRIPTION	TERM	PRIOR	1967	1968	1969	1970	1971	1972	1973	1974
COL.1-7			18-24	25-31	32-38	39-45	46-52	53-59	60-66	67-73	74-80
	HEADQUARTERS EXPENSE/MAN										
2303051	SALARIES	K $	•	•	•	•	•	•	•	•	•
2303052	TRAVEL	K $	•	•	•	•	•	•	•	•	•
2303053	TELEPHONE	K $	•	•	•	•	•	•	•	•	•
2303056	ALL OTHER	K $	•	25.000	25.000	25.000	25.000	25.000	25.000	25.000	25.000
	SALES TRAINING										
2303061	SALARIES/NEW HIRE	K $	•	1.200	1.000	1.000	1.000	1.000	1.000	1.000	1.000
2303062	TRAVEL/NEW HIRE	K $	•	•	•	•	•	•	•	•	•
2303063	ALL OTHER	M $	•	•	•	.100	•	•	•	•	•
	SALES MANAGEMENT										
2303072	SPECIAL PROJECTS	M $	•	•	•	•	•	•	•	•	•
2303073	ALL OTHER/FIELD MAN	K $	•	•	•	•	•	•	•	•	•
	SALES PROMOTION										
2303081	QUALIFYING SALESMEN	0/0	•	•	•	•	•	•	•	•	•
2303082	QUALIFYING BRANCH MANAGERS	0/0	•	•	•	•	•	•	•	•	•
2303083	GUESTS/QUALIFIED	0/0	•	•	•	•	•	•	•	•	•
2303084	CONVENTION COST/MAN	K $	•	•	•	•	•	•	•	•	•
2303085	OTHER SALES HELP, AMOUNT	M $	•	•	•	•	•	•	•	•	•
2303086	PER FIELD MAN	K $	•	.200	.200	.200	.200	.200	.200	.200	.200
	ADVERTISING										
2303091	REGULAR/RETAIL VALUE ORDERS	0/0	•	•	•	1.50	1.50	1.30	1.10	1.00	1.00
2303092	SPECIAL PROGRAMS	M $	•	•	•	.200	•	•	•	•	•
	TOTAL MARKETING EXPENSE OBJECTIVE (OPTIONAL)										
2303096	AMOUNT	M $	•	•	•	5.100	11.000	•	•	•	•
2303097	PRODUCT GROSS INCOME RATE	0/0	•	•	•	•	•	•	•	•	•

PSG - PLANNING SYSTEMS GENERATOR   11/15/68

- COMPANY CONFIDENTIAL -

Exhibit 9-11

Shipments, and 48.8M Value of Installed Equipment represent the planned level of marketing activity. The source of these business volume assumptions will be dealt with later.

A salesman's workload consists of selling, installing equipment, and maintaining good customer relations. Productivity is defined accordingly. A part of this workload may be carried by assistant salesmen. Field managers and district and headquarters personnel are related to field personnel. Expenses are related to manpower or specific marketing efforts or activities.

The reader is asked to inspect the worksheets which list all the decision variables in the marketing module of this sample divisional planning data system. Note especially the optional entry of a financial constraint and the resulting planning variance of −.175M in 1970, which needs to be managed away before the planned goals can become measurable objectives in an operating budget.

At the time the marketing module is executed the system sets up appropriate transfer records for other modules, such as total marketing expense to the P & L Summary. Since the system's design begins at the highest level of aggregation, the addresses for the transfer of supporting data are known. This is a most significant aspect of the approach to the design of a network of planning data systems. No general data bank is created and needs to be searched. Instead data are transferred directly and specifically. Please note in Exhibit 9-7 the "T" after the term column on line 2103021, Marketing, Amount. It signals that this entire line has been transferred from the marketing module and was not entered via a data card as defined on this worksheet for the P & L module.

The inputs to the marketing plan contain four lines about business volume. These are generated in the product plan and forecast module, which represents the next level of supporting source data.

PRODUCT PLAN AND FORECAST

At first this module may consist of no more than a statement of estimates about selling and billing quantities by product line and price assumptions by product per Exhibit 9-12. They must be sufficient to compute product gross income, retail value of orders, retail value of shipments, production and other volumes as required in the sales plan and other modules of the system.

Later on the product plan and forecast module may be expanded by the specification of econometric relationships between general business indicators, industry sales, and company share of market, depending upon assumptions about competitive products and price performance, demand elasticity, etc., sufficient to generate the quantities sold and leased by product or product line.

Computers are used extensively for market analysis and the generation of a variety of forecast data. But these computer programs are usually analytical models for the

DIVISION X PLANNING DATA   VIEW 2001

STRATEGIC PLAN SUBMITTED ....

PRODUCT LINE C

FORM 20-1   SUBSET 3

FORECAST-VOLUMES + PRICES

DESCRIPTION	TERM	1967	1968	1969	1970	1971	1972	1973	1974
SALES									
PRODUCT C 41	UTS			10000	20000	35000	50000	70000	90000
PRODUCT C 42	UTS			1000	2000	3500	5000	7000	9000
TOTAL	UTS			11000	22000	38500	55000	77000	99000
PRODUCTION									
PRODUCT C 41									
BILLINGS	UTS			9000	18000	32000	45000	60000	70000
OTHER DEMAND	UTS			4800	4800	5300	4900	3200	2800
TOTAL	UTS			13800	22800	37300	49900	63200	72800
PRODUCT C 42									
BILLINGS	UTS			900	1800	3200	4500	6000	7000
OTHER DEMAND	UTS			100	300	300	500	700	800
TOTAL	UTS			1000	2100	3500	5000	6700	7800
GRAND TOTAL	UTS			14800	24900	40800	54900	69900	80600
CUSTOMER SHIPMENTS	UTS			9900	19800	35200	49500	66000	77000
PRICES									
PRODUCT C 41	$/UT			1200	1500	1500	1500	1500	1500
PRODUCT C 42	$/UT			4000	4100	4100	4100	4100	4100
RETAIL VALUES									
ORDERS (SALES)	M $			16.0	38.2	66.9	95.5	133.7	171.9
SHIPMENTS (BILLINGS)	M $			14.4	34.4	61.1	86.0	114.6	133.7
OTHER DEMAND	M $			6.2	8.4	9.2	9.4	7.7	7.5
INSTALLED EQUIPMENT	M $			14.4	48.8	109.9	171.0	285.6	419.3
DISCOUNTS AND ALLOWANCES	M $			2.7	4.7	7.0	7.5	9.0	11.7
PRODUCT GROSS INCOME	M $			11.7	29.7	54.1	78.5	105.6	122.0

PSG - PLANNING SYSTEMS GENERATOR

- COMPANY CONFIDENTIAL -

Exhibit 9-12

11/15/68

benefit of professional forecasters and require in their use a great deal of evaluation or interpretation. Only in rare cases have they been defined in terms that make their inclusion in a business planning system feasible.

Returning to the P & L summary of product line C, let us move ahead to the other business functions and the respective sample displays of supporting data.

SERVICE

Exhibit 9-13 deals with service. Let us first verify the 1970 transfers to the P & L summary: Gross Income 3.498 M$, Gross Profit 1.032 M$. Income and workload are based on installed equipment and its coverage by service contracts or per call service. Service cost is either directly or indirectly related to workload. The number of decision variables in the service module of this division's planning data system are 26 by function and 30 by product within function. The reader may practice planning systems development by making up a listing of these variables himself and comparing it with the line items on Exhibits 9-14 to 9-17.

MANUFACTURING

The next example is from the Manufacturing Module. Workload is computed by product, considering the dynamics of manufacturing progress. A first subroutine determines declining workload and cost per unit as more units of the same type are manufactured. It also reflects lead time by operation and the decline of lead time to a target minimum commensurate with reasonable customer delivery schedules.

A second subroutine looks at total yearly workload in relation to capacity limitations, based on manpower, and determines a workload adjustment factor (WAF). This WAF is then used as shown in Exhibit 9-18 to bring capacity and workload into balance—using subcontracting as a buffer.

Based on this balanced workload, in-plant manpower and space are computed by product, summarized, and displayed, per Exhibit 9-19.

A third subroutine, see Exhibit 9-20, computes burden (overhead) for the adjusted in-plant workload by each cost center using fixed and variable cost rates. This takes into account the dynamics of cost as a function of plant utilization or total in-plant production. At the same time this subroutine computes purchase burden which is applied to both vendor purchases and contract work. The latter is the WAF buffer and a variable depending on plant capacity.

Finally, Exhibit 9-21 illustrates the summary display of all relevant cost data by product line. For product line C, the 1970 total cost is 13,194 K$. This amount is transferred to a gross profit subroutine where it is converted to unit cost and used in connection with LIFO and other valuation or adjustment logic to compute the 14.9 M product gross profit which is transferred to the P & L. To keep the number of exhibits

DIVISION X PLANNING DATA   VIEW 2001

STRATEGIC PLAN SUBMITTED ....

FORM 25-1   SUBSET 3

PRODUCT LINE C

SERVICE OPERATIONS BY PRODUCT

DESCRIPTION	TERM	1967	1968	1969	1970	1971	1972	1973	1974
EQUIPMENT INSTALLED									
SHIPMENTS	KUTS			9.900	19.800	35.200	49.500	66.000	77.000
ATTRITION	KUTS				.495	1.460	3.147	5.465	8.492
ADJUSTMENT	KUTS								
YEAR ENDING INVENTORY	KUTS			9.900	29.205	62.945	109.298	169.833	238.341
AVERAGE INSTALLED INVENTORY	KUTS			3.663	18.587	49.449	90.756	145.619	210.938
WARRANTY	KUTS			2.475	4.950	8.800	12.375	16.500	19.250
SERVICE POTENTIAL	KUTS			1.188	13.637	40.649	78.381	129.119	191.688
SELF SERVICE	KUTS							2.582	9.584
COMPETITION	KUTS							6.327	18.210
SERVICE CONTRACT UNITS	KUTS			.772	8.455	25.609	49.380	79.718	114.725
PER CALL SERVICE UNITS	KUTS			.416	5.182	15.040	29.001	40.492	49.168
OTHER	KUTS						.990	3.300	6.160
WORKLOAD PRODUCING REVENUE									
SERVICE CONTRACTS	K HRS			15.444	169.102	512.175	987.606	1594.356	2294.501
PER CALL SERVICE	K HRS			6.237	77.732	225.601	348.013	485.899	590.015
WORKLOAD CHARGED TO OTHER DEPARTMENTS									
GUARANTEE	K HRS			37.125	49.500	44.000	61.875	82.500	96.250
ENGINEERING CHANGES	K HRS			99.000	158.400	140.800	99.000	132.000	154.000
SALES CHARGES									
WARRANTY	K HRS			21.037	39.600	66.000	86.625	115.500	134.750
GOODWILL ASSISTANCE	K HRS			21.978	111.523	271.969	499.160	728.093	1054.688
DEMONSTRATORS	K HRS			45.000	52.500	60.000	60.000	60.000	60.000
TRADE INS	K HRS						4.950	16.500	30.800
FURNITURE + FIXTURES	K HRS			10.000	10.000	10.000	10.000	10.000	10.000
TRAINING	K HRS			50.000	50.000	10.000			
OTHER	K HRS								
TOTAL RECOVERY	K HRS			284.140	471.523	602.769	821.610	1144.593	1540.488
TOTAL WORKLOAD	K HRS			305.821	718.358	1340.545	2157.229	3224.848	4425.004
GROSS INCOME									
SERVICE CONTRACTS	M $			.216	2.410	7.299	14.814	26.307	37.859
PER CALL SERVICE	M $			.069	.933	2.707	4.872	6.803	8.260
BILLABLE PARTS	M $			.012	.155	.451	.870	1.215	1.475
OTHER	M $								
TOTAL	M $			.297	3.498	10.457	20.556	34.324	47.595
COST + RECOVERIES									
SERVICE CONTRACTS	M $			2.165	5.812	12.159	21.033	33.313	47.702
ESTIMATED INDIRECT COST	M $			.039	.423	1.280	2.963	4.783	6.884
CONTRACT PARTS	M $			.004	.047	.135	.261	.364	.443
PARTS SOLD	M $								
SPECIAL CHARGES	M $								
TOTAL RECOVERIES	M $			2.012	3.815	5.467	8.011	11.824	16.606
NET SERVICE COST	M $			.196	2.466	8.107	16.246	26.637	38.421
GROSS PROFIT	M $			.101	1.032	2.349	4.310	7.688	9.173
PROFITABILITY RATE	O/O			34.12	29.49	22.47	20.97	22.40	19.27

PSG - PLANNING SYSTEMS GENERATOR

- COMPANY CONFIDENTIAL -

11/15/68

Exhibit 9-13

DIVISION X PLANNING DATA   VIEW 2001

STRATEGIC PLAN SUBMITTED .....

FORM 25-8 (PRODUCT)   SUBSET 3

PRODUCT LINE C

SERVICE WORKSHEET 1 OF 2

CODE	DESCRIPTION	TERM	PRIOR	1967	1968	1969	1970	1971	1972	1973	1974
COL.1-7			18-24	25-31	32-38	39-45	46-52	53-59	60-66	67-73	74-80
	EQUIPMENT INSTALLED IN MARKET										
2503002	NEW SHIPMENTS	KUTS T	0.	0.	0.	9.900	19.800	35.200	49.500	66.000	77.000
2503003	ATTRITION, RATIO TO START INV	0/0	.	.	.	5.0	5.0	5.0	5.0	5.0	5.0
2503004	ADJUSTMENT	KUTS	.	.	.	.	.	.	.	.	.
2503005	TIME SCALE	0/0	.	.	.	37.0	45.0	60.0	60.0	60.0	60.0
2503006	WARRANTY	MONTHS	.	.	.	3.	3.	3.	3.	3.	3.
2503007	SELF SERVICE	0/0	.	.	.	.	.	.	.	2.0	5.0
2503008	COMPETITION	0/0	.	.	.	.	.	.	.	5.0	10.0
2503009	SERVICE CONTRACTS	0/0	.	.	.	65.0	62.0	63.0	63.0	63.0	63.0
2503010	TRADE-INS	0/0	.	.	.	.	.	.	2.0	5.0	8.0
2503011	DEMONSTRATORS	KUTS	.	.	.	1.500	1.750	2.000	2.000	2.000	2.000
2503012	FURNITURE + FIXTURES	KUTS	.	.	.	.500	.500	.500	.500	.500	.500
	WORKLOAD PRODUCING REVENUE										
2503031	SERVICE CONTRACTS	HR/UT	.	.	.	20.00	20.00	20.00	20.00	20.00	20.00
2503032	PER CALL SERVICE	HR/UT	.	.	.	15.00	15.00	15.00	12.00	12.00	12.00
	WORKLOAD NON-REVENUE PRODUCING										
2503033	GUARANTEE	HR/UT	.	.	.	15.00	10.00	5.00	5.00	5.00	5.00
2503040	ENGINEERING CHANGES	HR/UT	.	.	.	10.00	8.00	4.00	2.00	2.00	2.00
2503035	WARRANTY	HR/UT	.	.	.	8.50	8.00	7.50	7.00	7.00	7.00
2503037	GOODWILL SALES ASSISTANCE	HR/UT	.	.	.	6.00	6.00	5.50	5.50	5.00	5.00
2503038	DEMONSTRATORS	HR/UT	.	.	.	30.00	30.00	30.00	30.00	30.00	30.00
2503039	TRADE-INS	HR/UT	.	.	.	.	.	.	5.00	5.00	5.00
2503041	FURNITURE + FIXTURES	HR/UT	.	.	.	20.00	20.00	20.00	20.00	20.00	20.00
2503042	PRODUCT TRAINING	KHRS	.	.	.	50.000	50.000	10.000	.	.	.
2503045	OTHER	KHRS	.	.	.	.	.	.	.	.	.

PSG - PLANNING SYSTEMS GENERATOR

- COMPANY CONFIDENTIAL -

11/15/68

Exhibit 9-14

STRATEGIC PLAN SUBMITTED ....

FORM 25-8 (PRODUCT)   SUBSET 3

PRODUCT LINE C

SERVICE WORKSHEET 2 OF 2

CODE	DESCRIPTION	TERM	PRIOR	1967	1968	1969	1970	1971	1972	1973	1974
COL.1-7			18-24	25-31	32-38	39-45	46-52	53-59	60-66	67-73	74-80
	INCOME										
2503051	SERVICE CONTRACTS	$/UT	.	.	.	280.00	285.00	285.00	300.00	330.00	330.00
2503052	PER CALL SERVICE	$/HR	.	.	.	11.00	12.00	12.00	14.00	14.00	14.00
2503053	BILLABLE PARTS	$/UT	.	.	.	30.00	30.00	30.00	30.00	30.00	30.00
2503076	OTHER INCOME	M $	.	.	.	.	.	.	.	.	.
	COST + EXPENSE										
2503120	INDIRECT COST RATE (ESTIMATED)	$/HR	.	.	.	7.08	8.09	9.07	9.75	10.33	10.78
2503061	CONTRACT PARTS	$/UT	.	.	.	50.00	50.00	50.00	60.00	60.00	60.00
2503070	BILLABLE PARTS SOLD	O/O	.	.	.	30.0	30.0	30.0	30.0	30.0	30.0
2503077	SPECIAL CHARGES	M $	.	.	.	.	.	.	.	.	.

PSG - PLANNING SYSTEMS GENERATOR   11/15/68

- COMPANY CONFIDENTIAL -

Exhibit 9-15

DIVISION X PLANNING DATA   VIEW 2001   STRATEGIC PLAN SUBMITTED ....

FORM 25-9 (SUMMARY)   SUBSET 0

TOTAL DIVISION   SERVICE WORKSHEET 1 OF 2

CODE	DESCRIPTION	TERM	PRIOR	1967	1968	1969	1970	1971	1972	1973	1974
COL.1-7			18-24	25-31	32-38	39-45	46-52	53-59	60-66	67-73	74-80
	MANPOWER										
2500081	FIELD PRIOR YEAR	MEN	2400.	.	.	.	.	.	.	.	.
2500082	TRAINEES PRIOR YEAR	MEN	150.	.	.	.	.	.	.	.	.
2500083	AVAILABLE HOURS/MAN	HR/YR	.	1936.	1944.	1936.	1912.	1904.	1904.	1896.	1896.
2500084	OVERTIME	O/O	.	5.0	5.0	5.0	5.0	5.0	5.0	5.0	5.0
2500085	NON-PROD TIME/AVAIL HRS	O/O	.	15.0	15.0	14.0	14.0	14.0	14.0	14.0	14.0
2500086	PERFORMANCE FACTOR	O/O	.	100.0	100.0	100.0	100.0	98.0	99.0	101.0	103.0
2500087	BRANCH MGRS + FIELD	MEN	.	150.	160.	170.	180.	190.	200.	210.	220.
2500088	SUPERVISORS WORKLOAD	O/O	.	30.0	30.0	30.0	30.0	30.0	30.0	30.0	30.0
2500089	MANAGEMENT RATIO	RATIO	.	9.0	9.0	9.0	9.0	9.0	9.0	9.0	9.0
2500090	LOSS RATE ON FIELD MANPOWER	O/O	.	9.0	8.5	8.0	8.0	8.0	8.0	8.0	8.0
2500091	TRAINING PERIOD	MTHS	.	3.	3.	3.	4.	4.	4.	5.	5.
2500092	DISTRICT MANAGERS	MEN	.	20.	20.	20.	20.	20.	20.	20.	20.
2500093	HEADQUARTERS	MEN	.	28.	35.	47.	53.	60.	64.	71.	77.
2500094	PLANT	MEN	.	56.	76.	42.	84.	80.	115.	81.	89.

PSG - PLANNING SYSTEMS GENERATOR   - COMPANY CONFIDENTIAL -   11/15/68

Exhibit 9-16

TOTAL DIVISION   SERVICE WORKSHEET 2 OF 2

CODE	DESCRIPTION	TERM	PRIOR	1967	1968	1969	1970	1971	1972	1973	1974
COL.1-7			18-24	25-31	32-38	39-45	46-52	53-59	60-66	67-73	74-80
	DIRECT COSTING										
2500101	BR MANAGERS SALARY/MAN	K $	•	12.000	13.000	14.000	15.000	16.000	17.000	17.500	18.000
2500102	SUPERVISORS SALARY/MAN	K $	•	9.500	10.000	10.500	11.000	11.500	12.000	12.500	13.000
2500103	SERVICEMAN SALARY/MAN	K $	•	5.000	5.500	6.000	6.500	7.000	7.500	8.000	8.500
2500104	TRAINEES SALARY/MAN	K $	•	3.000	3.500	4.000	4.500	5.000	5.500	6.000	6.500
2500105	TRAVEL/REGULAR SERVICEMAN	K $	•	1.500	2.000	2.500	3.000	3.500	4.000	4.500	5.000
2500106	TOOL + REPAIR/RSM	K $	•	.150	.175	.200	.225	.250	.275	.300	.325
2500107	OTHER COST / RSM	K $	•	.200	.215	.230	.245	.260	.275	.290	.305
	OTHER COSTS										
2500111	BR OFFICE APPORTIONMENT	K$/MAN	•	.600	.700	.800	.900	1.000	1.100	1.200	1.300
2500112	DISTRICT EXPENSE	K$/MAN	•	50.000	52.000	55.000	60.000	65.000	67.000	75.000	80.000
2500113	HEADQUARTERS EXPENSE	K$/MAN	•	15.000	16.000	17.000	18.000	19.000	20.000	21.000	22.000
2500114	PLANT EXPENSE	K$/MAN	•	15.000	16.000	17.000	18.000	19.000	20.000	21.000	22.000
2500115	TRAINING EXPENSE	K$/MAN	•	.400	.400	.400	.550	.550	.550	.700	.700
2500117	MISCELLANEOUS CHARGES	M $	•	.200	•	•	•	•	•	•	•
2500118	GROSS COSTS TOTAL (OPTIONAL)	M $	29.000	29.900	33.900						

PSG - PLANNING SYSTEMS GENERATOR

- COMPANY CONFIDENTIAL -

11/15/68

Exhibit 9-17

DIVISION X PLANNING DATA   VIEW 2001   STRATEGIC PLAN SUBMITTED ....

PRODUCT LINE C   YEAR 1970

PRODUCTION WORKLOAD, MANPOWER, SPACE

DESCRIPTION	TOTAL WORKLOAD 000 HRS	DESIRED C P O/O	PLANNED WORKLOAD 000 HRS	IN PLANT MANPOWER	IN PLANT SPACE K SQFT	CONT PROC WORKLOAD 000 HRS	EQUIV C P MANPOWER	EFFECTIVE C P O/O
MACHINING	228.9	35.0	130.1	71.4	27.1	98.8	54.2	43.2
PROCESSING	22.1		22.1	12.1	9.3			
ASSEMBLY AREA I	759.9	20.0	531.3	291.6	40.8	228.6	125.5	30.1
ASSEMBLY AREA II	46.3	60.0	16.2	8.9	1.6	30.1	16.5	65.0
TOTAL	1057.2		699.7	384.0	78.8	357.5	196.2	33.8
LABOR REGULAR			683.5					
LABOR SPECIAL			16.2					
INDIRECT MANPOWER				307.2	55.5		157.0	
TOTAL				691.2	134.3		353.2	
WORKLOAD ADJUSTMENT FACTOR		87.4						

PSG - PLANNING SYSTEMS GENERATOR   - COMPANY CONFIDENTIAL -   11/15/68

Exhibit 9-18

DIVISION X PLANNING DATA   VIEW 2001

STRATEGIC PLAN SUBMITTED.....

SUBSET 0

TOTAL DIVISION

MANUFACTURING MANPOWER + SPACE

FORM 27-4

DESCRIPTION	TERM	1967	1968	1969	1970	1971	1972	1973	1974
MANPOWER (AVERAGE)									
DIRECT	MEN	1030	1000	1200	1400	1400	1400	1400	1400
INDIRECT	MEN	847	825	1004	1161	1155	1152	1149	1145
SUBTOTAL	MEN	1877	1825	2204	2561	2555	2552	2549	2545
ENGINEERING MANUFACTG	MEN	103	98	180	175	142	138	115	97
ENGINEERING PRODUCT	MEN	168	227	245	254	273	330	318	332
TOTAL FACTORY	MEN	2148	2150	2629	2990	2970	3020	2982	2974
DEVELOPMENT ENGINEERING	MEN	204	208	224	256	292	328	376	428
NON-MANUFACTURING	MEN	217	223	240	274	312	351	402	458
TOTAL LOCATION	MEN	2569	2581	3093	3520	3574	3699	3760	3860
SUPPLEMENTAL DIRECT	MEN	15							
SUPPLEMENTAL INDIRECT	MEN	12							
TOTAL SUPPLEMENTAL	MEN	27							
FACTORY NEW HIRES									
TO TOTAL FACTORY	MEN	112	99	610	511	129	201	111	141
	O/O	4.4	3.8	19.7	14.5	3.6	5.4	3.0	3.7
LABOR HOURS/MAN-YEAR	HOURS	1781	1746	1761	1822	1814	1814	1807	1807
SPACE (YEAR-END)									
PRODUCTION OPERATIONS									
MACHINING	KSQFT	70.9	66.2	82.9	100.1	100.5	101.4	100.5	101.8
PROCESSING	KSQFT	66.6	66.1	71.2	76.4	82.9	90.9	99.2	105.2
ASSEMBLY AREA I	KSQFT	83.2	75.5	94.9	113.8	115.7	116.0	115.7	116.8
ASSEMBLY AREA II	KSQFT	39.9	45.2	47.2	50.0	46.2	44.0	42.9	39.3
INDIRECT	KSQFT	155.0	149.0	181.2	209.5	208.5	207.9	207.4	206.7
SUBTOTAL	KSQFT	415.6	402.0	477.4	549.8	553.8	560.2	565.7	569.8
MFG + PROD ENGINEERING	KSQFT	51.5	61.8	80.8	81.5	78.9	88.9	82.3	81.5
DEVELOPMENT ENGINEERING	KSQFT	43.9	44.7	48.2	55.0	62.8	70.5	80.8	92.0
NON-MANUFACTURING	KSQFT	46.7	47.9	51.6	58.9	67.1	75.5	86.4	98.5
WAREHOUSE + MISCELLANEOUS	KSQFT	129.0	150.0	150.0	150.0	150.0	150.0	150.0	150.0
TOTAL LOCATION	KSQFT	686.7	706.4	808.0	895.2	912.6	945.1	965.2	991.6
SPACE AVAILABLE	KSQFT	750.0	750.0	875.0	1000.0	1000.0	1000.0	1000.0	1000.0
SPACE UTILIZATION	O/O	91.6	94.2	92.3	89.5	91.3	94.5	96.5	99.2

- COMPANY CONFIDENTIAL -

Exhibit 9-19

PSG - PLANNING SYSTEMS GENERATOR

11/15/68

SUBSET   0

FORM 27-5

TOTAL DIVISION   YEAR 1970   MANUFACTURING WORKLOAD AND BURDEN

DESCRIPTION	TERM	MACH	PROCESS	ASSBLY I	ASSBLY II	TOTAL BURDEN	CONTRACT PROCUREMENT	C P RATIO	PURCHASE BURDEN
TECHNOLOGY ONE									
PRODUCT D5X	K HRS	94.9	1.8	40.8	13.7	151.2			18.9
PRODUCT D6X	K HRS	64.0	1.7	28.5	9.4	103.6			7.8
TOTAL	K HRS	158.9	3.5	69.3	23.1	254.8			26.7
BURDEN COST	K $	867.0	30.2	561.1	166.1	1624.4			
BURDEN RATE	$/HRS	5.46	8.63	8.10	7.19	6.38			
O/O OF AVERAGE	O/O	85.6	135.3	127.0	112.7	100.0			
TECHNOLOGY TWO + THREE									
PRODUCT A1X	K HRS	147.0	61.4	281.2		489.6	276.4	36.1	579.7
PRODUCT A2X	K HRS	76.6	33.4	161.2		271.2	152.0	35.9	536.1
PRODUCT B3X	K HRS	54.3	41.6	326.0		421.9	282.5	40.1	409.7
PRODUCT C4X	K HRS	130.1	22.1	531.3	16.2	699.7	357.5	33.8	548.6
PRODUCT E7X	K HRS		.4	4.7		5.1	3.7	42.0	24.7
PRODUCT E8X	K HRS		5.5	155.9	299.4	460.8	324.2	41.3	911.5
SERVICE PARTS	K HRS	73.4	16.0	21.0		110.4	49.6	31.0	70.3
TOTAL	K HRS	481.4	180.4	1481.3	315.6	2458.7	1445.9		3080.6
BURDEN COST	K $	3025.3	1245.3	6029.9	2091.1	12391.6			
BURDEN RATE	$/HRS	6.28	6.90	4.07	6.63	5.04			
O/O OF AVERAGE	O/O	124.6	136.9	80.8	131.5	100.0			
GRAND TOTAL BURDEN		3892.3	1275.5	6591.0	2257.2	14016.0			

- COMPANY CONFIDENTIAL -

Exhibit 9-20

PSG - PLANNING SYSTEMS GENERATOR

11/15/68

DIVISION X PLANNING DATA   VIEW 2001

STRATEGIC PLAN SUBMITTED ....

FORM 27-6

SUBSET 0

TOTAL DIVISION

YEAR 1970

PRODUCTION COST SUMMARY

DESCRIPTION	PROD DEMAND	MFG BURDEN	LABOR	CONTR PROC	PURCHASE INC MATL	PURCH BURDEN	INT PLT TRANS	MFG ENG EXPENSE	TOTAL MFG COST
	*				000 $				
TECHNOLOGY ONE									
PRODUCT D5X	7420	935	196		2061	19		60	3271
PRODUCT D6X	1650	690	91		828	8		40	1657
TOTAL		1625	287		2889	27		100	4928
TECHNOLOGY TWO									
PRODUCT A1X	100.3	2016	1528	2196	4136	580	60	600	11116
PRODUCT A2X	37.0	1284	846	1288	4047	536	75	2000	10076
PRODUCT B3X	63.5	3533	1316	2665	1906	410		300	10130
TOTAL		6833	3690	6149	10089	1526	135	2900	31322
TECHNOLOGY THREE									
PRODUCT C4X	24.9	2341	2186	2407	3167	549	1244	1300	13194
PRODUCT E7X	470	19	16	34	205	25	195	400	894
PRODUCT E8X	4650	2576	1486	2864	5865	912	13837	1100	28640
TOTAL		4936	3688	5305	9237	1486	15276	2800	42728
SERVICE PARTS		621	344	498	80	70			1613
GRAND TOTAL		14015	8009	11952	22295	3109	15411	5800	80591

* PRODUCTION DEMAND IN INTEGER UNITS OR DECIMAL THOUSANDS

PSG - PLANNING SYSTEMS GENERATOR

- COMPANY CONFIDENTIAL -

11/15/68

Exhibit 9-21

within reasonable bounds, the input worksheets are not shown. There are a great variety of decision variables in manufacturing ranging from learning curve parameters by product, to labor rates, fixed and proportional burden rates, working hours, and downtime assumptions, etc.

In a way, a planning data system incorporates a scaled down standard cost manual, the emphasis being on scaled down. Resist the temptation to develop standard cost manuals for five years into the future. It is hard enough to keep today's standard costs in order.

Exhibit 9-22 covers the General and Administrative Function. Manpower is treated as variable with business volume plus a fixed base. Expenses are computed from manpower and distributed on the basis of product line revenue. Other product line oriented costs, such as certain personal property taxes, are computed from appropriate bases and factors. Please note that for 1970 the manpower-oriented expenses are 9.5M, of which 1.1M are distributed to Product Line C. The direct expense is added for a total allocation of 1.3M. This amount is transferred to the P & L.

These illustrations—and it will be of benefit to the reader to study them carefully— give tangible evidence about the architecture of a divisional planning system.*

Another look at the typical input structure and source data options in Chapter 7, Figures 6 and 7, might be helpful in rounding out the picture.

---

* The complete anatomy of logic and display for such a system is included in my dissertation "Business Planning by Computer," Western Reserve University, February 1965, available as publication #66–3035 from University Microfilms, Ann Arbor, Michigan.

DIVISION X PLANNING DATA   VIEW 2001

STRATEGIC PLAN SUBMITTED ....

FORM 29-1   SUBSET   0

TOTAL DIVISION

GENERAL + ADMINISTRATIVE

DESCRIPTION	TERM	1967	1968	1969	1970	1971	1972	1973	1974
MANPOWER - AVERAGE									
FINANCIAL	MEN	198	220	234	269	295	315	341	357
ADMINISTRATION	MEN	20	22	24	26	28	30	32	34
GENERAL MANAGEMENT	MEN	22	22	22	22	23	22	22	20
TOTAL	MEN	240	264	280	317	346	367	395	411
EXPENSE									
FINANCIAL	M $	6.9	8.2	9.7	11.7	13.3	14.7	16.3	17.6
ADMINISTRATION	M $	.5	.6	.7	.7	.8	.9	1.0	1.1
GENERAL MANAGEMENT	M $	.6	.6	.7	.8	.8	.9	1.0	1.0
TOTAL	M $	8.0	9.4	11.1	13.2	14.9	16.5	18.3	19.7
PRODUCT LINE DISTRIBUTION									
TO BE DISTRIBUTED	M $	6.3	7.2	8.0	9.5	10.7	12.0	13.5	14.6
DISTRIBUTION									
PROD LINE A	M $	2.9	3.1	3.1	3.6	3.6	3.7	3.8	4.1
PROD LINE B	M $	1.3	1.4	1.4	1.4	1.5	1.7	1.8	1.8
PROD LINE C	M $			.4	1.1	2.1	3.2	4.6	5.5
PROD LINE D	M $	.4	.5	.5	.6	.5	.6	.5	.6
PROD LINE E	M $	1.8	2.2	2.6	2.8	2.8	2.8	2.7	2.6
TOTAL DIRECT + DISTRIBUTION									
PROD LINE A	M $	3.1	3.4	3.5	4.0	4.2	4.2	4.4	4.6
PROD LINE B	M $	1.5	1.6	1.6	1.6	1.7	1.9	2.0	2.0
PROD LINE C	M $			.4	1.3	2.5	3.7	5.3	6.3
PROD LINE D	M $	.4	.5	.5	.6	.5	.6	.5	.6
PROD LINE E	M $	3.0	3.9	5.1	5.7	6.0	6.1	6.1	6.2
TOTAL EXPENSE	M $	8.0	9.4	11.1	13.2	14.9	16.5	18.3	19.7
O/O TO GROSS INCOME	O/O	4.3	4.5	4.8	4.7	4.6	4.5	4.4	4.4

PSG - PLANNING SYSTEMS GENERATOR

- COMPANY CONFIDENTIAL -

11/15/68

Exhibit 9-22

10

Planned Goals

The two preceding chapters contain a thorough description of a corporate planning data system backed up by a divisional planning data system for one typical division within that corporation. We must now proceed to demonstrate how these systems will actually be used in the process of originating planned goals. In this connection we also have to address the question of achievability, or more properly, the question of how assumptions about achievability enter into the process of originating planned goals in the first place.

The reader may wonder why so much pain has been taken in this book to show all this detail. It is, of course, much easier on both the writer—and the reader—to have to deal with only stylized examples. Unfortunately, in the reality of planning a business, it is exactly the degree of detail between the stylized examples for a proposed approach and the actual usefulness of the approach to management which becomes the key issue. While imagination is a cheap medium for the communication of an approach, the reality of implementation becomes very expensive or even untenable unless the medium fits the message.

Therefore, this book contains complete illustrations which, while by no means exhaustive, nevertheless cover sufficient substance to be realistic rather than stylized. As a matter of recommendation, the reader might try not to use imagination, but pencil and paper to list all the line items of information and related logic not covered. He may then wrestle with the question how all these additional specifications should be added for appropriate simultaneous consideration in a corporate or divisional planning exercise.

In the meantime, this chapter will deal with one such exercise at the corporate level. This will be a simple example involving the change of only one decision variable in the entire corporate planning data system. Though simple, the example is intended to demonstrate the system's power.

CORPORATE PLANNING EXERCISE

Let us assume to start with that the illustrative data which were used in the demonstration systems in Chapters 8 and 9 represent the agreed upon planned goals at a specific point in time, say, Nov. 15, 1968. Therefore, the year 1967 and prior are planning data which were extracted from the transaction data system and represent actual conditions. The years 1968 and 1969 represent the current operating budget, that is the latest agreed upon control data, against which progress is measured and evaluated, perhaps on a monthly or quarterly basis. The budgetary control process is not part of the planning system. The approved operating budget in the month of November would include an up-to-date reprojection of the current year's expected results and a detailed projection for all control accounts for next year is maintained within the transaction data system.

The operating budget is like a contract entered into by the various organizational units of the corporation and as such represents a business transaction. Therefore, budget data are business data in the conventional sense and become firm source information for the transaction data system. Changes in budget data follow the same procedures, being changes in the contractual agreements.

The years 1970 through 1974 represent genuine planning data as generated and documented through the planning data system.

The reader is asked to imagine himself a member of the corporation's management committee (CMC). Among other things, CMC's responsibility is to review and concur with strategic plans presented to it by the corporate or divisional managers, charged in turn with the responsibility to originate such plans. Let us assume that following an agreement between corporate management and the management of Division Y during the past several months, a major market research study had been undertaken in order to re-evaluate the market potential for Y's product line.

The last time such a thorough market study had been made, with the assistance— as is usually the case—of a consulting firm specializing in such studies, the consensus of opinions resulted in an input to the planning data system of 1320 Million $ for 1973 (see input line 0302201 on Form 03-9 Input Worksheet 1 of 7, Exhibit 8-12). In this manner the study's findings became an agreed upon basis for the development of a strategic plan.

The new study just undertaken points out that these previous estimates were "too conservative" and that in the best judgment of the researchers the market potential for 1974 could be expected to reach about $1.8 billions. As a parenthetical observation it seems to be general practice to offer conclusions in market research in such a way that comparability to previous similar studies is not immediately ascertainable, hence the new study addresses the year 1974 rather than the year 1973.

Before Division Y would be prevailed upon to recast their strategic plan through their divisional planning data system, the subset for Division Y within the corporate planning data system is used to take a quick look at what this new information might mean to the corporation as a whole. The exhibits at the end of this chapter show the output of the corporate planning data system in response to the change in market estimate for Division Y while keeping all other planning assumptions constant. This very rough examination of the consequences of a change in market assumptions would be available within hours following the CMC's decision to accept the new market research study as a basis for current strategic planning.

Among the output documents selected in this case, the reader will see:

(1) Corporate income analysis, Exhibit 10-1
(2) Updated charts for gross and net income comparison, Exhibits 10-2 and 10-3
(3) Income impact due to change in Division Y's market, Exhibit 10-4
(4) Division Y: Five pages of key planning data, Exhibits 10-5 to 10-9
(5) Input Worksheet, page 1 of 7, Exhibit 10-10, with the audit trail for the change in line 0302201 Market, Amount (the '0.' for 1973 cancels the previous estimate of 1320. Million $ and the entry of 1800. Million $ for 1974 establishes this new data in the system).

Note: Since no other changes were made in the planning assumptions, input worksheets 2 to 7 are not exhibited again. The reader is referred to the corresponding exhibits in Chapter 8.

The empty data cells between the new input and the 1969 market of 1124.9 millions are filled in by the system using linear interpolation. Other methods of interpolation are available in the system and may have been chosen instead. Anyway, the resulting change in market estimate for each year is as follows:

	1970	1971	1972	1973	1974
View 9001	1173.6	1222.4	1271.2	1320.0	1372.8
View 9002	1259.9	1394.9	1529.9	1665.0	1800.0
Change	86.3	172.5	258.7	345.0	427.2
Percent	7.4	14.0	20.4	26.1	31.1

This then is the quantified opinion regarding the "conservative" nature of the previous market research study.

XYZ PLANNING DATA SYSTEM VIEW 9002

CHANGE IN DIVISION Y'S MARKET

INCOME ANALYSIS

TOTAL CORPORATION

FORM 08-1

SUBSET 0

DESCRIPTION	1967 AMT	1967 O/O	1968 AMT	1968 O/O	1969 AMT	1969 O/O	1970 AMT	1970 O/O	1971 AMT	1971 O/O	1972 AMT	1972 O/O	1973 AMT	1973 O/O	1974 AMT	1974 O/O
DIVISION X																
GROSS INCOME	120.1	5.4	130.9	9.0	142.2	8.6	182.4	28.3	221.7	21.5	261.0	17.7	309.7	18.7	353.1	16.7
GROSS PROFIT	59.6	8.4	67.3	12.9	68.3	1.5	89.8	31.5	111.3	23.9	130.9	17.6	155.0	18.4	176.4	16.8
NET BEFORE TAX	18.6	3.9	20.3	9.1	8.7	-57.1	22.6	159.8	31.4	38.9	38.4	22.3	48.3	25.8	57.1	17.4
GROSS MARGIN	49.6		51.4		48.0		49.2		50.2		50.2		50.0		50.0	
NETBT MARGIN	15.5		15.5		6.1		12.4		14.2		14.7		15.6		16.2	
DIVISION Y																
GROSS INCOME	84.1	5.1	90.4	7.5	90.7	-.3	135.8	49.7	149.1	9.8	157.4	5.5	165.6	5.3	173.9	10.9
GROSS PROFIT	37.7	7.7	42.1	11.7	41.6	-1.2	68.1	63.7	74.6	9.6	78.0	4.5	81.3	4.3	84.7	12.3
NET BEFORE TAX	13.0	8.3	14.6	12.3	8.3	-43.2	27.8	234.7	30.4	9.5	31.6	3.8	33.2	5.2	34.8	15.1
GROSS MARGIN	44.8		46.6		45.9		50.2		50.0		49.6		49.1		48.7	
NETBT MARGIN	15.5		16.2		9.2		20.5		20.4		20.1		20.0		20.0	
DIVISION Z																
GROSS INCOME	36.0	5.9	40.5	12.5	39.7	-2.0	42.4	6.9	44.4	4.7	47.7	7.4	50.7	6.4	54.8	6.2
GROSS PROFIT	21.9	9.5	25.2	15.2	24.7	-1.9	26.1	5.5	27.8	6.8	29.5	6.0	31.6	7.0	34.3	6.6
NET BEFORE TAX	8.9	11.1	10.4	17.2	9.5	-8.5	10.0	5.2	11.3	12.6	12.2	7.7	13.7	12.7	15.1	7.9
GROSS MARGIN	60.8		62.3		62.3		61.5		62.7		61.9		62.2		62.6	
NETBT MARGIN	24.7		25.7		24.0		23.6		25.4		25.5		27.0		27.6	
SPECIAL PRODUCTS																
GROSS INCOME	-2.0		10.0		11.0	10.0	12.1	10.0	13.3	10.0	14.6	10.0	16.1	10.0	17.7	10.0
NET BEFORE TAX			-1.0	-50.0	.1	NA	.2	120.0	.8	230.0	1.5	83.3	2.1	43.0	2.7	NA
NETBT MARGIN			-10.0		1.0		2.0		6.0		10.0		13.0		15.0	
FOREIGN OPERATIONS																
GROSS INCOME	42.0	5.0	44.0	4.8	46.2	5.0	48.5	5.0	50.9	5.0	53.5	5.0	56.2	5.0	59.0	5.0
GROSS PROFIT	21.0	5.0	22.0	4.8	23.1	5.0	24.3	5.0	25.5	5.0	26.7	5.0	28.1	5.0	29.5	5.0
NET BEFORE TAX	8.4	5.0	8.8	4.8	9.2	5.0	9.7	5.0	10.2	5.0	10.7	5.0	11.2	5.0	11.8	5.0
NET AFTER TAX	4.2	5.0	4.4	4.8	4.6	5.0	4.9	5.0	5.1	5.0	5.3	5.0	5.6	5.0	5.9	5.0
GROSS MARGIN	50.0		50.0		50.0		50.0		50.0		50.0		50.0		50.0	
NETBT MARGIN	20.0		20.0		20.0		20.0		20.0		20.0		20.0		20.0	
NETAT MARGIN	10.0		10.0		10.0		10.0		10.0		10.0		10.0		10.0	
TOTAL CORPORATION																
GROSS INCOME	282.2	5.3	315.8	11.9	329.8	4.4	421.2	27.7	479.4	13.8	534.2	11.4	598.3	12.0	658.5	12.9
NET BEFORE TAX	46.9	2.2	53.1	13.3	35.9	-32.5	70.3	96.1	84.1	19.5	94.3	12.1	108.5	15.1	121.4	14.6
NET AFTER TAX	24.2	5.5	27.4	13.3	17.4	-36.6	34.0	95.1	40.6	19.5	45.5	12.1	52.3	15.1	58.5	13.4
RESEARCH	4.0	-2.4	3.8	-5.0	3.6	-5.3	4.1	12.7	3.6	-11.5	4.2	16.2	4.6	9.2	4.8	2.8
DEVELOPMENT	10.9	9.0	11.5	5.5	12.5	8.7	15.4	22.9	16.9	10.0	17.9	5.9	19.8	10.7	22.1	10.6
CHQ ADMIN.	13.4	9.8	15.2	13.4	17.8	17.1	22.6	26.9	26.6	17.7	30.5	14.9	34.7	13.6	39.4	16.6
O/O OF GROSS INCOME																
NET BEFORE TAX	16.6		16.8		10.9		16.7		17.5		17.7		18.1		18.4	
NET AFTER TAX	8.6		8.7		5.3		8.1		8.5		8.5		8.7		8.9	
RESEARCH	1.42		1.20		1.09		.96		.75		.78		.76		.73	
DEVELOPMENT	3.86		3.64		3.79		3.65		3.52		3.35		3.31		3.36	
CHQ ADMIN'ION	4.75		4.81		5.40		5.36		5.54		5.72		5.80		5.98	

NOTE - O/O COLUMN SHOWS YEARLY GROWTH RATE, EXCEPT FOR LAST YEAR, WHERE IT SHOWS COMPOUND GROWTH RATE OVER FIRST YEAR.

PSG - PLANNING SYSTEMS GENERATOR

- COMPANY CONFIDENTIAL -

12/16/68

Exhibit 10-1

FORM 08-2

XYZ PLANNING DATA SYSTEM   VIEW 9002

CHANGE IN DIVISION Y'S MARKET

SUBSET   0

TOTAL CORPORATION

COMPARISON OF GROSS INCOME

DESCRIPTION	TERM	REF.	1967	1968	1969	1970	1971	1972	1973	1974
TOTAL CORPORATION	M $	1	282.2	315.8	329.8	421.2	479.4	534.2	598.3	658.5
DIVISION X	M $	2	120.1	130.9	142.2	182.4	221.7	261.0	309.7	353.1
DIVISION Y	M $	3	84.1	90.4	90.7	135.8	149.1	157.4	165.6	173.9
DIVISION Z	M $	4	36.0	40.5	39.7	42.4	44.4	47.7	50.7	54.8
FOREIGN OPERATIONS	M $	5	42.0	44.0	46.2	48.5	50.9	53.5	56.2	59.0

PSG - PLANNING SYSTEMS GENERATOR

- COMPANY CONFIDENTIAL -

12/16/68

Exhibit 10-2

FORM 08-3

SUBSET 0

XYZ PLANNING DATA SYSTEM   VIEW 9002

TOTAL CORPORATION

CHANGE IN DIVISION Y'S MARKET

COMPARISON OF NET BEFORE TAX

DESCRIPTION	TERM	REF.	1967	1968	1969	1970	1971	1972	1973	1974
TOTAL CORPORATION	M $	1	46.9	53.1	35.9	70.3	84.1	94.3	108.5	121.4
DIVISION X	M $	2	18.6	20.3	8.7	22.6	31.4	38.4	48.3	57.1
DIVISION Y	M $	3	13.0	14.6	8.3	27.8	30.4	31.6	33.2	34.8
DIVISION Z	M $	4	8.9	10.4	9.5	10.0	11.3	12.2	13.7	15.1
FOREIGN OPERATIONS	M $	5	8.4	8.8	9.2	9.7	10.2	10.7	11.2	11.8

- COMPANY CONFIDENTIAL -

12/16/68

PSG - PLANNING SYSTEMS GENERATOR

Exhibit 10-3

CHANGE IN DIVISION Y'S MARKET

FORM 08-1   SUBSET 10   IMPACT ON TOTAL CORPORATION   INCOME ANALYSIS

DESCRIPTION	1967 AMT	1967 O/O	1968 AMT	1968 O/O	1969 AMT	1969 O/O	1970 AMT	1970 O/O	1971 AMT	1971 O/O	1972 AMT	1972 O/O	1973 AMT	1973 O/O	1974 AMT	1974 O/O
DIVISION X																
GROSS INCOME																
GROSS PROFIT																
NET BEFORE TAX																
GROSS MARGIN																
NETBT MARGIN																
DIVISION Y																
GROSS INCOME							45.7	50.4	51.0	.9	56.3	2.5	61.6	2.3	64.4	7.1
GROSS PROFIT							27.5	66.1	29.6	-1.2	31.8	1.8	33.9	1.7	34.6	8.1
NET BEFORE TAX							14.5	175.1	14.9	-7.3	15.8	1.9	16.5	-.6	16.6	10.2
GROSS MARGIN							5.0		4.2		3.8		3.5		2.9	
NETBT MARGIN							5.8		4.6		4.5		4.0		3.4	
DIVISION Z																
GROSS INCOME																
GROSS PROFIT																
NET BEFORE TAX																
GROSS MARGIN																
NETBT MARGIN																
SPECIAL PRODUCTS																
GROSS INCOME																
NET BEFORE TAX																
NETRT MARGIN																
FOREIGN OPERATIONS																
GROSS INCOME																
GROSS PROFIT																
NET BEFORE TAX																
NET AFTER TAX																
GROSS MARGIN																
NETBT MARGIN																
NETAT MARGIN																
TOTAL CORPORATION																
GROSS INCOME							45.7	13.9	51.0	-.3	56.3	-.1	61.6	-.3	64.4	1.6
NET BEFORE TAX							14.5	40.5	14.9	-4.4	15.8	-1.4	16.5	-2.1	16.6	2.4
NET AFTER TAX							7.0	40.1	7.2	-4.3	7.6	-1.4	7.9	-2.1	8.0	2.3
RESEARCH							.5	12.7	.5	2.9	.6	-1.0	.6		.6	2.1
DEVELOPMENT							1.8	14.6	2.0	.2	2.3	.6	2.5	.2	2.7	2.0
CHQ ADMIN.							2.9	16.2	3.3	-.6	3.7	-.1	4.1	-.6	4.4	1.9
O/O OF GROSS INCOME																
NET BEFORE TAX							1.8		1.4		1.2		1.0		.8	
NET AFTER TAX							.9		.7		.6		.5		.4	
RESEARCH																
DEVELOPMENT							.11		.06		.08		.09		.09	
CHQ ADMIN'ION									.10		.10		.09		.09	

NOTE - O/O COLUMN SHOWS YEARLY GROWTH RATE, EXCEPT FOR LAST YEAR, WHERE IT SHOWS COMPOUND GROWTH RATE OVER FIRST YEAR.

PSG - PLANNING SYSTEMS GENERATOR

- COMPANY CONFIDENTIAL -

12/16/68

Exhibit 10-4

XYZ PLANNING DATA SYSTEM   VIEW 9002

CHANGE IN DIVISION Y'S MARKET

DIVISION Y

INCOME AND EXPENSE SUMMARY

FORM 03-1   SUBSET 2

DESCRIPTION	1967 M$	1967 O/O	1968 M$	1968 O/O	1969 M$	1969 O/O	1970 M$	1970 O/O	1971 M$	1971 O/O	1972 M$	1972 O/O	1973 M$	1973 O/O	1974 M$	1974 O/O
BUSINESS VOLUME																
MARKET ESTIMATE	1040.0		1081.6		1124.9		1259.9		1394.9		1529.9		1665.0		1800.0	
SALES POTENTIAL	90.0		93.6		97.3		191.3		198.0		204.8		211.5		218.3	
O/O REPLACEMENT	5.0		5.0		5.0		5.0		5.0		5.0		5.0		5.0	
XYZ POSITION	250.0		240.0		249.8		277.2		306.9		336.6		366.3		396.0	
REMOVALS	11.0		11.5		12.0		12.5		13.9		15.3		16.8		18.3	
SHIPMENTS	21.0		21.5		21.8		39.8		43.6		45.1		46.5		48.0	
O/O XYZ POSITION	22.1		22.2		22.2		22.0		22.0		22.0		22.0		22.0	
XYZ REMOVALS	5.0		5.0		5.0		5.0		5.0		5.0		5.0		5.0	
XYZ SHIPMENTS	23.3		23.0		22.4		20.8		22.0		22.0		22.0		22.0	
GROSS INCOME																
PRODUCTS	45.8	54.5	48.2	53.3	48.4	53.4	88.4	65.1	96.7	64.9	100.0	63.6	103.3	62.4	106.6	61.3
SERVICE	37.2	44.2	41.0	45.4	41.4	45.6	46.0	33.9	50.9	34.2	55.9	35.5	60.8	36.7	65.7	37.8
SUPPLIES																
OTHER	1.1	1.3	1.2	1.3	.9	1.0	1.4	1.0	1.4	1.0	1.5	.9	1.5	.9	1.5	.9
TOTAL	84.1	100.0	90.4	100.0	90.7	100.0	135.8	100.0	149.1	100.0	157.4	100.0	165.6	100.0	173.9	100.0
GROSS PROFIT																
PRODUCTS	26.4	57.6	30.2	62.7	30.3	62.6	55.3	62.6	60.5	62.6	62.6	62.6	64.7	62.6	66.7	62.6
SERVICE	10.6	28.5	11.1	27.1	10.7	25.8	11.9	25.8	13.1	25.8	14.4	25.8	15.7	25.8	17.0	25.8
SUPPLIES																
OTHER	.7	63.6	.8	66.7	.6	66.7	.9	65.0	.9	65.0	1.0	65.0	1.0	65.0	1.0	65.0
TOTAL	37.7	44.8	42.1	46.6	41.6	45.9	68.1	50.2	74.6	50.0	78.0	49.6	81.3	49.1	84.7	48.7
EXPENSES																
RESEARCH	1.0	1.2	1.0	1.1	1.0	1.1	1.4	1.0	1.5	1.0	1.6	1.0	1.7	1.0	1.7	1.0
DEVELOPMENT	3.6	4.3	3.6	4.0	3.9	4.3	5.4	4.0	6.0	4.0	6.3	4.0	6.8	4.1	7.3	4.2
FIELD SALES	10.7	12.7	11.6	12.8	14.4	15.9	15.9	11.7	18.3	12.3	18.9	12.0	19.9	12.0	20.2	11.6
MKTG.SUPPORT	.9	1.1	1.1	1.2	1.3	1.4	1.8	1.3	1.9	1.3	1.8	1.2	1.8	1.1	1.9	1.1
ADMINISTRATION	3.1	3.7	3.4	3.8	3.5	3.9	5.4	4.0	5.7	3.8	5.7	3.6	5.6	3.4	5.6	3.2
OTHER	.7	.8	1.5	1.7	3.3	3.6	1.9	1.4	1.3	.9	1.8	1.1	1.4	.8	1.4	.8
APPORTIONMENTS	4.7	5.6	5.3	5.9	5.9	6.5	8.6	6.3	9.5	6.4	10.4	6.6	10.9	6.6	11.8	6.8
TOTAL	24.7	29.4	27.5	30.4	33.3	36.7	40.3	29.7	44.2	29.7	46.4	29.5	48.1	29.1	49.9	28.7
NET BEFORE TAX	13.0	15.5	14.6	16.2	8.3	9.2	27.8	20.5	30.4	20.4	31.6	20.1	33.2	20.1	34.8	20.0
NET AFTER TAX	6.8	8.0	7.6	8.4	4.0	4.4	13.3	9.8	14.6	9.8	15.2	9.6	15.9	9.6	16.7	9.6
EARNINGS/SHARE	2.25		2.53		1.33		4.44		4.87		5.05		5.31		5.56	

RATES OF CHANGE (O/O)

DESCRIPTION	1967	1968	1969	1970	1971	1972	1973	1974
MARKET ESTIMATE	4.0	4.0	4.0	12.0	10.7	9.7	8.8	8.1
XYZ POSITION	4.5	4.3	4.1	10.9	10.7	9.7	8.8	8.1
GROSS INCOME	5.1	7.5	-.3	49.7	9.8	5.5	5.3	5.0
GROSS PROFIT	7.7	11.7	-1.2	63.7	9.6	4.5	4.3	4.1
TOTAL EXPENSES	7.4	11.3	21.1	21.1	9.6	5.0	3.7	3.8
NET BEFORE TAX	8.3	12.3	-43.2	234.7	9.5	3.8	5.2	4.7
NET AFTER TAX	12.7	12.3	-47.5	234.7	9.5	3.8	5.2	4.7

PSG - PLANNING SYSTEMS GENERATOR

- COMPANY CONFIDENTIAL -

12/16/68

Exhibit 10-5

```
XYZ PLANNING DATA SYSTEM    VIEW 9002              CHANGE IN DIVISION Y'S MARKET

      DIVISION Y                                        SOURCE AND APPLICATION OF FUNDS
FORM 03-2        SUBSET  2
```

DESCRIPTION	TERM	1967	1968	1969	1970	1971	1972	1973	1974
NET CURRENT ASSETS 1-1	M $	40.0	41.1	45.1	45.8	24.4	28.7	35.0	41.1
NET EARNINGS	M $	6.8	7.6	4.0	13.3	14.6	15.2	15.9	16.7
DEPRECIATION ETC.	M $	3.4	4.6	3.3	4.9	6.3	6.2	5.9	5.7
FUNDS FROM OPERATIONS	M $	10.2	12.2	7.3	18.2	20.9	21.4	21.9	22.4
SALE OF STOCK	M $								
LONG TERM DEBT INCURRED	M $								
MISCELLANEOUS	M $								
TOTAL FUNDS PROVIDED	M $	10.2	12.2	7.3	18.2	20.9	21.4	21.9	22.4
TOTAL FUNDS AVAILABLE	M $	50.2	53.2	52.3	64.0	45.2	50.0	56.9	63.5
LAND AND BUILDINGS	M $	-.0	.0	.1	2.1	3.4	2.3	2.4	2.5
EQUIPMENT	M $	4.4	3.3	3.4	9.6	4.5	3.6	3.8	3.8
TOTAL INVESTMENTS	M $	4.3	3.3	3.5	11.7	7.8	5.9	6.2	6.3
LONG TERM DEBT REPAID	M $				20.0				
CASH DIVIDEND	M $	4.8	4.8	3.0	8.0	8.8	9.1	9.6	10.0
TOTAL FUNDS APPLIED	M $	9.1	8.1	6.5	39.7	16.6	15.0	15.8	16.3
NET CURRENT ASSETS 12-31	M $	41.1	45.1	45.8	24.4	28.7	35.0	41.1	47.1
ANALYTICAL RATIOS									
PLANT AND EQUIPMENT/TOTAL	O/O	47.5	41.1	53.9	29.4	47.1	39.5	39.3	38.7
EARNINGS PER SHARE	$	2.25	2.53	1.33	4.44	4.87	5.05	5.31	5.56
CASH DIVIDEND PAYOUT	O/O	71.0	63.2	75.3	60.0	60.0	60.0	60.0	60.0
RATES OF CHANGE									
FUNDS FROM OPERATIONS	O/O		19.3	-40.2	150.4	14.6	2.3	2.3	2.3
TOTAL FUNDS PROVIDED	O/O		19.3	-40.2	150.4	14.6	2.3	2.3	2.3
INVESTMENTS	O/O		-22.9	5.0	232.3	-33.0	-24.0	4.4	1.9
TOTAL FUNDS APPLIED	O/O		-10.9	-20.1	509.3	-58.2	-9.3	4.9	3.6
NET CURRENT ASSETS 12-31	O/O	2.6	9.8	1.7	-46.8	17.6	22.1	17.4	14.7
MANPOWER - CHANGES IN HEADCOUNT									
MANUFACTURING	MEN	14	-78	-94	479	-14	-67	-56	-47
ENGINEERING	MEN	17	3	15	81	29	18	25	26
MARKETING	MEN	19	26	97	67	108	19	43	16
SERVICE	MEN	28	16	25	-43	74	64	56	49
ADMINISTRATION	MEN	3	3	-8	48	-1	-6	-6	-6
TOTAL NET CHANGE	MEN	81	-30	35	632	196	28	62	37
TOTAL ON BOARD 12-31	MEN	4337	4307	4342	4974	5169	5197	5259	5296
INCREASE OVER PRIOR YEAR	O/O	1.9	-.7	.8	14.6	3.9	.5	1.2	.7

PSG - PLANNING SYSTEMS GENERATOR

12/16/68

- COMPANY CONFIDENTIAL -

Exhibit 10-6

DIVISION Y

BALANCE SHEET

FORM 03-3   SUBSET 2

DESCRIPTION	TERM	1967	1968	1969	1970	1971	1972	1973	1974
ASSETS									
CASH	M $	16.2	18.6	19.5	-1.2	.3	3.2	6.0	8.7
MARKETABLE SECURITIES	M $	7.0	8.0	8.4		.1	1.4	2.6	3.7
NOTES AND ACCTS. RECEIVABLE	M $	16.3	17.5	17.6	26.2	28.8	30.4	32.0	33.6
INVENTORIES	M $	27.6	28.7	29.7	41.5	45.7	48.5	51.3	54.1
PREPAYMENTS	M $	2.1	2.3	2.3	1.2	1.4	1.8	2.1	2.4
CURRENT ASSETS	M $	69.2	75.0	77.5	67.8	76.3	85.3	94.0	102.6
OTHER INVESTMENTS	M $								
LAND	M $	5.0	5.0	5.0	5.0	6.0	6.0	6.0	6.0
BUILDINGS	M $	6.1	6.1	6.2	8.3	10.6	12.9	15.3	17.8
NET LAND AND BUILDINGS	M $	5.6	5.1	4.7	6.2	8.9	10.4	11.9	13.3
FACTORY AND OFFICE EQUIPMENT	M $	19.4	22.7	26.1	35.7	40.1	43.8	47.6	51.5
NET FACTORY AND OFFICE	M $	10.6	10.1	10.9	16.4	15.4	13.8	12.9	12.3
PATENTS AND GOODWILL	M $	1.8	1.6	1.4	1.2	1.0	.8	.6	.4
TOTAL ASSETS	M $	87.2	91.8	94.5	91.6	101.6	110.3	119.3	128.5
LIABILITIES AND EQUITY									
INCOME TAXES	M $	1.6	1.8	1.1	3.6	4.0	4.1	4.3	4.5
ACCTS. PAYABLE AND ACCRUALS	M $	26.6	28.2	30.6	39.8	43.7	46.2	48.6	50.9
LOANS PAYABLE	M $								
CURRENT LIABILITIES	M $	28.1	30.0	31.7	43.4	47.6	50.3	52.9	55.4
DEFERRALS AND RESERVES	M $	20.0	20.0	20.0					
LONG TERM DEBT	M $								
TOTAL LIABILITIES	M $	48.1	50.0	51.7	43.4	47.6	50.3	52.9	55.4
EQUITY CAPITAL	M $	39.0	41.8	42.8	48.2	54.0	60.1	66.4	73.1
NUMBER OF SHARES OUTSTANDING	K	3000	3000	3000	3000	3000	3000	3000	3000
ANALYTICAL RATIOS									
CURR. ASSETS/CURR. LIAB.	O/O	246.0	250.5	244.7	156.2	160.2	169.6	177.7	185.0
CURRENT/TOTAL ASSETS	O/O	79.4	81.7	82.0	74.0	75.1	77.3	78.8	79.8
CURR. LIAB./TOTAL ASSETS	O/O	32.3	32.6	33.5	47.4	46.9	45.6	44.3	43.1
EQUITY PER SHARE	$	13.02	13.95	14.28	16.05	18.00	20.02	22.15	24.37
RETURN ON CAPITAL	O/O	11.4	12.3	6.3	27.7	27.0	25.2	24.0	22.8
CAPITAL TURNOVER RATIO	X	1.42	1.46	1.44	2.82	2.76	2.62	2.49	2.38
EARNINGS PER SHARE	$	2.25	2.53	1.33	4.44	4.87	5.05	5.31	5.56
RATES OF CHANGE									
CURRENT ASSETS	O/O	1.7	8.5	3.3	-12.6	12.6	11.8	10.2	9.1
NET LAND AND BUILDINGS	O/O	-8.8	-8.8	-7.9	32.7	43.5	17.1	14.1	12.2
NET FACTORY AND OFFICE	O/O	18.3	-5.0	8.1	49.9	-5.8	-10.3	-7.1	-4.7
CURRENT LIABILITIES	O/O	.4	6.5	5.8	37.0	9.7	5.6	5.3	4.8
EQUITY CAPITAL	O/O	8.5	7.1	2.4	12.5	12.1	11.2	10.6	10.0

PSG - PLANNING SYSTEMS GENERATOR

- COMPANY CONFIDENTIAL -

Exhibit 10-7

12/16/68

XYZ PLANNING DATA SYSTEM   VIEW 9002

CHANGE IN DIVISION Y'S MARKET

FORM 03-4   SUBSET 2

DIVISION Y

YEAR-END MANPOWER

DESCRIPTION	TERM	1967	1968	1969	1970	1971	1972	1973	1974
MANUFACTURING									
DIRECT	MEN	437	398	351	591	583	550	522	498
INDIRECT	MEN	437	398	351	591	583	550	522	498
TOTAL	MEN	874	796	702	1181	1167	1100	1044	997
GROWTH RATE	O/O	1.6	-8.9	-11.8	68.2	-1.2	-5.7	-5.1	-4.5
NEW HIRES	MEN	126	21	35	538	44	-12	-4	2
HIRING RATE	O/O	14.4	2.6	5.0	45.6	3.8	-1.1	-.4	.2
COST FACTOR PER MAN	K $	22.2	22.6	25.8	28.0	31.0	34.0	37.0	40.0
ENGINEERING									
PROFESSIONAL	MEN	131	133	143	197	216	228	245	262
SUPPORT	MEN	66	67	72	98	108	114	122	131
TOTAL	MEN	197	200	215	295	324	342	367	393
GROWTH RATE	O/O	9.2	1.5	7.5	37.6	9.8	5.5	7.4	7.0
NEW HIRES	MEN	20	7	19	87	35	25	33	34
HIRING RATE	O/O	10.4	3.5	9.0	29.3	10.9	7.3	8.9	8.6
COST FACTOR PER MAN	K $	23.4	23.1	22.8	23.0	23.0	23.0	23.0	23.0
MARKETING									
FIELD	MEN	516	542	639	704	807	825	866	881
SUPPORT	MEN	29	29	29	32	36	37	39	40
TOTAL	MEN	545	571	668	735	844	862	905	921
GROWTH RATE	O/O	3.6	4.8	17.0	10.1	14.7	2.2	5.0	1.8
NEW HIRES	MEN	63	66	137	104	150	62	88	62
HIRING RATE	O/O	11.5	11.6	20.5	14.2	17.8	7.2	9.7	6.7
COST FACTOR PER MAN	K $	21.3	22.2	23.5	24.0	24.0	24.0	24.0	24.0
SERVICE									
FIELD	MEN	2628	2644	2600	2525	2596	2658	2711	2759
SUPPORT	MEN			69	101	104	106	108	110
TOTAL	MEN	2628	2644	2669	2626	2700	2764	2820	2869
GROWTH RATE	O/O	1.1	.6	-.9	-1.6	2.8	2.4	2.0	1.8
NEW HIRES	MEN	265	241	239	167	290	285	282	279
HIRING RATE	O/O	10.1	9.1	8.9	6.4	10.7	10.3	10.0	9.7
COST FACTOR PER MAN	K $	10.1	11.3	11.5	13.0	14.0	15.0	16.0	17.0
ADMINISTRATION									
PROFESSIONAL	MEN	93	96	88	136	135	129	122	116
SUPPORT	MEN								
TOTAL	MEN	93	96	88	136	135	129	122	116
GROWTH RATE	O/O	3.3	3.2	-8.3	54.3	-.7	-4.6	-4.9	-5.3
NEW HIRES	MEN	4	4	-7	49	.3	-5	-5	-5
HIRING RATE	O/O	4.2	4.1	-8.1	36.2	.3	-3.8	-4.2	-4.6
COST FACTOR PER MAN	K $	33.3	35.4	39.8	40.0	42.0	44.0	46.0	48.0
TOTAL BUSINESS									
ON BOARD	MEN	4337	4307	4342	4974	5169	5197	5259	5296
GROWTH RATE	O/O	1.9	-.7	.8	14.6	3.9	.5	1.2	.7
NEW HIRES	MEN	477	339	423	945	520	355	393	372
HIRING RATE	O/O	11.0	7.9	9.7	19.0	10.1	6.8	7.5	7.0

PSG - PLANNING SYSTEMS GENERATOR

- COMPANY CONFIDENTIAL -

12/16/68

Exhibit 10-8

XYZ PLANNING DATA SYSTEM   VIEW 9002

CHANGE IN DIVISION Y'S MARKET

SPACE, BUILDINGS + LAND

FORM 03-5   SUBSET 2

DIVISION Y

DESCRIPTION	TERM	1967	1968	1969	1970	1971	1972	1973	1974
SPACE FORECAST									
PLANTS	KSQFT	159	145	128	215	212	200	190	181
WAREHOUSES	KSQFT	24	22	19	32	32	30	29	27
LABORATORIES	KSQFT	57	58	62	86	94	99	107	114
OFFICES	KSQFT	327	331	343	350	368	375	385	391
TOTAL	KSQFT	567	556	552	683	706	705	710	713
OCCUPANCY FACTORS/MAN									
MANUFACTURING	SQFT	260	260	260	260	260	260	260	260
MFG. EXTRA SHIFT RATIO	0/0	30.0	30.0	30.0	30.0	30.0	30.0	30.0	30.0
MFG. WAREHOUSING	0/0	15.0	15.0	15.0	15.0	15.0	15.0	15.0	15.0
ENGINEERING	SQFT	290	290	290	290	290	290	290	290
OTHER	SQFT	100	100	100	100	100	100	100	100
SPACE AVAILABILITY REVIEW									
PLANTS OWNED	KSQFT	128	128	128	128	128	128	128	128
LEASED	KSQFT	32	32	32	32	32	32	32	32
VARIANCE	KSQFT	-1	-15	-32	55	52	40	30	21
WAREHOUSES OWNED	KSQFT	4	4	4	4	4	4	4	4
LEASED	KSQFT	16	16	16	16	16	16	16	16
VARIANCE	KSQFT	4	2	-1	12	12	10	9	7
LABORATORIES OWNED	KSQFT	60	60	60	60	60	60	60	60
LEASED	KSQFT								
VARIANCE	KSQFT	-3	-2	2	26	34	39	47	54
OFFICES OWNED	KSQFT	33	33	33	33	33	33	33	33
LEASED	KSQFT	297	297	297	297	297	297	297	297
VARIANCE	KSQFT	-3	1	13	20	38	45	55	61
TOTAL OWNED	KSQFT	225	225	225	225	225	225	225	225
LEASED	KSQFT	345	345	345	345	345	345	345	345
REQUIRED (+)	KSQFT	4	3	15	113	136	135	140	143
BUILDINGS PLANNED AND REQUIRED									
PLANTS	KSQFT	-2.0			44.0	41.9	32.2	24.0	17.1
WAREHOUSES	KSQFT	.8	.3		2.4	2.4	2.0	1.7	1.4
LABORATORIES	KSQFT			2.2	25.6	34.0	39.2	46.5	54.0
OFFICES	KSQFT		.1	1.3	2.0	3.8	4.5	5.5	6.1
TOTAL (GROSS)	KSQFT	-1.2	.5	3.5	74.0	82.0	77.9	77.7	78.6
NET INVESTMENT IN BUILDINGS									
PLANTS	M $	-.0	.0		1.1	1.0	.8	.6	.4
WAREHOUSES	M $	-.0			.0	.0	.0	.0	.0
LABORATORIES	M $			.1	.9	1.2	1.4	1.6	1.9
OFFICES	M $		.0	.0	.0	.1	.1	.1	.1
TOTAL	M $	-.0	.0	.1	2.1	2.4	2.3	2.4	2.5
LAND HOLDINGS									
AREA ON HAND YEAR-END	ACRES	1000.9	1000.9	1000.9	1000.9	1500.9	1500.9	1500.9	1500.9
PURCHASES	ACRES					500.0			
NET INVESTMENT	M $					1.0			

PSG - PLANNING SYSTEMS GENERATOR

12/16/68

- COMPANY CONFIDENTIAL -

Exhibit 10-9

CODE	DESCRIPTION	TERM	PRIOR	1967	1968	1969	1970	1971	1972	1973	1974
COL. 1-7			18-24	25-31	32-38	39-45	46-52	53-59	60-66	67-73	74-80
	BUSINESS VOLUME ASSUMPTIONS										
0302201	MARKET, AMOUNT	M $	1000.0	.	.	.	.	.	.	0.	1800.0
0302202	OR GROWTH RATE	O/O F	.	4.0	4.0	4.0	.	.	.	.	.
0302203	REPLACEMENT AMOUNT	M $ O	.	.	.	.	.	.	.	.	.
0302204	FACTOR	O/O F	.	5.0	5.0	5.0	5.0	5.0	5.0	5.0	5.0
0302205	XYZ POSITION, AMOUNT	M $ F	220.0	230.0	240.0	.	.	.	.	.	.
0302206	OR GROWTH RATE	O/O F	.	.	.	4.1	.	.	.	.	4.0
0302207	OR SHARE OF MARKET	O/O F	.	.	.	.	22.0	22.0	22.0	22.0	22.0
0302209	XYZ REMOVALS, AMOUNT	M $ O	.	.	.	.	.	.	.	.	.
0302210	FACTOR	O/O F	.	5.0	5.0	5.0	5.0	5.0	5.0	5.0	5.0
	GROSS INCOME										
0302001	PRODUCTS, AMOUNT	M $ F	43.0	45.8	48.2	48.4	.	.	.	.	.
0302002	OR SHIPMENT FACTOR	O/O F	.	.	.	.	222.0	222.0	222.0	222.0	222.0
0302003	SERVICE, AMOUNT	M $ F	36.0	37.2	41.0	41.4	.	.	.	.	.
0302004	OR POSITION FACTOR	O/O F	.	.	.	.	16.6	16.6	16.6	16.6	16.6
0302005	SUPPLIES, AMOUNT	M $ O	.	.	.	.	.	.	.	.	.
0302006	OR POSITION FACTOR	O/O O	.	.	.	.	.	.	.	.	.
0302007	OTHER, AMOUNT	M $ F	1.0	1.1	1.2	.9	.	.	.	.	.
0302008	OR SHARE OF TOTAL INCOME	O/O F	.	.	.	.	1.0	1.0	1.0	1.0	1.0

NOTE - INPUT DATA SPECIFIED AS AN AMOUNT AND AS A RATIO ARE COMPLEMENTS UNLESS THE RATIO IS PREFACED BY 'OR.'

PSG - PLANNING SYSTEMS GENERATOR

- COMPANY CONFIDENTIAL -

12/16/68

Exhibit 10-10

PLANNING LOGIC

The examination of the operational consequences of this change in market potential is governed by the planning logic built into the Corporate Planning Data System. This has been explained in Chapter 8. In addition, it must be realized that all the dynamic relationships between market potential, sales, cost and expenses, manpower, space, investment, etc. had been taken from the last approved strategic plan. Furthermore, these dynamic planning factors were applied only to the years 1970 through 1974 since certainly in this first examination the approved operating budget was left unaffected.

The key point to be made here is that the origination of planned goals is a process going on step by step from rough cuts through many iterations until a comprehensive set of planning data emerges which does justice to the complexity of the entire business operation, is credible to the various teams of experts, and is acceptable to line management as an achievable goal to be accomplished by deliberate management action.

In this chapter we are showing only the first step in this process and we trust that the reader will use his imagination for the rest of the steps to be executed through the planning data system—first by changing additional planning assumptions in Division Y's subset and later on by a more thorough examination of the entire posture of Division Y through its own divisional system.

CHANGE IN BUDGET

However, no matter what refinements are applied to the evaluation for the years 1970 through 1974, one of the next iterations of the planning data system will have to pull out the stops on the data for the year 1969. This will be rather obvious when one sees the unrealistic jump in almost all the planning data series between 1969 and 1970. Such discontinuous behavior is very unlikely and the origination of planned goals requires that such discontinuities be thoroughly analyzed and examined if they are to become credible and acceptable. It is more likely that both the operating budget for 1969 and the longer-range objectives will have to be re-examined and adjusted in keeping with the new market potential estimate for 1974.

A discussion of some of the issues might be called for in order for the reader to appreciate the managerial reasoning encountered in the process of originating achievable planned goals. As a general rule, every participant in the objective setting game will try to be as noncommittal as possible. This is especially true when commitments may be interpreted as evidence for later sentencing. But even if the management climate is right for planning and there is a good understanding about the transitory nature of all planned goals, a variety of qualifying statements must preface each and every consideration of a planned goal. In fact, all commitments are conditional and complex. They may sound like a contract with a lot of clauses, for example:

Whereas the original agreed upon strategic plan contained a reasonable representation of the relationships between general business conditions, Division Y's revenue generating capabilities and operating ratios, and

Whereas these same relationships, revenue generating capabilities, and operating ratios are deemed achievable from 1970 through 1974 under a different assumption about Division Y's market potential, and

Whereas this change in market potential represents an increase of about 7½ percent in 1970 to as much as over 30 percent in 1974,

Then Division Y would, in the years 1970 and 1974, have a chance to

(1)   Produce additional gross income of around $50 Million a year and net before taxes of around $15 Million a year, thereby improving its net before tax margin by as much as 5 percentage points. The total corporation would gain around $7 Million in net after tax and improvement in its net after tax margin of close to 1 percent in 1970, declining to less than ½ percent by 1974.

(2)   Experience a substantial drain in cash reserves to the extent that in 1970, a year in which repayment of a long-term debt of $20 Million is due, some new sources of liquid funds must be found. Perhaps the cash flow of the other divisions will permit such financing to be internal to the corporation.

(3)   Encounter excessive manpower requirements and hiring needs for 1970. Almost 20 percent of the year-end manpower in 1970 would be new hires, and it is questionable whether this additional manpower could be absorbed by the organization without loss in operating efficiency. In manufacturing over 500 new people would have to be added to an organization which in the previous three years had been contracting rather than expanding. This would represent a sudden reversal of trend and a rate of absorption for new people of 45.6 percent, rather unlikely to succeed.

In engineering the situation does not look much better, the hiring rate being 29.3 percent. But the worst manpower problem seems to be indicated in general administration where the higher business volume and attendant administrative problems indicate an addition of some 49 (or 36.2 percent) new people. Since these are mostly promoted from departments in the functions rather than hired from the outside, the administrative manpower situation would tend to further aggravate the manpower problem in the functional departments.

(4)   Require substantial amounts of additional buildings. No provisions have been made in the approved strategic plan for an expansion of space. Therefore, everything would have to be added either by new construction or leasing. The estimates for net investment in buildings amount to over $2 Million per year starting in 1970, for gross space requirements among plants, warehouses, laboratories, and offices between 70 and 80,000 square feet.

Therefore, because of the lead times involved in building and expanding work forces, it seems inevitable that some activities be started almost immediately in order to make sure that the opportunity of maintaining the company's share in an expanding market not be missed. Unfortunately any preparatory expense of this nature will be impacting the year 1969 which, due to a number of conditions that have been carefully considered during the budgetary approval procedures, is a year of poor profit performance. Net profit is dropping from 8.4 to 4.4 percent and earnings per share from $2.53 to $1.33. Only a portion of this can be attributed to the increase in taxes from 48 to 52 percent. As a matter of fact net before taxes drops from 16.2 to 9.2 percent which is 43.2 percent, whereas net after taxes drops by 47.5 percent. The conditions which account for the unusually high expense for field sales (15.9 percent) as compared to a level of 12 to 13 percent in prior years, the jump in apportionment mostly due to an increase in institutional advertising by the corporation, and improvements in employee benefits need not be reiterated here.

In view of the above first findings it is recommended that the corporate planning data services department be requested to prepare a new strategic outlook based on the new market potential, including revised data for 1969. Two assumptions for an expected market development rate should be examined: From the 1968 starting position of $1,082 Million, the objective for 1974 of $1.8 Billion to be reached first by a digital progression and secondly by a constant growth rate progression. All operating factors and performance ratios for the year 1969 through 1974 to be left unchanged.

A meeting is scheduled for the day after tomorrow at 2 P.M. to discuss the results of this first strategic planning study with the Corporate Management Committee.

CORPORATE STAFF REVIEW

Let's assume that the Corporate Management Committee has reviewed the requested two new views of the future labeled View 9003 (digital progression) and View 9004 (constant growth rate progression). It has decided to accept the latter one as a valid goal to work at. It will now request that this View 9004 be checked out by each corporate staff department representing functional competence—such as manufacturing, marketing, service, engineering, etc. This process will perhaps result in several iterations of the corporate planning data system as well as some of its functional modules, which so far have not been brought into action since they are under the control of the respective functional departments. Through these modules the probable consequences of changes in business volumes are more thoroughly examined, analyzed, and evaluated and more realistic assumptions (performance ratios and planning factors) are generated ready for transfer into Division Y's summary module. This process should not take more than another few days, and within a week the Corporate Management Committee should be in a position to review a joint corporate staff proposal for a completely revised strategic plan for Division Y and the resulting revision of the corporate plan along with it.

DIVISIONAL PLAN REVISION

After this cursory review of a proposed revision for Division Y's plan which was prepared by corporate headquarters, the CMC will forward the resulting document to the line management of Division Y with the request to prepare a divisional plan which either lends support to the proposed corporate View 9025 (assuming that 21 iterations had been processed before the corporate staff arrived at a satisfactory proposal) or to show cause why a different plan should be adopted.

Of course, divisional management will use its own planning data system and its many modules to develop its own agreed upon and acceptable outlook based on the new market assumptions. Particular attention will be placed by the divisional management on specific action which would have to be taken in the immediate future and the impact of such action on the current operating budget. At the same time divisional management may use the procedural logic of the corporate planning system to which it has access, and use its own assumptions about performance ratios and time series progression which translate the Division's best judgment in the framework of corporate planning logic.

This process should take no more than one week, at the end of which either a reconciled position be presented for approval to the CMC or specific points of non-concurrence between divisional line management and corporate staff directors be argued before the CMC for final decision.

The agreed upon planning data will then be used to update the planning data bank and to issue appropriate reports by the system to all concerned as the new approved strategic plan for Division Y as well as the entire corporation.

DECISION VARIABLES

It might be well to summarize in this context the key elements in the decision-making structure under discussion. A change in one important economic variable (in this case an exogenous variable, namely, the marketplace in general) is being translated through a chain of relationships between activity levels and resource requirements. Figure 10 illustrates the logic structure. When an activity level changes one may assume that the amount of resources required to handle that activity will not change. This is commonly referred to as the phenomenon of fixed cost. In the short run most resources are capable of achieving a range of activities by either working a little harder or stretching the work. In practice it is extremely difficult to determine when the tempo of working a little harder becomes unhealthy and needs to be reduced by assignment of additional resources. Equally difficult is the determination of when stretching the work has reached the stage of so-called featherbedding requiring a reduction in resource allocation. Perhaps only in fully

DECISION VARIABLES

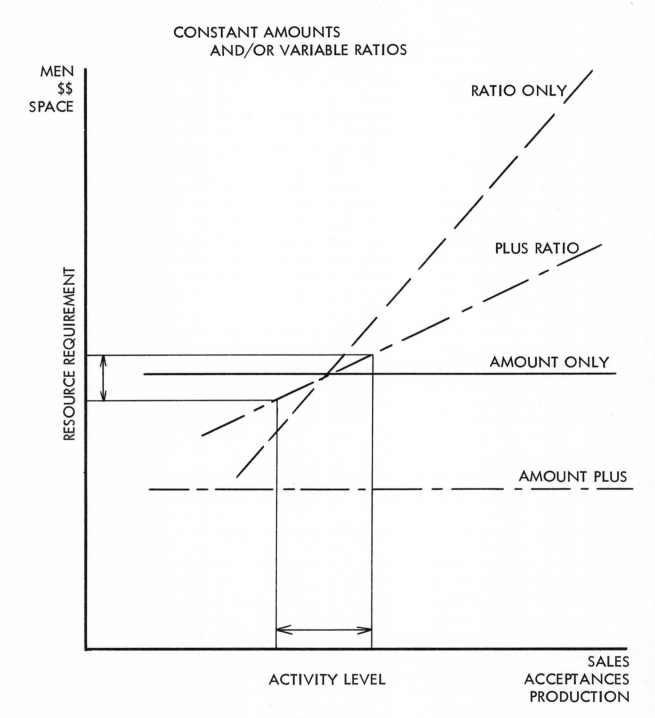

Figure 10

machine-paced operations does management have a fair chance through its industrial engineering studies to determine the productive capacity of an assigned resource. The more production is dependent upon human effort, the more productivity becomes a matter of dedication and commitment, and as such subject to bargaining.

The other extreme would be an assumption that as the activity level changes, resource requirements change proportionately with it. This is commonly called the variable cost relationship. Many business contracts are based on this assumption, for example prices, piecework rates, commissions, etc. However, complete proportionality seems to be on the way out. Prices get adjusted for quantity, piecework rates are supported by guaranteed minimum hourly wages, commissions are replaced by fixed salaries and complicated quantity bonus arrangements. Nevertheless many companies follow in their planning an implicit underlying assumption that most resource requirements are proportionate to their respective activity.

The reality lies somewhere in between. Therefore, the logic of a planning data system should allow management to express its opinion about the fixed or proportional nature of resource requirements with respect to changing activity levels as freely as possible. A decision variable which is intended to relate a resource requirement to an activity level should always have two dimensions, a fixed amount and a proportional ratio.

In turn the relationship between the amounts and ratios does not remain constant. In the short run and within the above discussed ranges of activity the fixed portion would be high. In the long run almost all fixed resource capacities, even when consisting of machine-paced operating capacities, can be converted to proportionality. This is a very important point for long-range strategic planning. It means that what is fixed and proportional in the year 1970 should not be carried forward into future years. Instead the fixed amount of a decision variable should be decreased from year to year. On the other hand, when time moves forward by a full year the fixed portions for the years 1970 through 1974 should be increased to reflect the fact that they are one year less capable of conversion to proportionality.

SPEED, ACCURACY, AND FLEXIBILITY

The availability of a system through which planned goals can be originated is well illustrated by the above example. No other but a computerized planning data system would be able to respond with arithmetic accuracy within two weeks to a major revision in a strategic plan, while allowing almost complete flexibility for the participants in this planning exercise to enter their assumptions about measurable planned goals. The resulting strategic plan for 1969 would then be transmitted to the budgeting department for further refinement and entry into the transaction data system, from which normal control reports against these planned goals will be issued to line management on a routine basis.

Under normal conditions it must be expected that such major revisions of the strategic plan do not happen too frequently. However, there are usually a number of minor occurrences at lower levels of aggregation which could be resolved in a number of different ways. There is a strong temptation to employ a strategic planning data system for the evaluation of operational options at too low a level of aggregation. This temptation must be resisted, especially at the corporate level. The corporate planning data system should not be designed for such a purpose. At best, the divisional planning system might be designed to include the capability of evaluating such things as specific product performance, marketing performance by geographic distribution or manufacturing workload distribution by plant location, etc. In contrast, the corporate planning system should concern itself mainly with business areas (product lines) as assigned to the various divisions (profit centers) and such business opportunities not yet assigned to a profit center, coming either from research activities or from other companies through merger and acquisition.

11

Sociopolitical Problems

Apparently there are a number of benefits to be derived from a system of business planning by computer, especially in relation to management decisions about planned goals and their achievement.

First of all, the computer forces the spelling out of planning logic. This alone may be a sufficient benefit to warrant the expenditure of designing such a system.* The development of planning logic is an exercise in applied industrial economics. It helps management become conscious of the interdependence of performance within the organization. For instance, the planning system of the IBM Office Products Division grew between the spring of 1962 and the fall of 1965 from about 1,000 to 4,000 yearly decision variables. This evolutionary expansion of the system in itself was a valuable

---

* $200,000 to $250,000 including initial programming and computer use charges.

143

contribution to the planning process and management's understanding of its own business.

The system asks questions about relevant quantitative planning assumptions in context, and is able to process the answers. It thereby facilitates simultaneous multiple factor analysis in the evaluation of alternative actions under consideration. The value of this needs no special brief.

The system assures that planned goals will be internally consistent and supported by auditable scource data. Such planning data can be expected to bring about management action based on more consistent thinking and more meaningful measures for performance against plan than the haphazard data usually generated in a coordinated but not systematized planning process.

The system provides for efficient documentation of agreed upon goals and their communication within the management team. In any large organization where bargaining is a critical element of the planning process, efficient documentation of agreements prevents or reduces ambiguity and misunderstandings.

Finally the system will serve as a framework for the application of advanced analytical techniques. This is a fundamental point. It will provide reasonable, clean, and consistent data for the parametric thinker and model builder with the clear-cut assignment to improve the quality, not the quantity of input. Most model builders do recognize the need for a system from which data can be drawn and through which analytical findings can be translated into terms which line management will deal with and accept. However, too often they underestimate the logistics problems of the system architect, and these problems are less technical than organizational or political.

SUBSETS AND DECISION VARIABLES

The selection of subsets and decision variables is a particularly relevant issue because bargains are usually struck in the aggregate, trusting that subset data can be found to support the aggregate objectives. This is, of course, fallacious reasoning and leads to the phenomenon of inconsistencies among various functions and among different levels of management.

A computerized planning system will allow the inclusion of more subsets and variables than any manual system, and thus facilitates bargaining at lower levels of aggregation. However, there are limits. Incorporation of departmental detail in a divisional planning system would signify a highly centralized organization. It is at this juncture that management philosophy and system's architecture have to be reconciled. As a matter of fact, the systems design process will assist management in resolving these organizational questions specifically and concretely.

When in operation, the planning system asks for data in a completely defined context. The answers are quickly processed by computer and resubmitted to management for review. This management review and approval process is a key feature of the planning system. It intends to provide for an orderly and systematic recording of managerial judgment, commitment, agreement, etc., as a planning data service relying for input on line management's free participation in decision making.

RESISTANCE TO CHANGE

The significant break with tradition which a system for business planning by computer introduces lies in the fact that a small group of professional planners with access to a high-speed computer can do more than was ever imagined possible in the way of collecting, processing, and disseminating relevant planning data throughout a large business organization.

However, this potential is not easy to realize because it has all the earmarks of a revolutionary upheaval of established practices and procedures. It crosses traditional organizational lines and is regarded as a threat by many people, even those in managerial positions. In today's civilized white-collar environment, the reaction is less violent than the Luddite riots in England 150 years ago, but organizational resistance is equally disconcerting and cannot be discounted. It exists even in a business where extensive computer usage is an accepted way of life. The real issue is not the computer but the new approach and procedure which the computer makes possible. Established power centers are afraid of losing control over the planning system and consequently over management decisions. The fear is like a superstition—hard to dispel because there is a trace of truth in it.

Confidence in the approach and, in this case a welcome healthy contempt requires familiarity with a real system and can come about only through direct exposure to it in actual operation. There is a danger that this stage is never reached. A planning system, like an aircraft, to get off the ground needs clearance from the control tower and a long enough runway. It may never get either.

This problem is by no means a new one. In 1513 A.D. Machiavelli wrote:

> "It must be considered that there is nothing more difficult to carry out, nor more doubtful of success, nor dangerous to handle, than to initiate a new order of things. For the reformer has enemies in all those who profit by the old order, and only lukewarm defenders in all those who would profit by the new order, this lukewarmness arising partly from fear of their adversaries, who have the laws in their favor; and partly from the incredulity of mankind, who do not truly believe in anything new until they have had actual experience of it. Thus it arises that on every opportunity for attacking the reformer, his opponents do so with the zeal of partisans, the others only defend him half-heartedly, so that between them he runs great danger." [1]

It is vital, therefore, that the development and operation of a system for business planning by computer be appropriately chartered and supported by top manage-

---

[1] Niccolo Machiavelli, *The Prince and the Discourses*, Modern Library, 1940/1950, Chapter VI, pgs. 21–22. Reprinted by permission of Oxford University Press.

ment. It must not be given the shadowy stature of "parallel operation" but must be established as the unifying assembly point for actual business planning. Most important, the relationship of the business planning system to the budgeting system must be clarified. The budget continues to be the procedure through which the organization authorizes action; in contrast, the business plan would be the procedure through which the organization establishes direction. It is, of course, essential that plan and budget are relatable so that direction and action can be reconciled.** This reconciliation is line management's responsibility. Sometimes the budget may have to be forced to conform to plan. On other occasions information developed in. the budgeting process will require a change of plan.

THE PLANNING CONDITION

Throughout this book we have explained and discussed decision variables, procedural logic, and documents of real computerized planning data systems. No claim is made that these definitions have universal theoretical validity. They are nothing more than a set of well-interconnected physical and fiscal goals against which achievements could be measured.

Why go to all this trouble when in the end we continue to be uncertain about the precision or correctness of the objectives established through the system and recorded by it, to say nothing about their achievability? This feeling of futility attacks every planner once in a while.

There is really no need to be discouraged by the complexity of the job to be undertaken and the political hazards involved. The computer has injected a mutational change into the business environment. The forces of evolution will take care of the rest. This book suggests an evolutionary approach to the building of a system for business planning in which the computer features as an intellectual catalyst. It recommends a sequence of modest steps that can be taken immediately to improve a less than satisfactory situation in comprehensive business planning.

The emergence of such a system gradually plays a contributing role in shaping the given historical and organizational environment from which it evolved. It does not proceed from the position that the environment must change first to suit an elegant theoretical construction.

What, then, was the historical background and organizational environment which sponsored the system described in this book. While some of it may be peculiar to IBM, e.g. ready access to a computer within walking distance of the planner, as well as familiarity with computer capabilities (and limitations) by most planners, the reader will realize that this is equally true in any larger corporation today.

** This is no new issue to budgeters who always struggle with compatibility between the budgeting and accounting systems.

THE STORY OF AN EVOLUTION

In 1956, the size to which the IBM Corporation had grown required the adoption of an organizational structure which separated various operating divisions from an advisory corporate staff. Before this change, the IBM Corporation had been organized by function across several product lines. It was this reorganization that created, among others, the fully integrated Office Products Division (then called Electric Typewriter Division) out of the sales, manufacturing, and service departments within the former functional organization. In turn administrative, planning, accounting, and control functions were set up within the Division, giving it the structure of a complete business of medium size.

In the years 1957 and 1958, business planning for the Division was carried on in terms of financial projections by the controller's office and in terms of new product development by product and marketing planners in cooperation with development engineers. The two planning efforts were not always compatible with each other and deliberations made in one found their way into the other only with a great deal of delay and often distortion. Anyway, the real decision-making process was tied in with the budgetary process and not with these longer-range planning efforts in financial, marketing or product planning. In recognition of the resulting dichotomy, in the summer of 1959, IBM established a corporate staff director for long-range planning with counterparts in each division for the purpose of developing internally consistent and comprehensive five-year plans. As far as the Division was concerned, this led within the next year to a conscious effort to coordinate the financial projections with the long-range product development and marketing plans. In June 1960 and 1961, a comprehensive and internally consistent five-year plan for the Division was developed and submitted to the Corporate Management Committee for approval. The 1960 Long-Range Plan represented an extension of the approved budget and treated new product developments and the respective incremental sales incomes and operating expenses as addenda. Of course, these addenda were not allowed to even show an impact on the budgeted years, typical for this approach to long-range planning as an extension of the budget. After lengthy technical discussions and political maneuvering, the 1961 Long-Range Plan was allowed to include all long-range business assumptions with respect to announced and planned new products and for the first time to deviate from the budget which had been approved the previous December. However, no authorization was given to change the budget in keeping with the long-range plan. As a matter of fact, a discussion of budgetary requirements was specifically barred from the deliberations about the long-range plan. Instead, it was suggested that "regardless" ways and means must be found to accomplish the plan without changing the approved operating objectives in the current budget. Writing about these intellectual acrobatics today, many years later, conjures up an almost incredible state of bureaucratic confusion.

PLANNING SYSTEM—NEED IDENTIFICATION

The experience in preparing these first two comprehensive plans taught management various lessons, the most important of which may be summed up as follows:

(1) The amount of detailed work and the length of time required to prepare a long-range plan for *only one set of assumptions* with regard to general economic activity, new product plans, and specific volume forecasts is out of balance with the value of the resulting plan in helping management make strategic decisions and establish measurable goals.

(2) The lack of a clear understanding of the purpose of the long-range plan, particularly as it related to the established accounting practices and procedures for operational planning and budgetary control, tends to create numerous conflicts and reconciliation problems. As a result, the task of long-range planning, which is a complex matter in itself, becomes further complicated by organizational and jurisdictional disputes.

During the two years of planning by traditional—i.e. by undefined—methods, discussions had been going on about ways of simplifying the planning process. However, simplification is usually viewed with suspicion—perhaps justifiably so—as an attempt to rationalize superficial thinking and haphazard guesswork in planning. During the second half of 1961, therefore, management came to the conclusion that the solution of the problem would require a new approach to planning which:

(a) Makes feasible the evaluation of alternate planning assumptions with regard to general economic activities, product line volumes, product mix, etc.

(b) Simplifies the analysis of long-range plans by connecting specific measurements of past performance with future managerial objectives in considerable detail.

(c) Facilitates the review procedures and working relationships between the various operating functions and corporate management by relying on clearly defined, reproducible planning logic.

Of course, the key to the implementation of this approach lies in the utilization of computers to carry out the required iterative calculations and documentations usually incurred in planning. In order to demonstrate the feasibility of the approach, the planning personnel in two functional areas of the Division started to work along the following schedule:

(1) Identify the planning documents that management feels are absolutely necessary.
(2) Learn how the data for these documents are currently being generated by predominantly manual methods.
(3) Identify the quantitative assumption from which this data is calculated.

(4) Specify in programming language the underlying input/output logic.

(5) Secure concurrence with these definitions from the responsible functional manager.

As a result of this preliminary work, which produced a few useful programs, in December of 1961, a staff report under the title of "Proposal for Mechanization of Planning" requesting manpower and funds for a full scale effort was submitted and approved by Division management.

By June 1962 the emerging business planning system had accomplished sufficient coverage to be of significant value in the 1962 strategic planning effort, especially in the evaluation of alternatives and the bargaining for agreement on divisional goals as well as the review and reconciliation process with corporate management.

The subsequent continued use and expansion of the system created a new environment and planning process.

It is significant to note that the sequence of events was:

(a) Prepare plans by any available methods.
(b) Specify planning logic and procedures.
(c) Computerize the processing of planning data.

Today, in retrospect, it seems more efficient to proceed from (b) to (c) and only then to (a). But in practice, every corporate planning effort known to the writer has been following the (a), (b), and (c) sequence.

SYSTEMS ANALYSIS

Back in 1961, it was assumed that in order to come up with a system which would be operational in the foreseeable future, functional planners could not be relied upon to develop logic specifications that would fit into the proposed integrated system. It was decided that systems analysis and definition would have to be done by the divisional planning staff group. Once the logic was defined, it would take a number of man-months to translate it into computer programs, debug them, and test them with real-life data before the system would become operational and useful for planning the business. It was also decided that no drastic changes could be made in the formats to which functional planners and management were accustomed. This gave some direction to the display of data, but left a wide field for applying skill and imagination in the generation of this data, especially since it was apparent that the existing, almost one for one input/output specifications in all their ramifications and detail could not possibly be accepted.

This opens up a lot of new controversial issues. The final output of the system was to be a view of the future which makes sense to the entire management, which means to those people who can take action (or refuse to take action). These are the people who effectively manage the business. If one visualizes a business employing 10,000 people including perhaps as many as 500 managers, it becomes quite difficult to see how the system could possibly make sense to all of them. The aspirations and motivations of various levels of management and different operating functions are not necessarily compatible with each other and even if they were compatible, they do not necessarily complement each other so that the business as a whole adds up to a successful operation.

Functional managers particularly are interested mainly in an excellent showing of their function, rather than the division or the business in its entirety. For example, no sales manager should be blamed for asking that the product he sells be underpriced and the salesmen who sell it be overpaid. It is the divisional or corporate manager's job to quantify the prefix "under" and "over" in relation to the successful performance of the entire business.

If we admit that functional interests are bound to take on independent power in the minds and actions of the respective managers, we cannot fail to see how an extension of the planning system to the department level manager would move us further away from the objective of building a system to assist divisional management in planning the entire business. The diffusion of interests and objectives would be unmanageable both in terms of information as well as in terms of measurable and achievable planned goals.

We may illustrate this point by reference to a contrast—an orchestra. Please note that there is a conductor who exercises direct supervision over all elements of the orchestra. There is no intermediate management, such as for instance, a foreman of the brass or a foreman of the strings, who would like to outshine his rival departments in the excellence of his department's performance (loudness?). Also, every member of the orchestra has in front of him the musical score (the plan) detailed as to his specific instrument, and except for a very limited scope within which he may add his interpretation to the score, he has to follow it under the guidance of the conductor. No member of the orchestra has any say-so with respect to what and how others in the orchestra should play. As a matter of fact, the whole musical score has been developed and written by someone who is not necessarily a member of the team (except for cases where a living composer may conduct the orchestra or play a soloist part). Even in jazz, particularly during a jam session, each musician has the right to improvise and develop new variations, but there is always the theme to be followed and someone who maintains strict discipline through rhythm.

In business the theme and rhythm are not furnished by a brilliant composer but by the forces of the market, by technology and innovation, and by the competitive actions of several management teams. Therefore, the score must be written with a sensitive ear for changes in key. Improvisation will have to be kept in line with the major theme of achievability. It does not appear unreasonable to compare business planning with the writing of a score that establishes this major theme. Without it there can be no true improvisation, in the sense of finding new means for achieving planned goals.

In view of the above, a conscious decision was made to approach the system's design from the top down, first resolving the system's requirements for senior management within the division, then proceeding into the functional areas, and finally including in the latter as much simulation of low order management decisions as possible. This required the introduction of so-called decisional logic, which is a first step in a practical approach towards optimization, and which every theoretician will uphold as an absolutely necessary function of a computerized business planning system. However, actual experience with decisional logic indicates that there are both practical and theoretical objections.

TYPES OF PLANNING LOGIC

It may be helpful to distinguish between:

(a) definitional logic, and
(b) decisional logic

The first type is the most common, whereas the second type represents certain challenges. Definitional logic relates inputs either in arithmetic or functional form to produce outputs. The computation is completely explained from the definitions of the decision variables (planning factors) involved. In the case of decisional logic, there are problems of choice as to how certain planning factors and resulting data are to be interpreted. In order to resolve an incompatible or contradictory condition, a decision rule must be specified.

Definitional logic involves mostly the selection of suitable inputs such as activity levels and resource requirement factors. Let us assume that the workload for the servicing of a certain product has been defined in terms of hours and appropriately computed for each plan year. The next step is to convert this workload (hours) into manpower (man-years). For this computation we would need a factor in terms of either hours per man-year or the reciprocal. Figure 11 illustrates a listing of the ingredients for this planning factor which also outlines the process leading to *its* definition.

Of course, instead of selecting hrs/yr as the input factor one could have stipulated calendar days, vacation days, and hrs/day as input variables and computed the available hrs/yr. This is strictly a matter of style and taste. Just as well, one might have started the input with net available hours.

The only rule to be applied is a practical one. Any planning factor which is likely to be subjected to frequent "what if" questions should be made available as a de-

MAINTENANCE SERVICE—WORKLOAD MANPOWER

Definition	Quantities		Selected Input
	Days/yr.	hours/yr.	Factor
Calendar	262		
Vacations & Holidays	19		
Gross available	243		
Hours per day	8	1944	hrs/yr
Personal, Sickness			
Lost time		194	% of hrs/yr
Overtime		97	% of hrs/yr
Net available		1847	(computed)
Indirect Workload			
Sales assistance		120	hrs per salesman
In-house equipment		10	hrs per unit installed
Engineering changes		60	hrs (transfer from product plan)
Training for new products		80	hrs (transfer from product plan)
Direct Workload		1577	(computed)

Figure 11

cision variable, i.e. as an input option. If there had been a lot of talk about more vacations and shorter working hours, the corresponding factors should be specified as separate input lines.

Decisional logic involves the selection of a suitable decision rule to resolve a condition of conflicting objectives. Let us assume that field sales manpower may properly be computed on the basis of workload and productivity objectives. We now have to determine the expense. Let us further assume that sales management has certain objectives as to the earnings each type of salesman ought to reach for the given productivity, while the controller has certain objectives as to the percentage of gross income available for salesmen's compensation. We may call the first objective "payroll demand" and the second "payroll fund." If payroll demand does not exceed the fund, everything is still explainable by definitional logic—payroll demand becomes the planned expense goal. The controller will be happy with the planning for lower marketing expense. But in a case where the payroll demand exceeds the fund, there is a choice. We may either persist on definitional logic by planning for the payroll demand while showing a planning variance between demand and fund, or we may introduce decisional logic by modifying productivity or earning levels of salesmen from the originally stated objectives in order to force a balance between payroll demand and fund. Of course, such an adjustment of original objectives would require appropriate notification in the form of a variance report. Figure 12 describes the planning specification involving decisional logic for the above example.

As shown in the above example of decisional logic, the planners had to choose one way of forcing a balance among otherwise conflicting objectives. The economic reasoning may run as follows: one cannot adjust payroll demand without either reducing earning levels or increasing productivity requirements. Reducing earnings per man might be simpler as it affects only expense and not manpower. But realistically, productivity requirements seem to be the more malleable factor. In other words, it appears to be an easier management task to ask men for more effort than to reduce their pay scale.

PLANNING VARIANCES

This type of decisional logic suits the economist and satisfies the business school graduate. However, functional planners tend to disagree with this reasoning and in particular with the automatic computation of adjustments. They object to the input of financial constraints in the sales program and want to have the payroll demand shown as their best responsible estimate in all cases. If adjustments are to be made to meet profitability objectives, so they argue, they should be carried out by changing the inputs, not by having the computer modify them.

Therefore, the use of decisional logic in planning encounters political objections, especially when it crosses functional organization boundaries.

No such objections are raised when the decision rules apply to conditions within the planning unit. For example, self-imposed constraints on space requirements, hiring rates, productivity improvement curves, etc. may be incorporated into the functional planning logic of a divisional system in order to compute resource requirements by function, but divisional resource constraints will not be accepted in

SALESMEN'S COMPENSATION ANALYSIS AND ADJUSTMENT

Payroll Demand

B1	Salesman Type A	Man-years x Earnings factor A
B2	Salesman Type B	Man-years x Earnings factor B
B3	Field Managers	Man-years x Earnings factor M
B9	Total	Payroll Demand

Payroll Fund

B11	Product Line I	
B12	II	
B13	III	Retail value of orders by product line
B14	IV	x Financial ratio (pricing factor)
B15	V	
B16	VI	
B19	Total	Payroll Fund

Decision logic $B20 = B9/B19$

If B20 $\leq$ 1.00, accept payroll demand as is

If B20 $\geq$ 1.01, multiply productivity factors by B20 and re-compute manpower, payroll demand, and payroll fund. Write:

PAYROLL DEMAND VARIANCE—Year ....

	Payroll Demand	Payroll Fund	Productivity		
	a	b	c	d	
	$/Man	% Revenue	Original	Adjusted	Term
Product I					Uts/Man
II					Uts/Man
III					000$/Man
IV					000$/Man
V					000$/Man
. . . . .					
Managers					% Salesmen

Figure 12

the functional planning system itself. Here is where the bargaining spirit of planning comes into play. The manager wants to be heard, not computed out of existence.

Interfunctional decision variables are best handled through the optional entry of constraints and the display of resulting planning variance (cf. Exhibit 9-8, second item from the bottom).

The reader is cautioned not to disregard the lesson to be learned from this seemingly trivial detail. The planning variance becomes an important item for discussion in plan review meetings, and is eventually resolved. But this resolution comes about by a process of reconciliation between responsible bargaining agents, speaking for their respective management units. This is consistent with the view that planning is bargaining, and a system for planning is to facilitate this process—not eliminate it.

In concept, decisional logic aims at the simulation of management—and its replacement by computer. In contrast, a system for business planning by computer is supposed to strengthen management. It is designed to assist managers in developing plans and making decisions by facilitating the manager's personal participation in a planning process. In the traditional planning process a manager becomes accustomed to delegating the planning work—and with it a certain amount of decisional responsibility. This is unavoidable because manual methodology and execution make a personal involvement by the manager an unreasonable and impractical proposition. A properly designed planning system by computer is supposed to be used by the manager himself.

Resistance to the system will not originate so much from the manager as from the functional planners. For them a computerized system of business planning represents a threat, and the incorporation of decisional logic into the system represents the most insidious feature of this threat. To a large measure, the job security of many functional planners depends upon the traditional workload of generating planning statistics by manual methods and providing liaison through personal contacts with all the departments in the function. The ensuing hustle and bustle creates a feeling of importance and belonging. It is rather unlikely that a person conditioned in this type of "busyness" can switch to a mode of operating which requires a fair level of abstract thinking.

This is the main reason why it would be impractical to assign the task of developing specifications for divisional or corporate planning logic to the functional planners, or to a systems and procedures staff who would have to depend again upon the functional planners. Instead, this task is best assigned to an independent business planning group at the divisional or corporate management level with the specific assignment to do a completed job. Only in this manner can more advanced configurations of planning logic be introduced into the functional specifications as fast as the functional manager is willing to accept them. Of course, where the functional manager delegates the responsibility for this acceptance to his functional planners, some of the momentum is again lost, at least for the time being.

EXCEPTION PRINCIPLE NOT APPLICABLE IN PLANNING

In management literature we find frequent proposals for improving management effectiveness through the exception principle. It is proposed that the manager should not review those aspects of his operation which have been standardized and operate within pre-established control limits. Instead, the manager should concentrate his attention on those aspects which are out of control as shown by suitable variance reports issued by the accounting system. How could the exception principle be applied in a planning system?

First of all the exception principle presupposes that standards of performance are available for all facets of normal operations. Anybody familiar with the theoretical questions and practical problems connected with the setting of standards for today's normal performance will agree that they should not be applied to the future. As a matter of fact, one of the most difficult problems in any standardization program is the careful specification of conditions for which the standard is valid, so that a change in conditions justifies a revision of standard.

In business planning the major concern is not the "norm" of current operating conditions, but the change in the norm either with or without a change in operating conditions. Therefore, the concept of normal operating conditions does not apply to a planning system. Of course, the planning factors may be interpreted by some as standards rather than self-imposed objectives. To counteract this notion, we must re-emphasize that each and every planning factor is completely variable at the discretion of the manager. That these planning factors are also shown for past years is only for the purpose of relating the planning logic of the future to the present. There is no attempt to project the future within the system on the basis of implied standards of performance. Each planning period requires its own set of inputs so that the manager may speculate about what could be done, rather than be faced with a prediction of what is going to happen according to someone else's judgment.

SYSTEMS DESIGN BY EVOLUTION, NOT REVOLUTION

Planning is a continuous process and it would be wrong to expect that a first planning system ought to be perfect or final. On the contrary, designing the planning logic is itself a method of learning and teaching managerial economics within a going business organization. It calls for a mature balance between theoretical perfection and useful application for the purpose of increasing managerial effectiveness. Of course, this educational give and take is not without difficulties. Traditionally, senior management is asking staff people for answers and recommendations in matters requiring special technical competence. It is not easy to convince top-level management that it is most important for them to get interested in how such answers and recommendations by staff are developed and what sort of reasoning is being used by the staff.

A complete planning system of the type described in this book will help greatly in overcoming the reluctance of senior managers to deal with procedural detail. No manager questions that validity and significance of a summary statement depend upon supporting data and logic. If no system is available, management makes a judgment about a summary statement by the so-called shotgun approach: it probes through random questions into lower level details to confirm its faith in the staff's competence and to assure itself that a thorough job has been done on the problem under consideration.

The time and effort that is consumed in this randomized analysis and evaluation of summary data, is most likely greater than the time and effort it would take for a manager to study and comprehend the reproducible logic of a planning system. He would from then on have to review only volume assumptions and planning factors and form a judgment about their validity and relevance to the problem under consideration. In addition, the review of input and logic would circumvent an important source of potential error in judgment which we might call "personality cult." It is the error generated by accepting as valid a statement well presented by personable and friendly associates of long standing because criticism tends to be interpreted as an attack on the person rather than the material presented.

The evaluation of plans between staff specialists and managers often resembles a detective game. Only after considerable digging is the "evidence" ready for a judgmental verdict. Had the planning process been specified and the evidence presented with the plan, most of the digging could have been eliminated and the evaluation directed immediately to those inputs which are themselves the expression of managerial judgment. The detective game would have taken place during the writing of the planning specifications in terms of reproducible logic and easily reviewable formats for quantitative evidence.

The need for an understandable language in which to express planning logic both for management and for the computer becomes obvious. In fact, development of such a planning language becomes a driving force behind the planning system itself.

Unless the manager is given a means to express himself directly to the computer the systems analyst or programmer remains the key man in the planning process.

Russell L. Ackoff in his thought-provoking article "Management Misinformation Systems" (*Management Science Magazine*, December, 1967) addresses this problem as follows:

"Managers suffer less from a lack of relevant information rather than from an overabundance of irrelevant information. Hence the most important function of an information system is filtration or evaluation and condensation. One cannot specify what information is required for decision making until an explanatory model of the decision process and the system involved has been constructed and tested. Since most MIS designers succeed in keeping managers ignorant and unable to evaluate the system as a whole, managers dele-gate the control of the organization to the systems designers and operators who may have many virtues, but managerial competence is seldom among them."

While Ackoff addresses the question from the point of view of operational decision and control systems these issues are even more pronounced in a system which deals with the origination of achievable goals. This is certainly an area in which adequate models are not easily constructed, if at all. The first order of business here is to de-termine what information is relevant. It certainly should be possible to make explicit the implicit model used by the decision maker and then treat it as a simulator for the comparison of proposed alternative solutions.

12

Technical Administrative Problems

Since this book is intended to offer some practical solutions to the complex managerial problem of originating and achieving planned goals, this last chapter will cover administrative practices and procedures and related technical issues. Of course, these will be related to the approach outlined in this book and the claim that planning for a business whose size requires several levels of management is inconceivable without an accounting system specifically designed for this purpose.

The design of such an accounting system is no easy task. Everybody knows that the installation of a transaction data system or traditional accounting system is a continuous job. It requires the attention of professional experts throughout the lifetime of a business organization. This is true in spite of the fact that traditional accounting systems have been with us for centuries and an extensive literature exists dealing with accepted accounting practices and procedures. The design of a suitable planning data system is equally a continuous job and equally requires the attention of professional experts throughout the life of the organization. This is even more true because planning systems cannot draw on an extensive literature for a body of established and accepted practices and procedures. The design of a planning data system is itself a creative act of innovation as a partial contribution to the wider field of management systems. Fortunately today's information technology provides the developer of planning data systems with the means to do the job in less time than the decades if not centuries it took accounting systems to mature. But it must be recognized that the job cannot be done overnight.

COMPUTERIZED PLANNING LOGIC

This book claims that planning for a business whose size requires several levels of management is inconceivable without the use of computers. There is, of course, no conclusive proof for this thesis, but it is hoped that the arguments and examples presented are a case of overwhelming circumstantial evidence. It is conceded that the computer is no more than a highly efficient printing calculator which accepts inputs and generates outputs in keeping with given instructions. There is no question that an army of clerks could theoretically be substituted for the computer. Let us briefly recall the main exhibits in this evidence.

Manual methods are not only very time consuming but fail to provide for the application of managerial economics in systematic and reproducible logic. This, however, is a critical and essential need when evaluating alternative courses of action.

The computer is not only more efficient but it also performs the important role of an unimpeachable disciplinarian. The writing of instructions to be followed by clerks and the organization needed to check compliance with instructions as well as numeric accuracy is a substantial administrative task. In practice, this tends to force a simplification of the procedures (planning logic) so that the instructions are intelligible to the clerks who have to carry out the calculations.

In contrast, such limitations in intelligibility do not apply to the computer. Therefore, the planning logic and instructions for computer operations can be tailored directly to the intellectual capacity of the manager whose responsibility it is to plan. Of course, as we pointed out on several occasions this remains a limitation, but one which is less restrictive and can be removed systematically. While it is impractical to incorporate into the first planning logic formulations which overtax the understanding of the responsible manager, subsequent cooperation between manager and staff planner will bring about a clearer definition of the managerial economics involved and a refinement of the computerized planning logic. In this feedback process between manager and planner the computer functions as a catalyst.

This is an important difference in approach from the usual simulation proposed by the management scientist who develops his system in a so-called ivory tower and is faced with the problem that only he has a full understanding of the power and usefulness of the simulation, while operating management views it with suspicion.

COMPUTER OPERATIONS

The design of a planning data system, i.e. its corporate and divisional subsystems with their many modules of managerial thinking is thoroughly intertwined with the machinery through which they are to be processed. Therefore, the selection of suitable machinery is of paramount importance. This amounts to answering the question: What type of computer installation is most conducive to get corporate and divisional planning off the ground? Several alternatives are available:

(1)   Assign time on an existing computer installation, such as one hour between 10 and 11 A.M. every day. This would be the case both at corporate headquarters and at divisional headquarters wherever they are located, assuming that each of these locations has sufficient computer power available.

(2)   Install a separate computer for each major planning unit dedicated to planning and other management science applications provided there is enough workload and sufficient economic justification for such a dedicated system in each location.

(3)   Install a dedicated system of sufficient power at one location, preferably corporate headquarters, and run it as a companywide planning service through remote entry terminals at each planning unit.

It is the writer's considered opinion that alternative (3) is by far the most desirable solution both from the point of view of successful development of planning data systems and from the point of view of making maximum computer power available at lowest possible cost to the user.

The Planning Systems Generator approach mentioned in Chapter 7 would require a computer installation with the following minimum configuration:

Memory	32K words or 128K bytes
Auxiliary	6 tapes or equivalent disc assignment
Input/Output	Card Reader-Punch, 132 chas. Printer

Operating System with Fortran IV compiler

The billing rate for such a system—operated as a cost center—would be in the range of 200 to 300 $/Hour. To this each subsystem user would have to add the cost of his terminal and the connecting lines, amounting to another 2,000 to 3,000 $/Month.

Monthly usage of the system would be accounted for somewhat like this:

Language development and maintenance   5 to 10 Hrs/Mth.

Planning data service by each terminal   10 to 30 Hrs/Mth.

Hence, the availability of say 20 Hours/Month from such a fully dedicated system with around ten terminals would cost the individual user from 300 to 450 $/Hour. Since work, i.e. planning data service, on the system would be calculated in terms of minutes, the really significant figure of cost to management is 5.— to 7.50 $/Min. A typical three-minute job executing a few modules within one of the subsystems would cost $20.—.

This would be the equipment—the machinery only. Next, we must discuss the question of personnel and other operating costs.

STAFFING

A corporation which is seriously interested in developing a planning data system will have to make a decision about how to develop a planning systems generator. It may either assign in-house resources to the task of designing it or subcontract this work to one of the many software development companies in the country. The architecture, efficiency, and teachability of the planning systems generator is of such importance, that the best talent both in the field of planning and in the field of systems design of the corporation must be assigned to this task, even if the actual programming is done outside.

Of course, there is a possibility of finding a completely operational planning systems generator, such as the one developed by IBM, and adopt it with minimum modifications to one's own management environment.

If this is not possible, an effort to design it from scratch would require at a minimum four man-years, two with planning competence and two with systems programming competence, all of the highest caliber. If actually six to eight people are assigned it is realistic to expect a first level planning systems generator to be operational within six months. This book, as a matter of fact, would be helpful to such an effort and might give the designers a considerable head start.

With an either homegrown or acquired planning systems generator available, the next step would be to teach it to the planning personnel at corporate headquarters and in each division or subsidiary. This teaching would include some initial assistance in debugging the first programs written by the prospective users. Depending upon the size of the organization at least one, perhaps as many as three people, must be permanently assigned to this task. They represent the hard core of a planning systems department. Then there will be some continuous need for the further development and maintenance of the planning systems generator as the various users gain experience and request additional facilities to be made available within this planning dialect. Unless there are major revisions in the language itself such additional programming may be easily subcontracted or handled by permanent members of the planning systems department.

Altogether if we exclude the development of the planning systems generator itself, the maintenance and internal support of its use in a diversified organization would require a permanent staff of from two to five professionals.

As to the number of actual users, that is managers and their assistants for planning, the only limitation would be how quickly they can be taught and how much computer time is available for the development of programs within each planning data subsystem. For a large division or subsidiary after a number of such programs have been developed and are in operation, it might become advisable to establish an individual with responsibility for coordination of the planning subsystem under development. If the division or subsidiary is in itself a highly complex and diversified operation a small planning systems department might emerge to provide for additional teaching and some programming assistance to the division's general and functional management. In this case it becomes extremely important to establish a clear-cut policy which insists on the use of one and only one planning systems generator. This must be carefully controlled in order to end up with a coordinated and internally compatible system. There is a strong tendency for divisional and subsidiary planning system departments to want to build their own systems including hardware and software packaging. If a corporation allows this to happen, the major benefit from the original effort to develop a planning systems generator in the first place is wasted and in addition future high costs of integration of incompatible systems will become necessary later on.

One simple and highly practical way of enforcing the use of a single common language is through the control of the source deck. This control is also facilitated if a central common computer is used for planning systems applications, in which case the planning dialect is stored on this central computer in object form accessible to all users through their respective terminals.

PLANNING DATA SERVICE

The above staffing represents an approach making maximum allowance for a completely decentralized management system in which each division or subsidiary represents a fully autonomous operating unit with its own procedures for originating and achieving planned goals. An alternative solution to this would be a centralized planning data service department with the responsibility of providing planning data processing and programming to the entire organization, divisional as well as corporate. However, even if this form of organization were chosen, it is important to emphasize the service characteristics of this setup. Within this planning data service department, divisional and corporate subsystems would continue to be operated as separate entities. In keeping with the philosophy that decisions about planned goals must be made by the management level responsible for their achievement, even a centralized planning data service would have to be so constituted as to rely upon input data through terminals at the various divisional and corporate headquarters locations. Under no circumstances should this department be run as a brain trust or mastermind for the origination of planned goals to be achieved by others.

The advantages of a centralized planning data service department consist mainly in the fact that the effectiveness of competent people in this area could be increased by bringing them together at one location. It is a well-known fact that talent in this area is rather limited and depends a great deal on continuous contact with professional colleagues. An isolated professional in a subsidiary or divisional organization may feel lost and his effectiveness may be completely dissipated.

There is such a thing as a critical mass of resources which have to be brought together in such an effort. Attacking the task with less than this critical mass will result in complete waste. It might as well not be undertaken at all.

The writer's experience indicates that a team of at least four professionals is required. On the other hand, the building of a planning data system is not something that can be forced or accelerated by assigning large resources. Therefore, there is not only a critical mass on the lower end of the scale, but also an upper limit. The planning data service department must work as a congenial group, and it seems that even the strongest leadership becomes overtaxed when there are more than ten professionals in the group.

It is one of the important characteristics of a computer-based planning data system that the computer functions in it as an extension of the human brain. Therefore, few but highly competent human brains can be tremendously effective unless their brainpower is usurped by less important matters, such as department politics and similar matters.

PLANNING DATA SECURITY

When planning data become meaningful expressions of managerial objectives and a road map for action, security becomes a relevant issue. This applies not only with respect to safeguarding this data from the inquisitive eyes of outsiders to the corporation but also within the organization, from those who don't have, as the term goes "a need to know." Centralized data banks represent an image which is contrary to creating a feeling of data security in the minds of the participants. This is one of the reasons why the planning systems generator described in this book is not approaching the problem from the concept of a centralized data bank. As a matter of fact, it has been the writer's experience that the facility of storing planning data on a centralized disk file with well-designed security via individual labels and identification codes has been a largely unsatisfactory feature of the system. There is no reluctance to store planning logic and report definitions centrally, even making them freely accessible to other management teams, but with regard to data the preferred operating mode has been to keep them either in card form or on tape, physically stored in lockable cabinets inside lockable rooms. In this manner they are under complete physical control of the user and entered into the system only in connection with a specific case of planning data processing.

GROUND RULES

To those who find the approach outlined in this book sufficiently valid to warrant some explanatory experimentation, a few important ground rules may be helpful:

(1) The objective is business planning. Don't get enamored with the computer. There will continue to be many aspects of planning which are better left outside the system.

(2) The target is usefulness as a function of the time available, not perfection. In other words, the sophistication of the system must be tailored to its delivery date. It is always better to arrange for continued improvement and refinement in the future than for an ultimate solution. There will never be an ultimate solution because a business planning system will turn into a process which will affect the art of planning by virtue of the feedback between staff planner and manager.

(3) Definitely start with the design of output displays to management and arrange for supporting data by stages of detail. This is the only way to find a practical answer to the question of "for whom" the planning is being done, and "how much" detail is really needed. Many attempts at the design of computerized planning systems have failed because the men in charge tried to live up to a standard of professional competence and theoretical validity which is beyond the current state of the art. Instead of designing a system for planning they were really doing research work in scientific management. This is a great danger and must be carefully guarded against because the men who will become enthusiastic about an assignment for designing a system for business planning by computer will be professionals of high competence and not easily satisfied with less than theoretically valid solutions.

(4) Insist on the use of a common language. This type of system cannot be developed by coordinating or integrating different systems independently developed in different organizational units.

PLANNING, BUDGETING, CONTROLLING

A long-range look at what might happen to the entire business planning and control process would reveal at least three tiers of systems:

(1) Corporate-divisional planning systems, as outlined in this book but more dynamic, i.e. equipped with a library of models by type of business and operating function.

(2) Functional-departmental planning systems with shorter time dimension, but greater segmentation and structure. These would embody the traditional budgeting system.

(3) Large and complex transaction recording systems containing data on history and current events. They would embody the traditional accounting system.

The interaction between these systems requires intelligence and is therefore not eligible for computerization—not now, and, I hope, never; certainly not as long as businessmen continue to be creative and resourceful individuals whose subjective aspirations have to be balanced against a choice of available alternative courses of action.

While it is conceivable that high-speed computers with tremendous memories would give rise to the vision that all facets of a business decision (views of the past combined with views of the future) might be ground through one gigantic management information system, its practicality is questionable. Even if such a system could be designed by a group of superhuman operations researchers and management scientists, the actual operations of the business would continue to require several levels of management. Only people can take action. How are people going to live with such a system?

The purpose of business planning is twofold: It is to inject the long-range view into the current management decision process and it is to establish an agreed upon direction for coordinated action.

While the future remains conjecture and expectation, it is necessary that a view of the future be maintained for every major business decision in the making. In this respect there is a surprising degree of unanimity among writers on the subject of business planning. To make major business decisions without the benefit of a pertinent view of the future is considered poor practice. In order to arrive at sound decisions a business must have not only a comprehensive view of the past, as furnished by the accounting system, but also a comprehensive view of the future. It is the purpose of the business planning system to furnish the view of the future. Computerization is needed because the future is uncertain and speculative. Alternate views must be made available to stimulate and rationalize the management decision process. Without the ability to look at alternatives in the context of the entire business, the decision-making process lacks an important perspective. Again, computerization becomes necessary when the uncertainties and speculations of a multilevel management must be brought together and reconciled.

The design of systems for business planning by computer is not an easy task, but it certainly is one of the more challenging and stimulating jobs available in any large organization. It deals with the problems of general management. The general manager needs the job done. More and more general managers begin to want the job done. Who will ask for and get the opportunity to do the job?

"It is precisely the human failure and inability to quantify all of the elements of the decision-making processes which make it—right now—impossible to provide systems which are consistent, flexible, and fair. But this doesn't mean that designers shouldn't try to design systems to take over some of the more mundane clerical work involved in the total process. And it doesn't mean that because a system isn't perfect, that it shouldn't be tried. The real tests are: is the new system better than the current system—or no system at all? And, does it free the human involved to spend more time on decisions which are so far beyond the scope of the computer and the systems designer?" [1]

---

[1] Reprinted with permission from *Datamation,* October, published and copyrighted 1965 by F. D. Thompson Publications, Inc., 35 Mason St., Greenwich, Conn. 06830.

APPENDIX

Print Specifications and Planning Logic for

Programs 03 and 08

(Corporate Planning Data)

```
            P S G   PROGRAM LIBRARY LISTING
   D E S C R I P T I O N S      TERM    *  L O G I C   S T A T E M E N T      *   SEQ.
      CARD COLUMNS 1 - 31       32-37        41 - 79                               NU.

)PROGRAM 03                                                                            1
)COMMENTS                                                                              2
      PROGRAM 3 - COMPREHENSIVE DIVISIONAL PLANS AND CORPORATE SUMMARY                 3
                                                                                       4
      IT IS THE OBJECTIVE OF PROGRAM 03 TO GIVE AN INTEGRATED REPRESENTATION           5
      OF I+E, MANPOWER, SPACE, SOURCE + APPLICATION OF FUNDS, AND BALANCE SHEET        6
      THE LOGICAL CONNECTIONS PROCEED IN THE FOLLOWING SEQUENCE                        7
          INCOME = F(MARKET POTENTIAL)                                                 8
          COST AND EXPENSE = F(INCOME)                                                 9
          MANPOWER = F(INCOME, COST, EXPENSE)                                         10
          SPACE, BUILDING REQ. = F(MANPOWER)                                          11
          SOURCE OF2FUNDS = F(INCOME, DEPRECIATION, NEW DEBT, ETC)                    12
          APPLICATION OF FUNDS = F(CHANGES IN INVENTORIES, A/R, A/P, ETC)             13
          INVENTORIES = F(INCOME, COST, EXPENSE)                                      14
          BALANCE SHEET = F(RESIDUAL ASSET AND LIABILITY VALUES)                      15
                                                                                      16
      SUBSET NUMBER '0' FOR CORPORATE SUMMARY                                         17
      SUBSET NUMBER '1' TO '6' FOR DOMESTIC DIVISIONS                                 18
      SUBSET NUMBER '7' FOR FOREIGN OPERATIONS                                        19
                                                                                      20
      FOR CORPORATE SUMMARY COPY ACCUMULATED DIVISIONAL DATA FROM C-MATRIX            21
      INTO B-MATRIX AND PROCEED TO RATIO CALCULATIONS. OTHERWISE GO DIRECTLY          22
      TO LOGIC FOR DIVISIONAL PLANNING DATA.                                          23
)END   COMMENTS                                                                       24
)NO DECIMALS (KSQFT,SQFT,MEN,K,KUTS)                                                  25
)TWO DECIMALS ($,X)                                                                   26
                                     IF SUBSET NE 0 THEN GO TO $301                   27
      FOR SUMMARY ONLY               COPY (C,B), ZERO(C), GO TO $302                  28
                                     $301                                             29
)FORM 1, DOUBLE COLUMNS,HEADING FORM 03-1 // INCOME AND EXPENSE SUMMARY               30
BUSINESS VOLUME                                                                       31
      MARKET ESTIMATE                B201=FILL(1,GRO(3,A201,A202)),            X      32
                                     BLANK=B205/A207*100                              33
      SALES POTENTIAL                B203=B201-B201P+B201P*A204/100+A203               34
      O/O REPLACEMENT                B204                                             35
                                                                                      36
XYZ POSITION                         B205=FILL(1,GRO(3,A205,A206)),            X      37
                                     BLANK=B201*A207/100,                      X      38
                                     BLANK=EXTEND(2,B205)                             39
      REMOVALS                       B209=B205P*A210/100+A209                         40
      SHIPMENTS                      B211=B205-B205P+B209,NEGATIVE=0                   41
O/O XYZ POSITION                     B206                                             42
      XYZ REMOVALS                   B210                                             43
      XYZ SHIPMENTS                  B212                                             44
                                                                                      45
)HEADING DOUBLE COLUMNS (M$,O/O)                                                      46
GROSS INCOME                                                                          47
      PRODUCTS                       B1=A1,BLANK=B211*A2/100        ,B2               48
      SERVICE                        B3=A3,BLANK=B205*A4/100        ,B4               49
      SUPPLIES                       B5=A5,BLANK=B205*A6/100        ,B6               50
      OTHER                          B7=A7,BLANK=B48/(1-A8/100)-B48 ,B8               51
          TOTAL                      B9=B1+B3+B5+B7                 ,B10              52
                                                                                      53
GROSS PROFIT                         /* FOR LOGIC SEE DO LOOP BELOW                   54
      PRODUCTS                       B11,B12                                          55
```

DESCRIPTIONS CARD COLUMNS 1 - 31	TERM 32-37	*	LOGIC STATEMENT 41 - 79	*	SEQ. NO.
SERVICE			B13,B14		56
SUPPLIES			B15,B16		57
OTHER			B17,B18		58
TOTAL			B19,B20		59
					60
EXPENSES			/* FOR LOGIC SEE DO LOOP BELOW		61
RESEARCH			B25,B26		62
CEVELOPMENT			B27,B28		63
FIELD SALES			B29,B30		64
MKTG.SUPPORT			B31,B32		65
ADMINISTRATION			B33,B34		66
OTHER			B35,B36		67
APPORTIONMENTS			B37,B38		68
TOTAL			B39,B40		69
					70
NET BEFORE TAX			B41=B19-B39,B42		71
NET AFTER TAX			B43=B41-B45,B46		72
EARNINGS/SHARE			B106		73
					74
)HEADING /RATE OF CHANGE (O/O)/					75
					76
MARKET ESTIMATE			B301		77
XYZ POSITION			B302		78
					79
GROSS INCOME			B303		80
GROSS PROFIT			B304		81
TOTAL EXPENSES			B305		82
NET BEFORE TAX			B306		83
NET AFTER TAX			B307		84
)END FORM, END PAGE					85
	GROSS PROFIT		DO L=11 TO 17 BY 2		86
			B(L)=A(L)+A(L+1)*B(L-10)/100		87
			B19=B19+B(L)		88
			END		89
	EXPENSES		DO L=25 TO 37 BY 2		90
			B(L)=A(L)+A(L+1)*B9/100		91
			B39=B39+B(L)		92
			END		93
SUBTOTAL GROSS INCOME, EX.OTHER			B48=B1+B3+B7		94
COST OF SALES + EXPENSES			B47=B9-B19+B39-B37		95
INCOME TAX			B45=B41*A45/100,BLANK=A46		96
EFFECTIVE TAX RATE			B46=PCT(B45,B41)		97
					98
MANPOWER BY FUNCTIONAL AREA					99
COST OR EXPENSE BY TYPE OF MANPOWER					100
MANUFACTURING			B140=B1-B11+B5-B15		101
ENGINEERING			B150=B25+B27		102
MARKETING			B160=B29+B31		103
SERVICE			B170=B3-B13		104
ADMINISTRATION			B180=B33		105
			DO L=140 TO 180 BY 10		106
PRIOR PERIOD TOTALS			B(L+4,1)=A(L+1,1)+A(L+3,1)		107
			B(194,1)=B(194,1)+B(L+4,1)		108
TOTAL PER MANPOWER FACTOR			B(L+1)=RATIO(B(L),A(L),1000)		109
FACTORED PLUS FIXED TOTAL			B(L+1)=B(L+1)+A(L+1)*(1+A(L+4)/100 X		110

DESCRIPTIONS CARD COLUMNS 1 - 31	TERM 32-37	*	LOGIC STATEMENT 41 - 79	*	SEQ. NO.
			+A(L+3)		111
FACTORED PLUS FIXED DIRECT			B(L+2)=B(L+1)/(1+A(L+4)/100)-A(L+3)		112
INDIRECT = TOTAL - DIRECT			B(L+3)=B(L+1)-B(L+2)		113
RESULTING TOTAL			B(L+4)=B(L+2)+B(L+3)		114
CHANGE IN YEAR			B(L+7)=B(L+4)-B(L+4,P)		115
HIRES FOR CHANGE AND ATTRITION			B(L+8)=B(L+7)+B(L+4)*A(L+9)/100	X	116
			+A(L+8)		117
GRAND TOTALS MANPOWER			B194=B194+B(L+4)		118
CHANGE IN YEAR			B197=B197+B(L+7)		119
NEW HIRES			B198=B198+B(L+8)		120
			END		121
					122
)FORM 4, SINGLE COLUMNS, HEADING FORM 03-4 // YEAR-END MANPOWER					123
MANUFACTURING					124
DIRECT	MEN	B142			125
INDIRECT	MEN	B143			126
TOTAL	MEN	B144			127
GROWTH RATE	O/O	B146			128
NEW HIRES	MEN	B148			129
HIRING RATE	O/O	B149			130
COST FACTOR PER MAN	K $	B145.			131
					132
ENGINEERING					133
PROFESSIONAL	MEN	B152			134
SUPPORT	MEN	B153			135
TOTAL	MEN	B154			136
GROWTH RATE	O/O	B156			137
NEW HIRES	MEN	B158			138
HIRING RATE	O/O	B159			139
COST FACTOR PER MAN	K $	B155			140
					141
MARKETING					142
FIELD	MEN	B162			143
SUPPORT	MEN	B163			144
TOTAL	MEN	B164			145
GROWTH RATE	O/O	B166			146
NEW HIRES	MEN	B168			147
HIRING RATE	O/O	B169			148
COST FACTOR PER MAN	K $	B165			149
					150
SERVICE					151
FIELD	MEN	B172			152
SUPPORT	MEN	B173			153
TOTAL	MEN	B174			154
GROWTH RATE	O/O	B176			155
NEW HIRES	MEN	B178			156
HIRING RATE	O/O	B179			157
COST FACTOR PER MAN	K $	B175			158
					159
ADMINISTRATION					160
PROFESSIONAL	MEN	B182			161
SUPPORT	MEN	B183			162
TOTAL	MEN	B184			163
GROWTH RATE	O/O	B186			164
NEW HIRES	MEN	B188			165

DESCRIPTIONS CARD COLUMNS 1 - 31	TERM 32-37	* LOGIC STATEMENT * 41 - 79	SEQ. NO.
HIRING RATE	0/0	B189	166
COST FACTOR PER MAN	K $	B185	167
			168
TOTAL BUSINESS			169
ON BOARD	MEN	B194	170
GROWTH RATE	0/0	B196	171
NEW HIRES	MEN	B198	172
HIRING RATE	0/0	B199	173
)END FORM, END PAGE			174
			175
OTHER MANPOWER (OFFICE SPACE)		B219=B164+B174+B184	176
MANUFACTURING PRIME SHIFT MANPOWER		B220=B144*(1-A220/100)	177
			178
SPACE AVAILABLE			179
PLANTS, TOTAL		B230=A230,BLANK=A232+A232*(1-A233/100)	180
WAREHOUSES, TOTAL		B234=A234,BLANK=A236+A236*(1-A237/100)	181
LABORATORIES, TOTAL		B238=A238,BLANK=A240+A240*(1-A241/100)	182
OFFICES, TOTAL		B242=A242,BLANK=A244+A244*(1-A245/100)	183
			184
)FORM 5, SINGLE COLUMNS, HEADING FORM 03-5 // SPACE REQUIREMENTS AND BUILDING PX			185
LANS			186
			187
SPACE FORECAST			188
PLANTS	KSQFT	B221=A221+A222*B220/1000	189
WAREHOUSES	KSQFT	B223=A223+A224*B221/100	190
LABORATORIES	KSQFT	B225=A225+A226*B154/1000	191
OFFICES	KSQFT	B227=A227+A228*B219/1000	192
TOTAL	KSQFT	B229=B221+B223+B225+B227	193
			194
OCCUPANCY FACTORS/MAN			195
MANUFACTURING	SQFT	B222	196
MFG. EXTRA SHIFT RATIO	0/0	B217	197
MFG. WAREHOUSING	0/0	B224	198
ENGINEERING	SQFT	B226	199
OTHER	SQFT	B228	200
			201
SPACE AVAILABILITY REVIEW			202
PLANTS OWNED	KSQFT	B231=A232+A233*A231/100	203
LEASED	KSQFT	B232=B230-B231	204
BALANCE	KSQFT	B233=B221-B230	205
WAREHOUSES OWNED	KSQFT	B235=A236+A237*A234/100	206
LEASED	KSQFT	B236=B234-B235	207
BALANCE	KSQFT	B237=B223-B234	208
LABORATORIES OWNED	KSQFT	B239=A240+A241*A239/100	209
LEASED	KSQFT	B240=B238-B239	210
BALANCE	KSQFT	B241=B225-B238	211
OFFICES OWNED	KSQFT	B243=A244+A245*A243/100	212
LEASED	KSQFT	B244=B242-B243	213
BALANCE	KSQFT	B245=B227-B242	214
TOTAL OWNED	KSQFT	B247=B231+B235+B239+B243	215
LEASED	KSQFT	B248=B232+B236+B240+B244	216
REQUIRED (+)	KSQFT	B249=B281+B282+B283+B284	217
			218
BUILDINGS PLANNED AND REQUIRED			219
PLANTS	KSQFT	B256=B231-B231P+B281*(1-B251)	220

DESCRIPTIONS CARD COLUMNS 1 - 31	TERM 32-37	*	LOGIC STATEMENT 41 - 79	*	SEQ. NO.
WAREHOUSES	KSQFT		B257=B235-B235P+B282*(1-B252)		221
LABORATORIES	KSQFT		B258=B239-B239P+B283*(1-B253)		222
OFFICES	KSQFT		B259=B243-B243P+B284*(1-B254)		223
TOTAL (GROSS)	KSQFT		B260=B256+B257+B258+B259		224
					225
NET INVESTMENT IN BUILDINGS					226
PLANTS	M $		B261=A261*B256/1000		227
WAREHOUSES	M $		B262=A262*B257/1000		228
LABORATORIES	M $		B263=A263*B258/1000		229
OFFICES	M $		B264=A264*B259/1000		230
TOTAL	M $		B265=B261+B262+B263+B264		231
					232
LAND HOLDINGS					233
AREA ON HAND YEAREND	ACRES		B274=B274P+B270		234
PURCHASES	ACRES		B270=A266+A267/43.56		235
NET INVESTMENT	M $		B278=B275+B276		236
)END FORM, END PAGE					237
					238
SPACE REQUIRED			/* SPACE SURPLUS NOT TRANSFERABLE		239
MANUFACTURING			B281=B233,NEGATIVE=0		240
WAREHOUSING			B282=B237,NEGATIVE=0		241
ENGINEERING			B283=B241,NEGATIVE=0		242
OFFICES			B284=B245,NEGATIVE=0		243
LEASED SPACE RATIOS, PLANTS			B251=B232/B230		244
WAREHOUSES			B252=B236/B234		245
LABORATORIES			B253=B240/B238		246
OFFICES			B254=B244/B242		247
COST OF LAND PER SQFT			B275=A266*A268/1000000		248
PER ACRE			B276=A267*A269/1000		249
					250
INVESTMENT IN EQUIPMENT PER AMOUNT					251
ENTERED AND ADDITIONAL REQUIREMENTS					252
PER INCREMENTAL EMPLOYEE			B279=A50+A51*B147/1000+A52*B157/1000	X	253
			+A53*(B167+B177+B187)/1000		254
PARTS INVENTORY			B71=A81+A82*B205/100		255
WORK IN PROCESS			B72=A83+A84*B211/100		256
TOTAL			B73=B71+B72		257
OTHER INVENTORIES			B70=A85+A86*B47/100		258
FIXED ASSETS AND DEPRECIATION					259
SHARES OUTSTANDING			B80=B80P+A73		260
LANDHOLDINGS			B81=B81P+B278		261
BUILDINGS			B82=B82P+B265		262
FACTORY AND OFFICE EQUIPMENT			B83=B83P+B279		263
PATENTS AND GOOD WILL			B85=B85P+A54		264
DEPRECIATION					265
BUILDINGS, STRAIGHT LINE			B61=DPR(1,B265,A62,0)+A61		266
EQUIPMENT, SUM OF DIGITS			B63=DPR(2,B279,A64,0)+A63		267
PATENTS ETC, STRAIGHT LINE			B65=DPR(1,A54,A66,0)+A65		268
TOTAL DEPRECIATION + OTHER NON CASH			B69=B61+B63+B65+A67		269
NET BOOK VALUES					270
BUILDINGS			B92=B92P+B278-B61+B265		271
PLANT + EQUIPMENT			B93=B93P+B279-B63		272
PATENTS AND GOOD WILL			B95=B95P+A54-B65		273
					274
)FORM 2, SINGLE COLUMNS, HEADING FORM 03-2 // SOURCE AND APPLICATION OF FUNDS					275

DESCRIPTIONS CARD COLUMNS 1 - 31	TERM 32-37	*	L O G I C S T A T E M E N T 41 - 79	*	SEQ. NO.
					276
NET CURRENT ASSETS 1-1	M $		B68=B105P+A101-A102		277
					278
NET EARNINGS	M $		B43		279
DEPRECIATION ETC.	M $		B69		280
FUNDS FROM OPERATIONS	M $		B97=B43+B69		281
					282
SALE OF STOCK	M $		B74		283
					284
LONG TERM DEBT INCURRED	M $		B75		285
					286
MISCELLANEOUS	M $		B77		287
TOTAL FUNDS PROVIDED	M $		B98=B97+A74+A75+A77		288
					289
TOTAL FUNDS AVAILABLE	M $		B99=B68+B98		290
					291
LAND AND BUILDINGS	M $		B100=B265+B278		292
EQUIPMENT	M $		B279		293
TOTAL INVESTMENTS	M $		B102=B100+B279		294
					295
LONG TERM DEBT REPAID	M $		B76		296
CASH DIVIDEND	M $		B103=A78*B80/1000,BLANK=A79*B43/100		297
TOTAL FUNDS APPLIED	M $		B104=B102+A76+B103		298
					299
NET CURRENT ASSETS 12-31	M $		B105=B99-B104		300
					301
ANALYTICAL RATIOS					302
PLANT AND EQUIPMENT/TOTAL	O/O		B107		303
EARNINGS PER SHARE	$		B106		304
CASH DIVIDEND PAYOUT	O/O		B109		305
					306
RATES OF CHANGE					307
FUNDS FROM OPERATIONS	O/O		B110		308
TOTAL FUNDS PROVIDED	O/O		B111		309
INVESTMENTS	O/O		B112		310
TOTAL FUNDS APPLIED	O/O		B113		311
NET CURRENT ASSETS 12-31	O/O		B114		312
					313
					314
MANPOWER - CHANGES IN HEADCOUNT					315
MANUFACTURING	MEN		B147		316
ENGINEERING	MEN		B157		317
MARKETING	MEN		B167		318
SERVICE	MEN		B177		319
ADMINISTRATION	MEN		B187		320
TOTAL NET CHANGE	MEN		B197		321
					322
TOTAL ON BOARD 12-31	MEN		B194		323
INCREASE OVER PRIOR YEAR	O/O		B196		324
)END FORM, END PAGE					325
TOTAL CAPITALIZATION			B218=B126+B128		326
LIQUID FUNDS LEFT OVER			B400=B105+B124-B115-B116-B117		327
					328
)FORM 3, SINGLE COLUMNS, HEADING FORM 03-3 // BALANCE SHEET					329
ASSETS					330

PSG PROGRAM LIBRARY LISTING

DESCRIPTIONS CARD COLUMNS 1 - 31	TERM 32-37	* LOGIC STATEMENT * 41 - 79	SEQ. NO.
CASH	M S	B119=B400, POSITIVE=B400-B118	331
MARKETABLE SECURITIES	M S	B118=B400*A96/100, NEGATIVE=0	332
NOTES AND ACCTS. RECEIVABLE	M S	B115=(A92*B1+A93*B3+A94*B5+A95*B7)/100 X	333
		+A91	334
INVENTORIES	M S	B116=B73+B70	335
PREPAYMENTS	M S	B117=A97*B105/100	336
CURRENT ASSETS	M S	B120=B115+B116+B117+B118+B119+A101	337
			338
OTHER INVESTMENTS	M S	B78	339
			340
LAND	M S	B81	341
BUILDINGS	M S	B82	342
NET LAND AND BUILDINGS	M S	B92	343
FACTORY AND OFFICE EQUIPMENT	M S	B83	344
NET FACTORY AND OFFICE	M S	B93	345
PATENTS AND GOOD WILL	M S	B95	346
			347
TOTAL ASSETS	M S	B121=B120+A98+B92+B93+B94+B95	348
			349
LIABILITIES AND EQUITY			350
INCOME TAXES	M S	B122=A99*B45/100	351
ACCTS. PAYABLE AND ACCRUALS	M S	B123=A105+A106*B47/100	352
			353
LOANS PAYABLE	M S	B79	354
CURRENT LIABILITIES	M S	B124=B122+B123+A107+A102	355
DEFERRALS AND RESERVES	M S	B125=A109+A110*B192/1000000	356
LONG TERM DEBT	M S	B126=B126P+A75-A76	357
			358
TOTAL LIABILITIES	M S	B127=B124+B125+B126	359
			360
EQUITY CAPITAL	M S	B128=B121-B127+A103	361
NUMBER OF SHARES OUTSTANDING	K	B80	362
			363
ANALYTICAL RATIOS			364
CURR. ASSETS/CURR. LIAB.	O/O	B130	365
CURRENT/TOTAL ASSETS	O/O	B131	366
CURR. LIAB./TOTAL ASSETS	O/O	B132	367
EQUITY PER SHARE	$	B133	368
RETURN ON CAPITAL	O/O	B129	369
CAPITAL TURNOVER RATIO	X	B134	370
EARNINGS PER SHARE	$	B106	371
			372
RATES OF CHANGE			373
CURRENT ASSETS	O/O	B135	374
NET LAND AND BUILDINGS	O/O	B136	375
NET FACTORY AND OFFICE	O/O	B137	376
CURRENT LIABILITIES	O/O	B139	377
EQUITY CAPITAL	O/O	B138	378
)END FORM, END PAGE			379
			380
MOVE CERTAIN LINES TO B-MATRIX		B74=A74, B75=A75, B76=A76, B77=A77	381
		B78=A98, B79=A107	382
ACCUMULATE DIVISIONAL DATA		DO L= 1 TO 300	383
		C(L)=C(L)+B(L)	384
		END	385

DESCRIPTIONS CARD COLUMNS 1 - 31	TERM 32-37	*	LOGIC STATEMENT 41 - 79	*	SEQ. NO.
ACCUMULATE SHARES OUTSTANDING ONCE			C80=B80		386
TRANSFER DIVISIONAL DATA TO PROGRAM 08			L=SUBSET*10		387
GROSS INCOME			TRAN(B9,8,0,L+1)		388
GROSS PROFIT			TRAN(B19,8,0,L+3)		389
NET BEFORE TAX			TRAN(B41,8,0,L+5)		390
DOMESTIC INCOME TAX RATE			IF SUBSET EQ 1 THEN TRAN(B46,8,0,198)		391
FOREIGN INCOME TAX RATE			IF SUBSET EQ 7 THEN TRAN(B46,8,0,199)		392
					393
FOR SUMMARY AND DIVISIONS			$302		394
CALCULATE RATIOS					395
REPLACEMENT RATE			B204=(B203-B201+B201P)*100/B201P		396
XYZ/MARKET			B206=PCT(B205,B201)		397
XYZ SHIPMENTS/SALES POTENTIAL			B212=PCT(B211,B203)		398
XYZ REMOVAL RATE			B210=B209*100/B205P		399
			DO L=1 TO 9		400
GROSS INCOME DISTRIBUTION			B(L+1)=PCT(B(L),B9)		401
GROSS PROFIT MARGINS			B(L+11)=PCT(B(L+10),B(L))		402
			END		403
			DO L= 140 TO 190 BY 10		404
COST FACTOR PER MAN			B(L+5)=B(L)*1000/B(L+4)		405
HIRING RATE			B(L+9)=B(L+8)*100/B(L+4)		406
			END		407
EARNINGS PER SHARE			B106=RATIO(B43,B80,1000)		408
DIVIDEND PAYOUT			B109=PCT(B103,B43)		409
FIXED/TOTAL INVESTMT			B107=PCT(B102,B104)		410
RETURN ON CAPITALIZATION			B129=PCT(B43,B218)		411
CURR. ASSETS/CURR. LIAB.			B130=PCT(B120,B124)		412
CURRENT/TOTAL ASSETS			B131=PCT(B120,B121)		413
CURR. LIAB./TOTAL ASSETS			B132=PCT(B124,B121)		414
CAPITAL TURNOVER RATIO			B134=RATIO(B9,B218,1)		415
EQUITY PER SHARE			B133=RATIO(B128,B80,1000)		416
MFG. EXTRA SHIFT RATIO			B217=100-B220*100/B144		417
MANUFACTURING			B222=B221*(1-B217*.01)*1000/B144		418
MFG. WAREHOUSING			B224=PCT(B223,B221)		419
ENGINEERING			B226=RATIO(B225,B154,1000)		420
OTHER			B228=RATIO(B227,B219,1000)		421
CALCULATE GROWTH RATES					422
MARKET ESTIMATE			B301=YGR(B201)		423
XYZ POSITION			B302=YGR(B205)		424
GROSS INCOME			B303=YGR(B9)		425
GROSS PROFIT			B304=YGR(B19)		426
TOTAL EXPENSES			B305=YGR(B39)		427
NET BEFORE TAX			B306=YGR(B41)		428
NET AFTER TAX			B307=YGR(B43)		429
LAND AND BUILDINGS			B100=YGR(B97)		430
TOTAL FUNDS PROVIDED			B111=YGR(B98)		431
INVESTMENTS			B112=YGR(B102)		432
TOTAL FUNDS APPLIED			B113=YGR(B104)		433
NET CURRENT ASSETS 12-31			B114=YGR(B105)		434
CURRENT ASSETS			B135=YGR(B120)		435
NET LAND AND BUILDINGS			B136=YGR(B92)		436
NET FACTORY AND OFFICE			B137=YGR(B93)		437
CURRENT LIABILITIES			B139=YGR(B124)		438
EQUITY CAPITAL			B140=YGR(B128)		439
MANPOWER MFG.			B146=YGR(B144)		440

DESCRIPTIONS CARD COLUMNS 1 - 31	TERM 32-37	* LOGIC STATEMENT * 41 - 79	SEQ. NO.
ENGINEERING		B156=YGR(B154)	441
MARKETING		B166=YGR(B164)	442
SERVICE		B176=YGR(B174)	443
ADMINISTRATION		B186=YGR(B184)	444
GRAND TOTAL		B196=YGR(B194)	445
TRANSFER SUMMARY DATA TO PROGRAM 08		IF SUBSET NE 0 THEN END	446
DEVELOPMENT		TRAN(B27,8,0,141)	447
RESEARCH		TRAN(B25,8,0,143)	448
APPORTIONMENTS		TRAN(B37,8,0,145)	449
			450
)FORM 9, WORKSHEET, HEADING FORM 03-9 // INPUT WORKSHEET 1 OF 7			451
BUSINESS VOLUME ASSUMPTIONS			452
MARKET, AMOUNT	M $	A201	453
OR GROWTH RATE	0/0	A202	454
REPLACEMENT AMOUNT	M $	A203	455
FACTOR	0/0	A204	456
XYZ POSITION, AMOUNT	M $	A205	457
OR GROWTH RATE	0/0	A206	458
OR SHARE OF MARKET	0/0	A207	459
XYZ REMOVALS, AMOUNT	M $	A209	460
FACTOR	0/0	A210	461
GROSS INCOME			462
PRODUCTS, AMOUNT	M $	A1	463
OR SHIPMENT FACTOR	0/0	A2	464
SERVICE, AMOUNT	M $	A3	465
OR POSITION FACTOR	0/0	A4	466
SUPPLIES, AMOUNT	M $	A5	467
OR POSITION FACTOR	0/0	A6	468
OTHER, AMOUNT	M $	A7	469
OR SHARE OF TOTAL INCOME	0/0	A8	470
)IMAGE NOTE - INPUT DATA SPECIFIED AS AN AMOUNT AND A RATIO ARE COMPLEMENTS UNLX			471
ESS THE RATIO IS PREFACED BY 'OR'.			472
)END PAGE			473
)FORM 9, WORKSHEET, HEADING FORM 03-9 // INPUT WORKSHEET 2 OF 7			474
GROSS PROFIT			475
PRODUCTS AMOUNT	M $	A11	476
GROSS INCOME RATIO	0/0	A12	477
SERVICE AMOUNT	M $	A13	478
GROSS INCOME RATIO	0/0	A14	479
SUPPLIES, AMOUNT	M $	A15	480
GROSS INCOME RATIO	0/0	A16	481
OTHER, AMOUNT	M $	A17	482
GROSS INCOME RATIO	0/0	A18	483
EXPENSES			484
RESEARCH AMOUNT	M $	A25	485
GROSS INCOME RATIO	0/0	A26	486
DEVELOPMENT, AMOUNT	M $	A27	487
GROSS INCOME RATIO	0/0	A28	488
FIELD SALES AMOUNT	M $	A29	489
GROSS INCOME RATIO	0/0	A30	490
MKTG.SUPPORT, AMOUNT	M $	A31	491
FIELD SALES RATIO	0/0	A32	492
ADMINISTRATION, AMOUNT	M $	A33	493
GROSS INCOME RATIO	0/0	A34	494
OTHER EXP.OR INC.AMOUNT	M $	A35	495

DESCRIPTIONS CARD COLUMNS 1 - 31	TERM 32-37	*	LOGIC STATEMENT 41 - 79	*	SEQ. NO.
GROSS INCOME RATIO	O/O		A36		496
APPORTIONMENTS, AMOUNT	M $		A37		497
GROSS INCOME RATIO	O/O		A38		498
CORPORATE TAX RATE	O/O		A45		499
OR TAX AMOUNT	M $		A46		500
)REPEAT IMAGE					501
)END PAGE					502
)FORM 9, WORKSHEET, HEADING FORM 03-9 // INPUT WORKSHEET 3 OF 7					503
CHANGE IN FIXED ASSETS					504
EQUIPMENT, AMOUNT	M $		A50		505
MANUFACTURING PER MAN	K $		A51		506
ENGINEERING PER MAN	K $		A52		507
OTHER PER MAN	K $		A53		508
PATENTS AND GOODWILL	M $		A54		509
WORKING CAPITAL FACTORS					510
CURRENT ASSETS (PRIOR ONLY)	M $		A101		511
CURRENT LIABILITIES (PRIOR ONLY	M $		A102		512
A/R AMOUNT	M $		A91		513
OF GROSS INCOME — PRODUCTS	O/O		A92		514
SERVICE	O/O		A93		515
SUPPLIES	O/O		A94		516
OTHER	O/O		A95		517
SECURITIES/DISPOSABLE FUNDS	O/O		A96		518
PREPAYMENTS/NET CURRENT ASSETS	O/O		A97		519
SUNDRY ASSETS	M $		A98		520
INCOME TAXES PAYABLE/TAXES DUE	O/O		A99		521
A/P AND ACCRUALS, AMOUNT	M $		A105		522
COST + EXPENSE FACTOR	O/O		A106		523
LOANS PAYABLE	M $		A107		524
DEFERRALS AND RESERVES, AMOUNT	M $		A109		525
MANPOWER FACTOR	$		A110		526
)REPEAT IMAGE					527
)END PAGE					528
)FORM 9, WORKSHEET, HEADING FORM 03-9 // INPUT WORKSHEET 4 OF 7					529
DEPRECIATION FACTORS					530
BUILDINGS, AMOUNT	M $		A61		531
BOOKLIFE	YRS		A62		532
EQUIPMENT, AMOUNT	M $		A63		533
BOOKLIFE	YRS		A64		534
PATENTS AND GOODWILL, AMOUNT	M $		A65		535
BOOKLIFE	YRS		A66		536
OTHER NON-CASH, AMOUNT	M $		A67		537
OTHER FUNDING AND INVESTMENTS					538
EQUITY CAPITAL (PRIOR ONLY)	M $		A103		539
SALE OF CAPITAL STOCK (CO)	M $		A74		540
NUMBER OF SHARES ISSUED	K		A73		541
INCREASE IN LONG TERM DEBT	M $		A75		542
REDUCTION IN LONG TERM DEBT	M $		A76		543
MISCELLANEOUS	M $		A77		544
INVENTORIES					545
PARTS, AMOUNT	M $		A81		546
POSITION FACTOR	O/O		A82		547
WORK IN PROCESS, AMOUNT	M $		A83		548
SHIPMENT FACTOR	O/O		A84		549
OTHER INVENTORIES, AMOUNT	M $		A85		550

D E S C R I P T I O N S CARD COLUMNS 1 - 31	TERM 32-37	* L O G I C S T A T E M E N T 41 - 79	* SEQ. NO.
COST + EXPENSE FACTOR	O/O	A86	551
)REPEAT IMAGE			552
)END PAGE			553
)FORM 9, WORKSHEET, HEADING FORM 03-9 // INPUT WORKSHEET 5 OF 7			554
DIVIDEND POLICY			555
CASH DIVIDEND, AMOUNT/SHARE	$	A78	556
OR PAYOUT/NET EARNINGS	O/O	A79	557
YEAREND MANPOWER			558
MANUFACTURING COST/MAN	K $	A140	559
DIRECT	MEN	A141	560
INDIRECT	MEN	A143	561
RATIO	O/O	A144	562
ATTRITION	MEN	A148	563
RATIO	O/O	A149	564
ENGINEERING. COST/MAN	K $	A150	565
PROFESSIONAL	MEN	A151	566
SUPPORT	MEN	A153	567
RATIO	O/O	A154	568
ATTRITION	MEN	A158	569
RATIO	O/O	A159	570
MARKETING COST/MAN	K $	A160	571
FIELD	MEN	A161	572
SUPPORT	MEN	A163	573
RATIO	O/O	A164	574
ATTRITION	MEN	A168	575
RATIO	O/O	A169	576
)REPEAT IMAGE			577
)END PAGE			578
)FORM 9, WORKSHEET, HEADING FORM 03-9 // INPUT WORKSHEET 6 OF 7			579
YEAREND MANPOWER CONTINUED			580
SERVICE COST/MAN	K $	A170	581
FIELD	MEN	A171	582
SUPPORT	MEN	A173	583
RATIO	O/O	A174	584
ATTRITION	MEN	A178	585
RATIO	O/O	A179	586
ADMINISTRATION COST/MAN	K $	A180	587
PROFESSIONAL	MEN	A181	588
SUPPORT	MEN	A183	589
RATIO	O/O	A184	590
ATTRITION	MEN	A188	591
RATIO	O/O	A189	592
SPACE FORECAST			593
MANUFACTURING, AMT.	KSQFT	A221	594
PER MAN	SQFT	A222	595
EXTRA SHIFT RATIO	O/O	A220	596
WAREHOUSING, AMT.	KSQFT	A223	597
TO MFG. SPACE	O/O	A224	598
ENGINEERING, AMT.	KSQFT	A225	599
PER MAN	SQFT	A226	600
OTHER, AMT.	KSQFT	A227	601
PER MAN	SQFT	A228	602
)REPEAT IMAGE			603
)END PAGE			604
)FORM 9, WORKSHEET, HEADING FORM 03-9 // INPUT WORKSHEET 7 OF 7			605

D E S C R I P T I O N S CARD COLUMNS 1 – 31	TERM 32-37	*	L O G I C S T A T E M E N T 41 – 79	*	SEQ. NO.
SPACE AVAILABLE					606
PLANTS, TOTAL	KSQFT		A231		607
OWNED, AMT.	KSQFT		A232		608
RATIO	O/O		A233		609
WAREHOUSES, TOTAL	KSQFT		A235		610
OWNED, AMT.	KSQFT		A236		611
RATIO	O/O		A237		612
LABORATORIES, TOTAL	KSQFT		A239		613
OWNED, AMT.	KSQFT		A240		614
RATIO	O/O		A241		615
OFFICES, TOTAL	KSQFT		A243		616
OWNED, AMT.	KSQFT		A244		617
RATIO	O/O		A245		618
BUILDING COST PER SQFT					619
PLANTS	$		A261		620
WAREHOUSES	$		A262		621
LABORATORIES	$		A263		622
OFFICES	$		A264		623
LAND PURCHASES (CO)					624
ACREAGE	UTS		A266		625
SQ. FOOTAGE	KUTS		A267		626
LAND ACQUISITION COST (CO)					627
PER ACRE	$		A268		628
PER SQ. FOOT	$		A269		629
)REPEAT IMAGE					630
)END PAGE, END FORM, END PROGRAM 03					631

DESCRIPTIONS CARD COLUMNS 1 - 31	TERM 32-37	* LOGIC STATEMENT 41 - 79	# SEQ. NO.
)PROGRAM 08			1
)COMMENTS			2
PROGRAM 8, INCOME ANALYSIS BY PRODUCT DIVISION WITH DIFFERENCE CALCULATION			3
FOR ALTERNATIVE PLANS IN SUBSET 10.			4
)END COMMENTS			5
PLANNING VARIANCE		IF SUBSET EQ 10 THEN GO TO $801	6
INCOME DATA PER DIVISION		DO L=11 TO 81 BY 10	7
GROSS INCOME PER AMT OR GRT		B(L)=GRO(3,A(L),A(L+1))	8
GROSS PROFIT PER AMT + MARGIN		B(L+I)=A(L+2)+A(L+3)*B(L)/100	9
NET BEFORE TAX PER AMT + MARGIN		B(L+J)=A(L+4)+A(L+5)*B(L)/100	10
CORPORATE TOTAL FOR GROSS INCOME		B181=B181+B(L)	11
NET BEFORE TAX		B185=B185+BL(L+4)	12
GROSS PROFIT MARGIN		B(L+202)=PCT(B(L+2),B(L))	13
NET BEFORE TAX MARGIN		B(L+204)=PCT(B(L+4),B(L))	14
		END	15
NET AFTER TAX DOMESTIC		B177=(B185-B75)*(1-A198/100)	16
FOREIGN		B77=B75*(1-A199/100)	17
TOTAL		B187=B177+B77	18
NET AFTER TAX MARGIN FOREIGN		B277=PCT(B77,B71)	19
TOTAL		B387=PCT(B187,B181)	20
SUPPORT OPERATIONS		DO L=141 TO 149 BY 2	21
		B(L)=A(L)+A(L+1)*B181/100	22
RESPECTIVE RATIOS TO GROSS INCOME		B(L+200)=PCT(B(L),B181)	23
		END	24
GROWTH RATES		DO L= 11 TO 187 BY 2	25
YEARLY GROWTH RATES		B(L+1)=YGR(B(L))	26
COMPOUND GROWTH RATES		B(L+1)=CGR(B(L),1,8)	27
		END	28
PREPARE FOR COMPARATIVE ANALYSIS		DO L=11 TO 387	29
COPY B- INTO C-MATRIX		C(L)=C(L)+B(L)	30
PREVENT TRANSFER OF ITERATIVE VIEW		IF SWITCH EQ 1 THEN END	31
TRANSFER ORIGINAL VIEW ONLY		TRAN(8,10,L)=B(L)	32
		SWITCH=1	33
		END	34
)FORM 1, DOUBLE COLUMNS (AMT,O/O), HEADING FORM 08-1 // INCOME ANALYSIS			35
DIVISION X			36
GROSS INCOME		B11 , B12	37
GROSS PROFIT		B13 , B14	38
NET BEFORE TAX		B15 , B16	39
GROSS MARGIN		B213	40
NETBT MARGIN		B215	41
			42
			43
DIVISION Y			
GROSS INCOME		B21 , B22	44
GROSS PROFIT		B23 , B24	45
NET BEFORE TAX		B25 , B26	46
GROSS MARGIN		B223	47
NETBT MARGIN		B225	48
			49
DIVISION Z			50
GROSS INCOME		B31 , B32	51
GROSS PROFIT		B33 , B34	52
NET BEFORE TAX		B35 , B36	53
GROSS MARGIN		B233	54
NETBT MARGIN		B235	55

DESCRIPTIONS CARD COLUMNS 1 - 31	TERM 32-37	*	LOGIC STATEMENT 41 - 79	*	SEQ. NO.
					56
SPECIAL PRODUCTS					57
GROSS INCOME	B61	,	B62		58
NET BEFORE TAX	B65	,	B67		59
NETBT MARGIN	B265				60
					61
FOREIGN OPERATIONS					62
GROSS INCOME	B71	,	B72		63
GROSS PROFIT	B73	,	B74		64
NET BEFORE TAX	B75	,	B76		65
NET AFTER TAX	B77	,	B78		66
GROSS MARGIN	B273				67
NETBT MARGIN	B275				68
NETAT MARGIN	B277				69
					70
TOTAL CORPORATION					71
GROSS INCOME	B181	,	B182		72
NET BEFORE TAX	B185	,	B186		73
NET AFTER TAX	B187	,	B188		74
RESEARCH	B143	,	B144		75
DEVELOPMENT	B141	,	B142		76
CHQ ADMIN.	B145	,	B146		77
O/O OF GROSS INCOME					78
NET BEFORE TAX	B385				79
NET AFTER TAX	B387				80
RESEARCH	B343				81
DEVELOPMENT	B341				82
CHQ ADMIN'ION	B345				83

```
                                                                            84
IMAGE NOTE - O/O COLUMN SHOWS YEARLY GROWTH RATES EXCEPT FOR LAST COLUMN WHICH X   85
SHOWS COMPOUND GROWTH RATE OF LAST OVER FIRST YEAR.                          86
)END FORM, END PAGE                                                         87
   COMPUTE PLANNING DIFFERENCE FROM      $801    DO L=11 TO 387             88
ORIGINAL DATA IN A-MATRIX AND NEW DATA   B(L)=C(L)-A(L)                     89
IN C-MATRIX. WEED OUT MINOR VARIANCES.   IF (ABS(B(L)) LT 0.05 THEN B(L)=0  90
                                         END                                91
)FORM 2, INDEX(5), HEADING FORM 08-2 // GROSS INCOME COMPARISON            92
TOTAL CORPORATION              M $      B181                                93
DIVISION X                     M $      B11                                 94
DIVISION Y                     M $      B21                                 95
DIVISION Z                     M $      B31                                 96
FOREIGN OPERATIONS             M $      B71                                 97
)END FORM, END PAGE                                                        98
)FORM 3, INDEX(5), HEADING FORM 08-3 // NET BEFORE TAX COMPARISON          99
TOTAL CORPORATION              M $      B185                               100
DIVISION X                     M $      B15                                101
DIVISION Y                     M $      B25                                102
DIVISION Z                     M $      B35                                103
FOREIGN OPERATIONS             M $      B75                                104
)END FORM, END PAGE                                                        105
)FORM 4, INDEX(4), HEADING FORM 08-4 // ANALYSIS OF SUPPORT OPERATIONS     106
CORP.PRETAX NET                M $      B185                               107
RESEARCH                       M $      B143                               108
DEVELOPMENT                    M $      B141                               109
CHQ ADMINISTRATION             M $      B145                               110
```

P S G PROGRAM LIBRARY LISTING

DESCRIPTIONS CARD COLUMNS 1 - 31	TERM 32-37	*	LOGIC STATEMENT 41 - 79	*	SEQ. NO.
)END FORM, END PAGE					111
)FORM 9, WORKSHEET, HEADING FORM 08-9 // INPUT WORKSHEET 1 OF 2					112
DIVISION X					113
GROSS INCOME AMOUNT	M $		A11		114
OR GROWTH RATE	O/O		A12		115
GROSS PROFIT AMOUNT	M $		A13		116
GROSS INCOME RATIO	O/O		A14		117
NET BEFORE TAX AMOUNT	M $		A15		118
GROSS INCOME RATIO	O/O		A16		119
DIVISION Y					120
GROSS INCOME AMOUNT	M $		A21		121
OR GROWTH RATE	O/O		A22		122
GROSS PROFIT AMOUNT	M $		A23		123
GROSS INCOME RATIO	O/O		A24		124
NET BEFORE TAX AMOUNT	M $		A25		125
GROSS INCOME RATIO	O/O		A26		126
DIVISION Z					127
GROSS INCOME AMOUNT	M $		A31		128
OR GROWTH RATE	O/O		A32		129
GROSS PROFIT AMOUNT	M $		A33		130
GROSS INCOME RATIO	O/O		A34		131
NET BEFORE TAX AMOUNT	M $		A35		132
GROSS INCOME RATIO	O/O		A36		133
)IMAGE NOTE - INPUT DATA SPECIFIED AS AN AMOUNT AND A RATIO ARE COMPLEMENTS UNLX					134
ESS THE RATIO IS PREFACED BY 'OR'.					135
)END PAGE					136
)FORM 9, WORKSHEET, HEADING FORM 08-9 // INPUT WORKSHEET 2 OF 2					137
SPECIAL PRODUCTS					138
GROSS INCOME AMOUNT	M $		A61		139
OR GROWTH RATE	O/O		A62		140
NET BEFORE TAX AMOUNT	M $		A65		141
GROSS INCOME RATIO	O/O		A66		142
FOREIGN OPERATIONS					143
GROSS INCOME AMOUNT	M $		A71		144
OR GROWTH RATE	O/O		A72		145
GROSS PROFIT AMOUNT	M $		A73		146
GROSS INCOME RATIO	O/O		A74		147
NET BEFORE TAX AMOUNT	M $		A75		148
GROSS INCOME RATIO	O/O		A76		149
SUPPORT OPERATIONS					150
RESEARCH AMOUNT	M $		A143		151
GROSS INCOME RATIO	O/O		A144		152
DEVELOPMENT AMOUNT	M $		A141		153
GROSS INCOME RATIO	O/O		A142		154
CHQ ADMINISTRATION AMOUNT	M $		A145		155
GROSS INCOME RATIO	O/O		A146		156
INCOME TAXES					157
TAX RATE, DOMESTIC	O/O		A198		158
FOREIGN	O/O		A199		159
)REPEAT IMAGE					160
)END PAGE, END FORM, END PROGRAM 08					161

Index